D0450115

GAME LOADS AND PRACTICAL BALLISTICS FOR THE AMERICAN HUNTER

Bob Hagel

GAME LOADS AND PRACTICAL BALLISTICS FOR THE AMERICAN HUNTER

Alfred A. Knopf
New York · 1978

This is a Borzoi Book
Published by Alfred A. Knopf, Inc.

Published in the United States by Alfred A. Knopf, Inc., New York, and simultaneously in Canada by Random House of Canada Limited, Toronto. Distributed by Random House, Inc., New York.
Library of Congress Cataloging in Publication Data
Hagel, Bob. (date)
Game loads and practical ballistics for the American hunter.
Includes index.
1. Ballistics. 2. Cartridges. 3. Hunting.
I. Title.
SK274.3.H33 1978 639'.1 77-21053
ISBN 0-394-40397-5
ISBN 0-394-73482-3 pbk.
Manufactured in the United States of America
First Edition

To all hunters everywhere,
and especially to those
big game hunters who load their own
hunting ammunition.

Contents

Introduction

The dominant reason for writing this book is to give the American hunter the information needed to make clean, humane kills with a single shot the rule rather than the exception at all practical hunting ranges on all species of North American game. Whenever a shot is missed or an animal wounded, and several more shots are required to bring it to bag, something did not work out quite the way the hunter intended, or at least not as well as may have been possible. This does not mean that if the advice given in these pages is faithfully followed, no more shots will be missed or more game wounded. Any hunter who has killed much game has missed some and wounded an occasional animal, and if he does much more hunting it will happen again in the future. It is hoped, however, that the information presented here will serve to make both the hunter and the ammunition used more efficient, or at least furnish the knowledge needed to develop that efficiency.

As far as cartridges for varmint hunting are concerned, they have been covered quite thoroughly as to the where and why some are better than others for certain types of hunting. The performance of the cartridge and the great variety of available bullets are discussed so that the varmint hunter who has not used them all will know what to expect from them and how to get the most they have to offer by reloading them to their highest potential. But varmint hunters do a great deal more shooting than big game hunters; they become much more familiar with their rifles, cartridges, and loads, and if they miss completely, or place a shot poorly, it is of little consequence. The shot that misses damages only the hunter's ego, or shows him he did something wrong either in loading his ammunition or in shooting it, and very few good varmint bullets that connect at all fail to kill.

With the big game hunter the story is completely different, and if the load used fails to perform correctly, or he doesn't know its limitations or he misjudges the range for one reason or another, the hunt may be a failure because there is no second chance. This being the case, it is vital that the hunter know not only what cartridge and load is the best for the various kinds and sizes of game under various hunting conditions, but how to put the bullet in the right spot to do the most good no matter what the hunting conditions may be.

Perhaps the main purpose of this book is to tell the big game hunter what cartridge and load is best suited to various kinds of game and hunting. It is, of course, a fact that any North American game animal can be killed with any cartridge suited to big game hunting if conditions are right, but this does not make that cartridge ideal for the job. It must also be remembered that the rifle and the cartridge it fires do not directly kill the game; it is the bullet that either succeeds or fails to take care of that chore. While factory ammunition does a reasonably good job in most hunting situations if the hunter selects it carefully for the kind of hunting to be done, few big game hunters will argue that it is as good as handloads made up especially for a specific purpose. The hunter/handloader has the option of using any case/powder/bullet combination that fills his needs, and he can also tailor that load to bring out the best accuracy *his rifle* has to offer.

While this is not a book on handloading per se, we have given a lot of information on hunting handloads and what the reloader should strive for in making up the most efficient hunting loads. Also included are tables of handloads for most of the popular varmint and big game cartridges. These tables are by no means intended to be complete, but consist of the loads that have been found to give the highest velocity from each bullet weight with safe, trouble-free performance in hunting rifles. To enlarge on these load tables it is suggested that any or all of the reloading manuals be purchased and studied. No attempt has been made here to go into the beginner basics of handloading, as the various reloading manuals take care of that very well, but the Appendix of this book does enlarge on much of what the manuals say, as well as give some of the finer points of reloading that are of more value to the hunter than to other shooters.

Of course, the most accurate rifle, the flattest shooting and most potent load, and a bullet that performs correctly to take advantage of all the things rifle and cartridge have to offer, are of little value if the hunter fails to hit the animal. We have endeavored to tell the hunter how to sight his rifle so that a big game animal can be hit in the vital area at the longest possible range with the least amount of guesswork. There are also many things that cause shots to miss that the average hunter never gains experience enough to become aware of. Many of these aspects of hunting have been delved into so that the hunter will know what to look for and what to expect, and how to make a vital hit in a situation that is otherwise likely to cause a miss.

I do not claim to have all the answers as to the best cartridge or load for any or all game and all hunting situations. I am also fully aware that there are other hunters who have killed a wider variety of North American big game, in many more places, than I. And certainly many have taken more game of some species, and perhaps killed larger numbers combined, and their experience is respected here whether they agree or disagree with what I have written. But there is a vast difference in the amount of knowledge gained by those who hunt purely for the pleasure of hunting, and those who hunt not only because they love hunting and the game but have a burning desire to study the game and the hunting, and use every instance where an animal is either missed, wounded, or killed cleanly to find out what happened and why.

From the time I started shooting big game more than forty-five years ago, cartridge and bullet performance has intrigued me. From the day I killed my first big game animal, which happened to be a black bear, I have been digging bullets and taking notes on how they performed, as well as the cartridges and loads behind them. As a guide and outfitter back at the time when there were sections of the West where the only pack string seen on a hunting trip was your own, and having hunted here and there where the country and game are still wild and plentiful even today, I have seen many hundreds of game animals killed, in all colors, shapes, and sizes. And as a writer on guns and hunting it has been my privilege to use every new cartridge that has appeared in the past twenty-five years or so, and the rifles that fired them, along with all the older numbers and many wildcats. From those hundreds of animals I have dug the bullets fired by all these cartridges, and in cases where the bullet made exit, the wound channel it left was carefully examined. From that experience some hard conclusions have been formed regarding cartridge and bullet performance. And it is on that experience that the thought, discussion, and suggestions of this book are founded.

Bob Hagel
Gibbonsville, Idaho
March 1977

GAME LOADS AND PRACTICAL BALLISTICS FOR THE AMERICAN HUNTER

1

Game Loads and Practical Ballistics for the American Hunter

There are many reloading manuals available to the American hunter who likes to load his own ammunition, and there have been a number of books written on the subject, but I know of none that were written with the American hunter specifically in mind. It might be well to point out at the start that this is not a reloading manual per se, although the Appendix gives reloading information that is pertinent to hunting reloads. Neither will this book give the basic A-B-C steps of reloading that are so well covered in the many excellent reloading manuals. Instead, this book is written for the hunter, whether he snipes tiny ground squirrels at unbelievably long ranges or clobbers Alaskan moose and brown bears in brush so thick he hardly has room to lift his rifle. It also includes a great deal of information on commercial ammunition that has been gained by many years of testing in the hunting country.

By and large, varmint hunters are much better informed on loads and ballistics than are big game hunters, but, if the queries that come to me as a gun writer and hunting editor are interpreted correctly, even this knowledgeable clan of accuracy bugs runs into many tangles that they are unable to unravel. It isn't that they don't always know what they are doing, but they have neither the time nor the equipment to carry on the kind of experiments, both in the lab and in actual hunting, that it takes to find the answers.

It seems that in varmint hunting the criterion usually used is extreme accuracy. This is, to a point, as it should be, because if you can't hit 'em you can't kill 'em, but there is more to it than that.

If your load is accurate enough to win a benchrest match, it won't be a good varmint load if the velocity is too low to give the flatness of bullet flight so vital to long range varmint shooting. Neither will it give quick, clean kills if the bullet does not expand violently at the ranges at which the varmint is shot.

Varmint hunters, like other reloaders—or people who do many other things not remotely related to reloading or hunting—often get in a rut; they may get so entrenched in using certain bullets, powders, or cartridges that they fail to realize the potential of new developments. On the other hand, there are those who get carried away with everything new that comes along and think it must be better than those things that have been proved reliable and highly effective. In this work we intend to point up the good and bad points of what the new and the old have to offer the hunter. If the new is better for some reason, we'll try to show not only that it is but why it is, and how to use it to take advantage of what it has to offer the hunter. Some of the new powders and bullets hold certain advantages over the old ones for certain cartridges, while not being as good for others, but the average varmint hunter does not have the time or the equipment to find this out for himself.

The varmint hunter is interested in one thing, the end result. We'll dig deep into all the many aspects of varmint cartridges, loads, and bullets, and into the actual hunting, to try to show the varmint hunter how to attain the best results.

Going deeper into the varmint hunting picture, there is a great deal of confusion regarding the so-called varmint cartridges of over .224 caliber. When bullet diameter increases to 6mm (.243) or over, I personally consider the cartridge a combination varmint/big game cartridge. These cartridges, the various 6mm's, .25s, and probably the 6.5mm's, form a group of cartridges that are very popular with a great many hunters who do a lot of varmint hunting, and a little big game hunting for deer, antelope, and other game of similar size. The confusion comes in where bullets are concerned, and where actual drop at practical hunting ranges, either varmint or big game, is considered. There is also the matter of wind drift between the various bullet weights used in these larger calibers, and also between these calibers and the .22 varmint cartridges.

To anyone who knows something about what he is doing, and

with much experience in both big game and varmint shooting, it soon becomes obvious that no one bullet is right for both. Even so, it is amazing to find how many hunters try to use one bullet weight and design for "everything." They also believe that because the larger calibers use heavier bullets, they automatically shoot flatter and are less affected by wind than are the lighter .22 bullets at similar velocity. We'll take a hard, no-myth look at all these things as we go along and explain why the answers come out the way they do.

We'll show what can be expected of these same varmint/big game cartridges when the hunter uses them on game that is larger than deer. Is he justified in using them for heavier game? If so, or when necessity leaves no alternative, what bullet weight and design should be used, under what circumstances, and where should he place that bullet to do the most good?

Progressing further into the big game hunting field, there is that great majority of cartridges from .270 to .35 or even larger in the so-called standard case, which are simply cases with less powder capacity than that of the big belted cases referred to as "magnum." These cases have a great deal of virtue and probably form the backbone of American hunting cartridges. Here again, some powders are much more desirable than others with bullets of various weights, and while accuracy is less important, velocity, flat bullet flight, retained energy at long range, and especially bullet performance are highly important.

In looking at this class of cartridges we find that they have the widest choice of suitable powders. These cartridges are also perhaps used for a wider range of shooting than all others. Many hunters use a .270 or .308 Winchester, or the venerable old .30-06, for varmint shooting during the summer, then use the same rifle for everything from antelope to moose in the fall hunting season. This practice is certainly to be commended, because the hunter gets a lot of much-needed practice with his big game rifle, and he'll do a much better job when he makes contact with a bull, buck, billy, or ram. It is normal for these hunters to pick the lightest bullets for varmint shooting, and these bullets are designed for that purpose, so everything works out well. But when it comes to big game hunting, they seem all too often to get hung up on some kind of mental block and forget that for all these cartridges there are bullets that are designed for game of different sizes. I've known big game hunters who insisted on using a 150 gr. bullet in the .30-06 for everything from whitetails to elk and moose, and others who thought the 220 gr. was *the* answer, regardless of the size of the game or of the range. They also forget, or don't know, why different point designs exist, or go by what some joker told them who knew even less.

It is next to impossible under today's hunting conditions for the average once-a-year hunter to gain enough experience to know a great deal about bullet performance on various kinds of big game under the wide variety of conditions they will be seen and shot. All too often the big game hunter sees a single example of bullet performance and animal reaction to that performance, and from that forms an opinion that sticks with him throughout his hunting career. In scientific circles they say that "a single instance does not necessarily prove a point," and this is never truer than in shooting big game. All too few hunters ever spend the time it takes to do the messy, smelly job of following the bullet's path to see what it did, and to do some mental calculation to try to understand why the animal reacted the way it did. It is all too common for the hunter to say, "Well, it killed him, didn't it?" and let it go at that. The next time, under similar circumstances, it may not kill him and you'll never know why.

Going on up the line to the magnum cartridges—those cartridges that deliver a bit more power than their "standard" counterparts—the situation is much the same as with the less-potent big game cartridges, only it is more complicated. It is less complicated as far as powder choice is concerned, because there are fewer suitable powders to choose from, but the bullet department is a different story.

The problem arises from the fact that in most instances the big cases use all the same bullets as the smaller ones, but they squirt them out at higher velocities. This situation is fine as far as flat trajectory is concerned, which means ease of hitting at longer ranges, but this same higher velocity raises merry old hell with expansion control of most bullets. Bullets that deliver good performance from the standard capacity cartridges are usually too fragile to stand up under the increased velocity of magnum cartridges. They expand violently in the same manner as a varmint bullet. If the game is on the small side, and sometimes if it isn't, they are inclined to make messy, bloodshot hamburger of a lot of good meat. They also lack penetration for large animals when and where it is needed. If the range is long enough they may work quite well, but we usually have little choice as to range, except possibly to edge closer, which, in this case, is the wrong direction.

What is almost always needed for shooting big game with the magnum cartridges is a bullet especially designed for that use—and, better yet, a premium quality bullet designed with high velocity cartridges, certain but controlled expansion, and deep penetration as the criteria.

It matters little how good the bullet is and how well it performs if it doesn't hit the animal. Whenever an animal is beyond the point-blank range of the cartridge, most hunters are hard pressed to know how to make a vital hit. There are dozens of trajectory and sighting-in tables and charts, but few if any give the hunter the information on bullet drop and sighting to compensate for that drop, which would be of value in the field with a nervous ram on the far side of the canyon. Straight trajectory figures are almost completely worthless to the hunter in hunting country. Most hunters associate trajectory with drop but do not know how to use it. Actual bullet drop figures are also useless, because they do not consider sights and sighting. Factory trajectory/bullet drop/sighting dope sheets are getting better every day, but they still leave a lot to be desired for use by the hunter in hunting country. He doesn't have a lot of time to think about it when all the chips are down, and he needs to be sighted to realize the full trajectory potential of the cartridge he is using. Granted, he may not wish to use the same sighting for all cartridges for all kinds of shooting, but he should know where, how, and why different sightings are necessary.

Judging range is, of course, the cause of more misses by good game shots than any other reason. Few hunters spend time enough in game country to learn to judge range accurately, but if a hunter's rifle is sighted correctly to take full advantage of the trajectory of the cartridges it fires, a lot of the range problem is eliminated. Also, if you know how to go about judging range and know what conditions can foul up your best efforts, you will have progressed far in the right direction.

Light conditions vary a great deal in different types of hunting country. Atmospheric conditions encountered at sea level and at 10,000 feet are far from the same, and things look different. Haze, fog, rain, and snow change the perspective so much that the average hunter who does not spend much time in hunting country is completely confused. There are, however, general rules of thumb that are gained by long association with all kinds of terrain and light conditions that are very helpful, and we'll attempt to tell you how to apply them.

It has always seemed to me that when it comes to long range shooting and ballistics that apply to and control rifle-cartridge performance, hunters are inclined to run to the extreme in one of two directions: either they oversimplify it or they try to get too technical. Oversimplification is not conducive to accurate results, and if too much emphasis is put on technicalities, the game will be long gone before you figure it out. Actually, the hunter must generalize to a point, because in long range shooting, for example, a great many factors over which he has no control enter into the picture—factors like altitude, barometric pressure, and humidity. There are no hard-and-fast rules in hunting country.

On the opposite end of the stick, the hunter who will hunt in areas where the shots are mostly at close range in the timber, but who wishes to use only one rifle and cartridge for both types of hunting, needs to know how to get the most out of that cartridge. Or, if a cartridge is selected especially for timber hunting, how to select it and a load for it, and what the limitations of that load will be. There are good brush cartridges and some fair brush bullets, but will they really plow through brush? Will they perform as well as hunters have been led to believe?

It is my intention to explain all these things so that the hunter will know what I am talking about and how to apply what he or she has learned. There is little or no theory in anything written here, and if any of the information given has not been proved or disproved by me, I have stated so. The charts and tables are from data collected and tested by me unless otherwise stated, and the text that refers to those charts and tables explains the circumstances under which they were compiled.

It will be noted that the load tables do not attempt to cover all powders and bullet weights. This information is available in the various reloading manuals. Only the powders that give the best results for the particular cartridge and bullet weight are listed, as others would afford only supplementary data and would be superfluous. These load-data tables do, however, include not only nearly all of the most useful powders for the cartridges mentioned, but bullets of various brands. This is something that few reloading manuals do, because most of them are produced by the various powder and bullet companies and therefore show loads using only their own powders or bullets. The *Lyman Reloading Handbook* is an exception. The velocities, and the powder charges that it takes to attain those velocities, will often vary from those found in the various reloading manuals, but so do the charges and velocities of the different manuals vary a great deal. It should be remembered that all the load/velocity data listed here was taken from standard factory or custom rifles, the kind hunters use in hunting country, and not from special pressure guns with chambers and barrels cut to much closer tolerances than are usually found in hunting rifles. Actually, this is what the hunter is interested in—a clear-cut idea of what *his rifle* is producing.

I think that while the various reloading manuals are excellent in every respect (the writer has been involved with some of them in various capacities) and the several books written on reloading are of great value to any reloader, the American hunter has been shortchanged in many ways. In the following chapters I hope to remedy this situation and offer the hunter information that is badly needed and that has never been available to him before under one cover.

2

Varmint Cartridges and Loads

To start the discussion on varmint cartridges it might be well to point out that varmint hunting does not necessarily call for varmint cartridges. True, varmint cartridges are designed to be used for varmint hunting for the most part, but some, the .222 Remington for example, have set accuracy records that no other cartridge in commercial form has equaled. It is also possible to reduce the load to the point where they may be used for taking small game for the table, and some hunters have used them for shooting larger game like deer and antelope. But their primary purpose is varmint shooting.

On the other hand, varmint hunting is very often done with some pretty unlikely cartridges. I have done a good deal of varmint hunting with handguns in the class of the .357 Magnum to the big .44 Magnum, and even some with the old .45 Colt. I've also shot uncounted numbers of chucks and jackrabbits with various 7mm and .300 magnum cartridges. Some of this was done when the big cartridge was the only thing I happened to have along when some exceptional varmint shooting was encountered. At other times I was testing bullets designed for varmint hunting with these cartridges. I also know big game hunters who do not even own a varmint rifle, yet do a lot of varmint shooting with their big game rifles, usually something like the .270 or .30-06. Which all goes to show that varmint hunting is regularly done with something other than a varmint cartridge, but that a true varmint cartridge is designed with varmint shooting as the criterion of its performance.

Actually, it is a little hard to say when varmint shooting first started or what cartridges were used. One thing is certain: for many years the great majority of what was then referred to as "pest" shooting was done with whatever was at hand, mostly .22 rimfire rifles that were kept in nearly every home, often with .22 Short cartridges because Long and Long Rifle cartridges were too expensive, especially when we consider that most of the pest shooting was done by farm lads who might tend to pop off a few extra rounds on occasion. Few adults took time out from the serious business of raising the crops and livestock that the varmints fed on to hunt them down.

Later, when cartridge development advanced and the big bore started giving way to smaller caliber cartridges, gun buffs began experimenting with smaller cases and light bullets of small caliber, such as .25 to .32 diameter. These experiments resulted in such cartridges as the .32-20, the .25-20 single shot, and a few others of less popularity during the 1880s and '90s. Later the .25-20 repeater and the .22 Winchester Centerfire appeared, along with the .22 Savage High-Power. The latter was considered a big game cartridge at the time, but it fulfilled the requirements of a varmint cartridge much better.

These cartridges worked fairly well and, except for a few wildcats of small caliber, were the only varmint cartridges available. They were, however, drastically limited in their effectiveness by lack of velocity, as well as by varmint bullets of undesirable shape and structure. This lack of velocity and poor bullet shape caused bullet drop to be so great that hits at much over 100 yards were confined either to those varmint hunters of long experience who did a huge amount of shooting, or to luck. And even when the bullet did find the mark at extended ranges, the chance of a clean, quick kill was small indeed.

The Modern Varmint Cartridge Is Born

The first really effective varmint cartridge in .22 caliber was the .22 Hornet that evolved from the black powder .22 Winchester Center fire (WCF) case. The Hornet arrived on the scene in about 1930 in commercial form and immediately took over as *the* varmint cartridge of the day. While not a spectacular performer by today's standards, it was a long step forward in varmint cartridge history. The Hornet proved very accurate even in light sporter barrels, and with the 45 gr. bullet of good ballistic shape stepping along at nearly 2700 fps, it shot flat enough to make hits fairly consistent out to well over 150 yards. Also, the little bullets were designed with jackets that expanded well at these longer ranges and gave almost certain kills even with marginal bullet placement.

The advent of the Hornet also triggered the development of what was to become a long line of .224 caliber varmint bullets, as well as handloading to derive the most from the cartridge and those bullets. This handloading-bullet development trend was given a further boost when the .220 Swift appeared some five years after the birth of the Hornet, and was followed closely by the appearance of the .219 Zipper and .218 Bee, which were made with lever action rifles specifically in mind.

While factory-loaded ammunition gave good accuracy and bullet performance in all these cartridges, handloads with both factory- and self- or custom-made bullets gave even better results. However, handloading and the better varmint bullets, and the advent of new powders that gave better velocity and accuracy, which was turning handloading of varmint cartridges into a highly sophisticated art, were just getting started to roll when World War II came along and set it all back by several years. However, at war's end the interest in all shooting and hunting, including varmint hunting, rose to an unprecedented high, which has continued unabated. The fact that few components were available to the handloader during the first postwar years caused bullet-making firms to spring up where none had existed before, and most of them produced varmint bullets that were superior to any that had existed before.

When these bullet-making firms, like Speer, Hornady, and Sierra, started producing bullets for varmint hunting, they did a great deal of experimenting that led to the development of better bullet shape. This in turn gave much flatter trajectory for long range shooting at very small targets. But it was also discovered that the original .224 bullets of 40–48 gr. had very poor ballistic coefficient no matter how good the form factor. Even when started at .220 Swift velocities of over 4000 fps, they soon slowed to a trot,

These are examples of true varmint cartridges. *From left:* .22 Hornet; .17 Rem.; .222 Rem.; .223 Rem.; .222 Rem. Mag.; .224 Wby.; .225 Win.; .22-250; .220 Swift.

which caused energy, velocity, and their initial explosive effect to drop off badly. Shortly all of these companies started making bullets of from 50 gr. up to 60–63 gr. to overcome this deficiency.

These bullets took various forms, but most were of spitzer shape with small pointed noses of soft lead. Nearly all of these companies also produced at a somewhat later date cavity point bullets in 52–53 gr. weights. The soft points were intended primarily as varmint hunting bullets, while the HP bullets were designed mostly with high velocity and target accuracy in mind.

These various bullet styles and weights were produced with the many different .224 caliber varmint cartridges in mind. As far as the Hornet cartridge was concerned, it was at its best with bullets of 45–50 gr. for all kinds of shooting, so most of the new bullets were of little use for it. But for the .220 Swift and the several wildcats like the .22 Varminter, later to become the .22-250 Remington, these new bullets broadened the field of use and gave better results than had ever been attained before.

Actually, it mattered little that these newer bullets of heavier weight were unsuitable for the .22 Hornet, because about the time the varmint-bullet-making business got well under way, Remington introduced the .222 Remington in 1950. The new entry to the .22 varmint cartridge line, the "baby .30-06," as it was dubbed by some gun buffs, proved to be one of the smartest moves Remington ever made, because it probably sold more rifles and rounds of ammunition than any other varmint cartridge. It is possible that the .22-250 has outstripped it in rifle sales today, but it will take a long time, if ever, for it to catch up in overall sales.

The great boom in .22 varmint cartridges did not come, however, until the late 1950s and up until the mid-'60s. Two more cartridges on the .222 head size case were produced by Remington in the form of the .222 Remington Magnum and the military-commercial .223 Remington or 5.56mm. Larger commercial cartridges that could surely be classed as magnum .22s came from several sources: the .224 from Weatherby; the .225 from Winchester; and the wildcat .22-250 commercialized by Remington. These were all good varmint cartridges, and all gave higher velocity than the .222 Remington and less than the .220 Swift. But only the .223 and .22-250 were to gain great popularity. In fact, when Winchester chambered the .225 in the Model 70 and dropped the .220 Swift, they apparently made a classic mistake, because the .225 chambering lasted only a short time and was replaced by the .22-250 along with the older commercial .222 in M-70 rifles.

But to backtrack to the advent of the .222 Remington, the commercial load was and still is a 50 gr. bullet at a listed velocity of 3200 fps. Maybe the factory load churned up this much velocity in some of the original rifles with 26″ barrels, and it no doubt did in minimum-tolerance pressure test barrels, but I have yet to chronograph any brand of .222 ammunition that gave the 50 gr. bullet 3100 fps. Mostly it runs around 3000 fps. However, there are a number of powders that will give the 50–52 gr. bullets a muzzle velocity of 3300 fps from a 24″ barrel. For example, 26.5 gr. of BL-C2 will give a 50 gr. bullet an MV of 3392 fps, and 21.5 gr. of Reloader 7 will start it at 3353 fps from the 24″ barrel of a standard sporter. And 55 gr. bullets can be pushed along at higher velocity than factory loads give the 50 gr. from the same barrel length. Even so, the .222 proved to be an extremely good varmint cartridge for everything up to and including chucks and jackrabbits out to 200 yards with good factory ammunition. Most factory bullets expanded quite well up to that range even on varmints as small as ground squirrels. Some factory ammunition lacked sufficient accuracy for consistent hits on targets as small as ground squirrels and magpies* at over 100 yards, but other ammunition by the same maker proved highly accurate.

Varmint Bullets

An example of this is Remington factory ammunition loaded with soft point and Power-Lokt cavity point bullets. In using hundreds of rounds of both I don't recall ever shooting average five shot groups of much under 1 1/2" at 100 yards with the soft point load in any rifle, but the Power-Lokt bullet factory load will shoot groups almost as tight as the same bullet will give from good handloads in a good varmint rifle. This means from 1/2" to no more than 3/4" at 100 yards. This bullet is also very effective on even the smallest varmints out to over the 200 yard mark in the 50 gr. weight intended for the .222. It is not only highly accurate but has good ballistic coefficient for a .224 50 gr. bullet, and it is completely explosive out to as far as the trajectory of the .222 makes hits reasonably certain. Any of the heavier weight bullets are quite effective in the .222, and I have even used the Speer 70 gr. with good results on jackrabbits out to 150 yards or so, but in spite of what some rcloading manuals show, the .222 is at its best with bullets of not over 55 gr. I have found that when one feels a heavier bullet is needed, a larger cartridge is a better choice.

As for being able to hit small targets with the .222, the various 52–53 gr. hollow.point bullets give the best results in most rifles. However, there is a fly in the soup here as far as the .222 is concerned. While most of the 52–53 gr. HP bullets are made with target accuracy in mind (some of them have been used to win hundreds of benchrest matches), they work quite well on varmints of all sizes if velocity is high enough. They work very well at quite long ranges in the larger cartridges that develop higher velocities, but lack sufficient expansion at .222 velocities at much beyond 150 yards. One exception to this is the 52 gr. Speer varmint bullet. Its large cavity point causes it to expand violently at the ranges where the .222 is effective, but that same large cavity point reduces ballis-

*Magpies and crows are now under federal migratory bird regulations, with different seasons for various sections, and are no longer subject to year-round hunting in most areas.

tic coefficient far below that attained by some of the other brands, so hits are not as easy, because of greater drop.

Hornady makes a couple of bullets that are exceptionally well suited to the .222 in their 50 and 55 gr. SX (super explosive) style. Sierra also makes the 50 gr. Blitz that is designed to give extreme explosive effect at fairly low velocity. These bullets all have good ballistic shape to flatten trajectory for easier hits at long range, and give good varmint accuracy in most rifles with the right powder and charge.

The .222 Remington Magnum is built on the same basic case as the .222 but is a bit longer and has more powder capacity. It was originally designed as a military round but was never accepted. At a later date Remington did succeed in interesting the military in the .223, which is almost identical in body size but has a shorter neck. In fact, there is so little difference in the performance of these two cartridges that loads for one will likely do quite well in the other. There is less than 1 gr. difference in case capacity of a ball powder like BL-C2 in favor of the .222 Remington Magnum. Both cases hold 3.5–4.5 gr. more powder than the .222 does, depending on the capacity of the brand and lot of cases used.

Either one of these larger cases will give an average of about 200 fps with all bullet weights over .222 velocities at similar pressures from the same barrel length. Most of the reloading manuals show the .223 as giving very little more velocity than the .222, but a close look at the rifle data will show that .222 velocity was usually taken from 26″ barrels while the .223 loads were clocked from the 20″ barrels of semiauto military and sporter rifles. I have also found that in a good bolt action rifle the .223 will stand somewhat hotter loads without showing pressure pains.

Generally speaking, the same powders work well in both the original .222 Remington and the later .222 Rem. Mag. and .223, with slightly slower powders being better in the two larger cases to give the high velocity so desirable in varmint hunting. The same bullets are effective in the larger cases, but they will handle the heavier bullets better, due to the increase in velocity. Either one of these cartridges will add 50–100 yards to the effective varmint range of the .222, either from the ease in making sure hits or because the same bullets will expand that much farther away.

While the .224 Weatherby and the .225 Winchester both show

somewhat lower velocity than the .22-250 when all are loaded to full throttle, there probably isn't enough difference to cause the varmint hunter much concern or to go very deeply into their respective performances. Actually, the .225 has a slight edge on the .224, averaging near 100 fps higher velocity, but this isn't enough to be of any great consequence. Further, few rifles other than Winchester or Weatherby were ever chambered for either one, and Winchester has dropped chambering the .225 completely. Weatherby still chambers the .224 in the excellent miniature Mark V rifle, but they also chamber the .22-250.

If the varmint hunter already owns one of these rifles for either cartridge, there would be little reason to change unless factory ammunition is used exclusively, and then the better choice would be the .22-250, because ammunition for it is available anywhere.

I have used both cartridges extensively for varmint hunting from magpies to coyotes with many bullet styles and weights. It was found that with good handloads there wasn't enough difference between the two, or between them and the .22-250, to cause much concern in either the hitting or killing departments.

There is little doubt that the .22-250, both as a wildcat and as a commercial number, is one of the finest varmint cartridges ever developed. It is exceeded in velocity in the .224 commercial cartridge line only by the .220 Swift, and only the .222 head size cartridges give better average accuracy, and then not by enough to matter to the varmint hunter. As far as I'm concerned, the .22-250 and the .220 Swift are the ultimate for straight varmint shooting, regardless of caliber. There are exceptions to this, as we'll see later, but for average varmint hunting situations on everything from ground squirrels, magpies, and crows on the small end, to coyotes and bobcats on the large side, I know of no cartridges that are more efficient.

These two cartridges, and wildcats of similar case capacity, handle the heavier .224 bullets more efficiently than do the smaller cases. It is in these cases that bullets of over 55 gr. are at their best —bullets like the 60 gr. Hornady soft point and hollow point, and the 63 gr. Sierra. For example, either the .22-250 or the Swift will push the 60–63 gr. bullets along at 300–400 fps faster at the muzzle than the .222 will start the 50 gr.! When the difference in the ballistic coefficient between the 50 gr. and the 60–63 gr. bullets is considered, it is not hard to see how much more efficient the two big cases are for the longest range varmint shooting.

When anyone mentions these two cartridges together, the point is always raised as to which is the most desirable varmint cartridge, and no discussion of varmint cartridges would be complete without some comment on this controversial subject. An appraisal of any varmint cartridge hinges mostly on its accuracy, ability to shoot flat over the longest varmint shooting ranges to ensure ease in bullet placement, and the velocity required to do that and also give the violent bullet expansion so necessary for quick, clean kills.

The Swift has more than 100 fps advantage over the .22-250, so flat trajectory and long range killing ability are somewhat better with the same bullet. As far as accuracy is concerned, any difference of importance to the varmint hunter would be in the rifle, not the cartridge. This leaves only one possible advantage in favor of the .22-250: it burns less powder. The difference of 3–4 gr., depending on the powder, certainly isn't enough to matter much as an economic factor, but it is claimed by some that it makes a good deal of difference in barrel life in favor of the .22-250. There is probably some difference, but it is unreasonable to assume it is great. The Swift got the reputation of burning out barrels when it first appeared, and writers have been repeating it ever since without actually knowing if they were right. I've read of where barrels were washed out in 300–500 rounds, which could be true if the rifle was shot too fast so that the barrel heated excessively, but I've seen a number of Model 70 Swift rifles that had fired many thousands of rounds and still shot very small groups from barrels that showed little wear. Today's barrel steels also hold up better.

The big disadvantage today is that Winchester no longer loads ammunition for the Swift. The last I knew, Norma still loaded a 50 gr. load, but Norma ammunition is not found in every corner hardward store. Both W-W and Norma still make cases, however, which pretty well limits the Swift to a handloader's cartridge. Also, Ruger and Savage are the only American-made rifles chambering the Swift cartridge today. The Ruger offering is in their Model 77 bolt action magazine rifle, while Savage offers it in their modified single shot 110 action known as the 112V. Both rifles have varmint weight barrels and give excellent accuracy.

As for handloading being the only way to obtain ammunition for the great old cartridge, it makes little difference to anyone who will use the Swift. If it is chosen over the .22-250, the user is buying it because he wants the ultimate in a .22 varmint cartridge for long range shooting. This being the case, he will want to realize the full potential of the cartridge. And there is only one way to get it—load your own ammo. While the original Swift ammunition gave good accuracy, the 48 gr. bullet left much to be desired. Accuracy was good at 100 yards and held up very well out to about 300 yards, then seemed inclined to drop off badly in all shooting I did at over that range. Even though the bullet was listed as starting at over 4100 fps, the light, short bullet with its poor ballistic coefficient slowed down rapidly. Also, the last ammunition loaded by Winchester showed less than 4000 fps at the muzzle of the 26″ Ruger M-77 barrel.

When the Swift is capable of starting a 55 gr. bullet at up to 3900 fps, and the 60–63 gr. at 3700 fps, it seems unlikely that anyone would wish to use a 48 gr. for varmint shooting. However, with the 52–53 gr. hollow point bullets made mostly for match shooting, I have found that the Swift velocity of 4000 fps will expand them at extremely long ranges for explosive effect. Starting at that velocity, these very accurate bullets with their high ballistic coefficient are perhaps the most efficient of all as far as sure hits are concerned. These are the bullets the real accuracy bug should experiment with for both target and varmint shooting.

Reading these remarks about the .220 Swift, one might get the impression that my personal opinion is that it is a far superior cartridge to the .22-250. To be completely candid, I do feel it is the top of the line of .22 varmint cartridges in commercial form, but to say it is very far ahead of the .22-250 would not be completely true. At the very most, there isn't more than 50 yards sure killing range in favor of the Swift with the same bullets, and this would likely be cut even further if both were used in the same barrel length. All of my own work with the .22-250 has been done with a 24″ barrel and with a 26″ tube in Swift chambering.

I suppose the longest range varmint shooting I ever did with a .22 varmint cartridge was done with a Model 70 Swift, but this wasn't necessarily because I was using that cartridge, but because of conditions. The shooting was across a plowed field at a range that was unknown at the time of shooting but was estimated at near

500 yards. The varmints were young rockchucks, about half grown, that were feeding on new grain shoots. We were so far away that the chucks paid no attention whatever to the distant sound and did not spook at bullets impacting the ground nearby. As I recall, it took me three shots to dope the elevation and wind to find the first one. Even though it was quite calm, with perhaps a little more breeze on the side of the field where the chucks were, I found I had to hold about three "chuck lengths" into the breeze. Drop was even more difficult because a half-grown chuck sticks up very little when flattened out, feeding. Anyway, after the dust of bullet impact gave the hold needed, I made about three hits from every five shots. Could I have done it with a .22-250? My hunting partner was using one, and he connected about half as often as I did.

We later paced the distance to approximately 500 yards, and found that the Sierra 50 gr. bullets we both were using were expanding some but had lost their explosive effect. (My load was 41 gr. of 4064 for an MV of 4109 fps, and his, as I recall, was 36.5 gr. of 4320 that probably gave about 3775 fps.) Actually, that is too far to shoot chucks with that bullet in either cartridge. I have, however, killed many chucks at ranges of 350–400 yards with a .22-250 and Speer HP 52 gr. bullets loaded to near 3800 fps. At that range they will expand well on large chucks, but not as well on small ones.

Loading for Accuracy and Velocity

Up to this point we have looked at .22 varmint cartridges as a whole, and while we have not attempted to cover them all individually, we have pretty well covered them in the groups in which they fit. We've also shown why some are better than others for all-around varmint shooting, but there are other aspects of varmint shooting that require explanation if the varmint hunter is to get the most from these cartridges, which will also make him or her a better varmint hunter.

First of all, a bit of advice on loads might not go amiss. As has been pointed out, accuracy is a necessity for any serious varmint load, but it must also give the bullet it uses enough velocity to shoot flat and kill cleanly to the limit of the range of the cartridge.

Some powders may give excellent accuracy but fall short in the velocity department, while others attain high velocity at the sacrifice of accuracy. Neither situation is desirable, and, where possible, the two should be combined, or at least a compromise made. A look at the charts in this book will indicate which powders give the highest velocity with maximum loads that give trouble-free shooting for hunting use. A study of one of the reloading manuals will also give clues to the best powders. But neither the charts nor the manuals will tell you if those loads will give the kind of accuracy you need in *your rifle.* Even if the group size were given with every load, it would be next to meaningless in another rifle. Rifles are as individual in temperament as people are, and while there are loads that give good accuracy in *most* rifles, they do not apply to *all* rifles.

However, one thing I can tell you is that for the .222, .223, and .222 Magnum cartridges, the spherical powders are generally the best. The main reason for this is that most of the stick-type powders are too bulky if you are looking for maximum velocity. This is especially true of the .223 and .222 Remington Magnum, and particularly with the heavier bullets. You'll need a powder funnel with a long drop tube and then you'll have to sift the powder very slowly from the scale pan. A powder measure will not work for some of the heavier loads because the case will run over. Just as an example of what may be expected, BL-C, 748, and Reloader 7 give good velocity and accuracy in the .222, while 748 and H-335 do extremely well in the .223 and .222 Mag. The latter is the most outstanding performer of all I have used with any bullet weight in these two cases.

When going to the larger capacity cases from the .224 Weatherby to the .220 Swift, powder capacity is no problem with any bullet weight if you use any suitable powder in either spherical or tubular form. Also, these cases deliver outstanding velocity with many of the older powders like 4320, 4064, and 4895, and even slow burning 4350 in the Swift with heavy bullets. But some of the newer powders like Norma 204 and 203 in stick form, or the newer ball powders like W-W 760, give outstanding performance. In fact, Norma 203 and W-W 760 are probably the best powders for all bullet weights from the standpoints of accuracy and velocity.

A great deal has been said and written regarding the type of

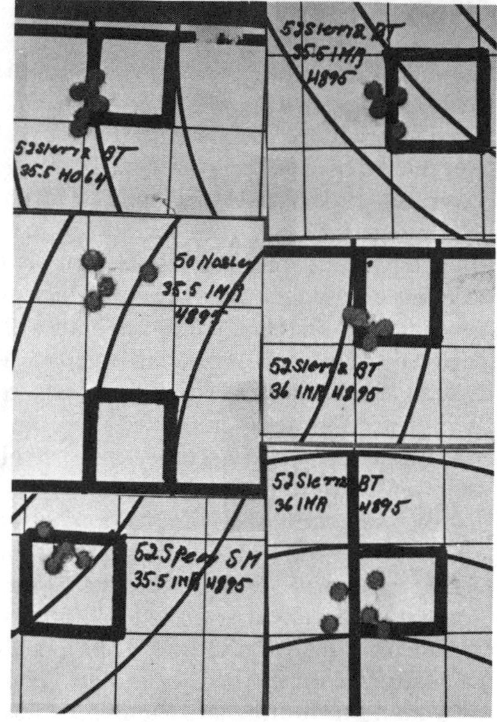

These groups were all fired at same time from Savage 112V rifle chambered for .22-250. They show how different loads and bullets often change point of impact; how different powders and charges and bullets can affect accuracy. Also, the kind of accuracy it takes for long range varmint shooting. Squares subtend 1″. Fired at 100 yards from bench.

primer it takes to give the best results with the two different powder types, ball and stick. We have been led to believe that to properly ignite the ball powders a magnum primer is needed. Generally speaking, this is not true with any of the .22 cases mentioned here. I have just completed running tests with all the primers readily available to the American reloader, and find that with either small or large rifle primers there is little difference in velocity or uniformity between the magnum and standard types with ball powders. In fact, some magnum primers give *less* velocity and *less* uniformity in shot-to-shot velocity than do standard strength primers. Use whatever you have at hand that gives an accurate load.

One more point we might add to the reloading angle is that while it is generally felt that a load a grain or two below maximum will give the best accuracy, it isn't necessarily so. I have usually received the best accuracy from the .222 with loads of about 3000 fps with 52 gr. bullets, but some of the benchrest boys load those same bullets just as hot as the case will stand and break records with them! It is not news to most users of the .220 Swift that the best accuracy often comes at the highest permissible pressure. In working up a load for your rifle, don't assume anything, try it both ways. If the hot load happens to be the most accurate, it will be just that much more effective for varmint shooting.

At this point someone might ask how much accuracy is actually needed for a good varmint load. The simple answer to that would be—all you can get! But that isn't completely true either, because it does make a little difference what kind of varmints are being shot, and under what conditions. Generally speaking, any rifle and load that will not group within 1" at 100 yards is not adequate for varmint shooting. Take the feathers off a magpie and you'll find that a 2" circle will cover the vital area. A crow will spread this area by not more than 1". A cross section of an average ground squirrel will show only about 2", while a prairie dog is a bit larger. Obviously, if your rifle and load will not stay in 1" or less at 100 yards, you have little chance of hitting any of these varmints consistently at the 200 yard mark. And this doesn't allow for errors. A chuck or a jackrabbit affords a much larger target, up to 5" the small way, so a load that will print into 1 1/2" at 100 yards is adequate out to 250 yards or so. But we also have to consider that a chuck, even a big one, flattened out on top of a rock, or feeding in the grass, cuts this area nearly in half. It must also be remembered that both the bunnies and chucks are often shot at 300–400 yards. Here again, the 1 MOA (minute of angle, or approximately 1") is absolutely mandatory, and tighter grouping loads will give more certain kills.

For coyote hunting with any of these .22 caliber cartridges, the 1 1/2" accuracy criterion will do very well. The vital shoulder-lung area of a coyote will run in excess of 6" the small way even on a small coyote. A load that will shoot into 1 1/2 MOA will land a bullet in the vital area out to 400 yards if you do your part, and the .22 varmint cartridges, even the mighty Swift, are not adequate for coyotes at beyond that range even if you are capable of hitting them.

While it can't be classed as normal varmint shooting, the calling of coyotes and bobcats is a completely different game and requires no high degree of accuracy. For this kind of shooting, accuracy can be pretty sloppy, but bullet performance should be considered if the hide is the object of the hunt, as we'll see later.

To cut the matter of accuracy even finer, a point that is not often considered is that not all .22 varmint cartridges require the same degree of accuracy. This is actually a rather sad state of affairs, because the cartridges that require the least degree of accuracy are the ones that will, on the average, shoot the tightest groups. There is no doubt that the .222 is consistently the most accurate, with the .223 and .222 Magnum running in close second place. Yet velocity and consequent bullet drop and performance limit their use to around 200–250 yards. The degree of accuracy needed at this range is not the same as that required at the 350–400 yard ranges which the larger .22 caliber varmint cartridges make possible. This is not to say that the larger cartridges like the .22-250 and the Swift do not have sufficient accuracy for these ranges with good loads, but it does show that the accuracy pattern is reversed somewhat.

Aspects of Bullet Performance from Ground Squirrels to Coyotes

When all the chips are on the table, the ace in the hole for any cartridge used for any kind of hunting is the bullet. There is a vast difference, however, between the ideal performance of bullets used for shooting big game and those used for varmints. A big game bullet often requires controlled expansion to be effective, but not so for the varmint bullet. To be thoroughly effective a varmint bullet must be designed to completely disintegrate on anything it hits; anything with more resistance than a sunbeam. This in itself is not too difficult to attain, but it must also have high ballistic coefficient so as to retain sufficient velocity to give this same explosive effect at the longest range at which it will be used. This total disintegration is desirable for more reasons than one. First, to be completely effective on even the smallest of varmints, there must be enough explosive effect to kill cleanly even if the hit is "around the edges." This kind of bullet action will kill a chuck, jackrabbit, or ground squirrel just as quickly with a hit in the paunch as in the shoulders or lungs. Second, if the bullet misses the target it will completely break up on contact with the ground.

This point is especially critical when hunting in areas where there are people and/or livestock. While a bullet that does not completely come apart on contact with varmint or ground may kill quite well, it may also ricochet to strike some faraway object like man or beast.

The varmint hunter should be especially sensitive to total bullet blowup when shooting crows perched above the ground. A miss, or a bullet that remains partially intact, can travel a great distance before it later makes contact with some other object. The hunter will at least know the direction in which the bullet that misses will travel, but the one that passes through the varmint will likely take an angle that causes it to strike something the hunter can't even see. Of course, the solution to this problem is not to shoot unless you are certain of the background, but it is and will be done, and the bullet that leaves no pieces to fly over the countryside is good insurance.

Like the accuracy problem, the bullets that have the best potential for shooting flat do not always expand the best at long range. The various hollow point bullets have the best long range and wind bucking shape, but they also must have *small* cavities to have good long range form. As this style of point depends on the air, fluid, or other substance trapped in the cavity to expand the point of the jacket and start it ripping apart, the velocity must be higher than with the conventional soft point to make it perform properly. It all boils down to the fact that the HP bullets are a little easier to hit with at long range, but the soft points are better killers. What usually happens is that as range increases, the performance of the HP bullet tends to become erratic; one will expand to the point of violent blowup, while the next may not expand at all. A few examples will not prove the point here, and only experience will tell you which bullet will best fill your need for the kind of varmint shooting you are doing.

This brings us around to another problem that has cropped up recently since the prices of coyote and bobcat pelts have reached an undreamed-of high. When the varmint hunter shot coyotes mostly for sport and for predator control, he cared little if his bullet left a hole in the far side of the carcass big enough to stick his head in without getting his ears bloody; his only concern was a quick, sure kill. This is not so today. With good coyote pelts worth forty bucks or so, that kind of tear can cut the price in half, so the varmint-pelt hunter has been doing some serious head-scratching. In the past couple of years I've had dozens of letters asking for advice on how to avoid this. Actually, there is no surefire solution to the problem. Most bullet makers are producing fully metal-jacketed bullets in .224 and .243 calibers by popular demand from coyote, fox, and bobcat hunters who think they are the answer to hole-free hides. Not so. True, the solid bullet that does not expand will leave only a bullet-size hole on both sides, but the animal with that tiny wound is very likely to run off into the brush and die miles away unless its brain or spine has been hit. It will suffer, and you won't recover the hide, either. Better to leave a big hole in the hide than to have that happen.

There are also a couple of other drawbacks to using these "solids." One is the fact that if they are started at very high velocity they are inclined to expand unless the range is long enough so that the velocity has dropped off. My experiments have proved this, and the people who make them will tell you the same thing. In fact, Joyce Hornady told me that their 55 gr. FMJ .224 bullets were almost certain to expand if velocity exceeded 3000 fps. The other side of the coin shows that if they do not expand, but work as the coyote hunter intends them to, they will slice on through and go merrily on their way until they run out of steam or strike something else, like the rancher's cow! It goes without saying that a miss will cause a ricochet on contact with the ground.

Just because a coyote is not very large and bobcats and foxes are even smaller, never think for a minute that they can't take a lot of punishment and keep going. To make certain of instant kills, the bullet has to tear up a lot of the internal mechanism that pumps life into the animal. The best solution I know of for sure, clean kills without ruining the hide is to use the most explosive bullet you can get, and in fairly light weight—something like the 50 gr. Hornady SX or the Sierra Blitz. These bullets usually will not make exit and will kill instantly because they blow up completely. Hornady does not recommend that the 50 gr. SX be loaded to velocities of more than 3500 fps, because of possible blowup before reaching the target due to the very thin jacket. However, I have loaded them to around 3650 fps with no problem, but did get an occasional key-hole at 3800 fps. To further ensure that they will not exit, try to wait for a head-on or a quartering shot; or, if the animal is broadside and there's no time to wait for it to turn, place it in the shoulder. Try to avoid broadside lung shots, because the bullet is more likely to exit, taking a hand-size hunk of hide with it.

There are a couple of other aspects of varmint shooting that give food for thought to most varmint hunters who choose one of the .222 varmint cartridges. One is the economy angle. The .222, .223, and .222 Magnum are somewhat cheaper to shoot in the large quantities that most varmint hunters use. True, the bullets will cost the same, but the big cases are more expensive and they use more powder. And if you use factory ammunition there is a lot of difference. Also, these three cartridges will handle the major part of varmint hunting.

If you are hunting in populated areas where noise is a factor, the smaller cases may also prove desirable. The added noise of the larger cartridge, although it isn't too great, may bother people more, and farmers are inclined to think more noise means more danger to their livestock. If you are out in the wide open spaces where much of the varmint hunting in the West is done and ranges run on the long side, then the bigger cartridges may be your dish. They are certainly easier to hit with when ranges run over the 200 yard mark, and they are a much better choice for the coyote hunter because they pack more punch way off in the sage, greasewood, or cactus.

Sighting and How to Hit Varmints of All Sizes at Various Ranges

This brings up the all-important aspect of hitting small objects at long range. Any hunter, whether he hunts jackrabbits or mountain goats, soon learns that by far the greatest reason for misses is misjudging the range. And all the rangefinding gadgets that can be carried around by a varmint hunter are about as useless as mammary glands on a slab of bacon. Varmints do not come in the right sizes and shapes to lend themselves to mechanical rangefinding techniques, and any optical rangefinder that is small enough to carry only serves to confuse the issue. The best solution is to sight your rifle to take full advantage of the cartridge and load you are using.

But before going into how to sight your rifle to get the most out of your load without doing too much guessing as to bullet drop and mid-range trajectory arc, one thing should be cleared up: there are no hard-and-fast rules that apply to all loads and all hunting situations. We can tell you how to come close to knowing where your bullet will land at a given range, but not exactly, and neither can anyone else. Ballistic tables that give you bullet drop at a certain range in fractions of an inch are calculated for a certain bullet with a known ballistic coefficient and a known muzzle velocity, and which is fired under assumed atmospheric conditions at a certain elevation above sea level. And the ballisticians who figure out the ballistic coefficients of the various bullets don't always completely agree, either.

To start with, unless you have your own chronograph you won't know exactly what the muzzle velocity of the load is in *your rifle.* The load velocities given here or in any other table may miss the velocity of the same load in your rifle by as much as 50 fps or even more either way. If you don't believe that, compare some of the reloading manuals. A second point is that all bullets of a certain weight with shapes that are similar may have significantly different ballistic coefficients. Third, the elevation above sea level with its attendant change in air density affects bullet drop a great deal. Other atmospheric conditions like barometric pressure and humidity also upset the picture somewhat. A good chronograph will also show a day-to-day change in velocity of several fps with ammunition from the same box in the same rifle, and altitude will have more affect on muzzle velocity also. These are intangibles to a great extent, but they are there, and they will cause misses if you depend completely on paper figures.

However, there are rules of thumb that work well, and with a little personal experimenting you can learn enough about the load you are using to make hits that seem almost impossible. However, for consistent hits under varied hunting conditions, you should have your rifle sighted so that the bullet will be as high at the high point of its mid-range trajectory curve as it can be and still stay within the vital area of the varmint being fired at. Obviously, this will be less for a ground squirrel than for a chuck. The average varmint hunter may shoot both in the same day, with a few magpies and crows thrown in, so the best idea is to try to compromise, remembering that not all ground squirrels, sod poodles, and chucks stand up to be shot at; at least half will be flattened out, feeding.

When a Columbian ground squirrel sits erect, the bullet can strike up to 4" or so above or below point of aim and kill cleanly if it is explosive and at high velocity, but more than 1" to either side will give a miss.

At least half of the ground squirrels shot will be feeding and so will offer little more than a 2" vertical target. A varmint rifle sighted to place its bullets over 1" high at 100 yards will overshoot with center hold. For ground squirrels, magpies, and other small varmints, the 1" high 100 yard sighting is ideal, and it works equally well on chucks and jackrabbits.

One boon to the varmint shooter is that nearly all the well-shaped .224 bullets of 50–63 gr. will have similar drop out to about 400 yards if all are loaded full-throttle. In spite of what has often been said to the contrary, the difference in velocity will take care of the difference in ballistic coefficient. Check the Hornady or Sierra charts and you'll see that this is near enough to being correct that other factors will have more effect on hits and misses.

As it is often impractical to sight a rifle at 200 yards or more, 100 yard sighting is the best procedure. Using the .222 loaded to near maximum for a velocity with the 50–53 gr. bullets of the best pointed shape at 3250–3300 fps MV, it is about ideal to sight 1 1/2" high at 100 yards.* The bullet will then be right on the point of aim at just over 200 yards, about 2" low at 250 yards, and down only about 6" at 300 yards. This sighting will also work out to similar figures with the .223 and .222 Magnum, but slightly flatter with only about a 4"–4 1/2" drop at 300 yards and about zero at 225 yards. What this amounts to for the varmint hunter is that he can forget about range out to about 225 yards with the .222 and hold center of a feeding chuck out to that range and get a vital hit. On a ground squirrel with all four feet on the ground, or with a crow, he should hold near the bottom at 100–125 yards for a center hit, but if he forgets and holds center, a kill will probably be made anyway. You can stretch this sure hitting range to about 250 yards with the .223 and .222 Magnum. On the other hand, if you use most brands of factory-loaded .222 ammunition in hunting rifles with 24" barrels, the 1 1/2"-plus sighting at 100 yards will put the bullet about on the point of aim at 175 yards and about 7" low at 300 yards.

When you go on up to the class of the .22-250 and .220 Swift that will start the 50–53 gr. bullets at around 3800 fps or more, the sure hitting range with a center hold increases a good deal. Using the same 1 1/2" high sighting at 100 yards, the bullet will still land nearly that much high at 200 yards and close to 2" up at 150 yards, but it will be only about 2"–2 1/2" low at 300 yards. On a chuck or a jackrabbit, a center hold will give a kill right out to around 300 yards. For smaller varmints like ground squirrels, prairie dogs, and

*These figures are for scopes with reticle approximately 1 1/2" above center of bore; they will vary for larger scopes and target mounts.

crows, it is usually better to sight about 1" high at 100 yards, because if you sight much higher the bullet may be a bit too high to stay on target at around 150 yards. With the 1" high sighting at 100 yards, zero will come at about 220 yards, with an impact of about 4" low at 300 yards. Personally, I like the 1"-plus 100 yard sighting for the smaller varmints, and the 1 1/2" high sighting for everything from chucks to coyotes. In fact, on coyotes in open country where ranges are likely to be up to as far as you can hit them and your load is capable of killing them, a 275 yard zero is about right with the .22-250 or Swift. You can hold center of an average coyote and get a vital hit out to 320 yards. If you hold half of the width of the coyote's body over his back, the bullet will land in the vital area at 400 yards. It is well to remember, however, that the vital broadside area of an average coyote is little more than 5" in depth, while what you see, which includes the hair, will measure nearly 10". The Swift will, of course, have a little advantage in range over the .22-250, but not much. You'll have to do your own long range drop testing to be able to take advantage of it with the load you will use.

Again, I'd like to reiterate that these figures are only averages for bullets of good ballistic coefficient. The ones you use may vary somewhat and make slight changes. As an example, the 60 gr. Hornady Spire Point–soft point bullet has a listed ballistic coefficient of .269, while the Hornady 60 gr. hollow point shows .299. This will not make much difference, but it does make some.

Wind drift is more important in varmint hunting than in any other type of hunting. The reason is that most of it is done in open country, especially rockchuck, jackrabbit, and coyote hunting in the West, where winds are usually present to some extent, and the targets are so small that the slightest drift will cause a miss. If you want to face the facts and forget the frills, wind drift charts, no matter how accurate, are of little use. It may be of some value to know how much a certain bullet will drift when the wind is blowing at a certain velocity, but applying it in hunting country is something else. One example is that a spitzer 50 gr. bullet starting at 3800 fps will drift about 3 1/2" at 200 yards in a 10-mile-per-hour crosswind; the drift will be about 7", or double, if wind velocity picks up to 20 mph, and more than triple at 30 mph. If it seems that, knowing this, you will know how much to allow for wind drift at 200 yards with the average pointed 50 gr. .224 bullet at 3800 fps, you are wrong, for several reasons. First, I have yet to see the man who can tell me exactly what wind velocity is. Second, to be correct, the wind must be blowing at a right angle (90°) to the line of fire. And if this isn't enough to upset your calculation, it may be blowing at about your estimate where you are, but it may be calm, half that much velocity, or moving in a different direction where the varmint is. This is especially true in long range cross-canyon shooting.

For instance: You are wandering around on a sage flat and a jackrabbit takes off through the bushes and finally stops in an opening at what you think is 250 yards. With the right sighting you won't have to worry much about bullet drop, but the wind is trying to unseat your hat. That bunny isn't going to sit there more than a few seconds and you have to use some of that time to get in a steady sitting position. Obviously you don't have time to try to figure out how fast the wind is moving, or if it is blowing at 90° to the line of fire or anything between that and maybe 45°. The only solution is to allow what you think is the right amount, touch it off, and hope you guessed right!

The general consensus is that if you were using a heavier bullet, like a 60–63 gr., the problem of finding the bunny with the bullet would be much simplified. But the answer is that it wouldn't help enough to be of any practical value. Seeing that the 50 gr. pointed bullet starts at around 3800 fps and the 60–63 gr. at 3600 or less, there will be only about 1" difference in impact with a 20 mph wind on that 250 yard jack, and this only if the wind is at 90° to bullet travel.

I can now hear someone saying the answer to that problem is to use something like the .243 that will buck the wind a lot better. This sounds good and has produced some effective advertising, but a hard look at the facts shows that at 300 yards, the 75 gr. HP pointed .243 bullet starting at 3500 fps will drift nearly *1/2" more* in a crosswind than will the 60–63 gr. .224 bullet at 3600 fps! Again, this will depend on the ballistic coefficients of the various bullets in both calibers, and the velocities at which they are actually started. But it doesn't take a computer to figure out that there is little advantage in using the larger caliber as far as wind drift is concerned.

Sure, the boys who punch one-hole groups in a benchrest target dope the wind mighty close, and so do a lot of varmint hunters I know, but this comes from long experience and not from the book. Also, the guy at the benchrest isn't too concerned about the target getting up and running off while he tries to dope the wind.

About the only suggestion I have to offer, aside from experience gained from trial and error and close observation while practicing on distant rocks or paper, is to observe closely what the breeze is doing over where the game is. As mentioned earlier, there may be a 20 mph wind where you are and either more wind or less where the target is. To check this, take note of the movement or lean of grass, brush, or tree branches at your position, and check that against what is going on at target location. You can also check wind direction at the same time. Of course, you will not have time for this unless the varmint is sitting still and not likely to go anywhere.

Before we leave the .22 caliber cartridges that I consider strictly varmint cartridges, and go to those that may be referred to as varmint/big game cartridges, perhaps we should give brief coverage to the latest addition to the varmint cartridge line, the .17 caliber.

.17 Caliber Facts and Fancies

The .17 caliber had its beginning in the form of a number of wildcat experiments dating to as early as the 1940s, but didn't really build up a full head of steam until the mid-'60s, when a rash of them appeared. Most of them were based on the small .22 caliber cases: .222 Remington, and .223 and .222 Magnum, with modification of neck and body length and shoulder angle. The .17 had more than a few growing pains, most of them due to the tiny bore being difficult to make so accuracy was attained and fouling kept down when it was achieved. Many of the first barrels delivered very good accuracy for a few shots, then went completely sour. Part of this was due to what the smallest imperfection did to the tiny bore, and part to a lack of bullets suitable to the small bore and high velocity of the light bullets.

There is little use in going into these different wildcats, as few of them exceeded the performance of the commercial .17 Remington they preceded. Anything we say about the .17 Remington will pretty well hold true of the wildcats.

While the .17 was still in the wildcat stage, and for a short time after the Remington offering appeared, some pretty wild tales floated around regarding its performance. It was claimed to be a super cartridge with some kind of mystic power that was "chain lightning and sudden death" on everything from white-footed mice to Alaskan brown bears. Velocity was touted as being the highest of all commercial cartridges, which was partially true, because American companies no longer loaded the .220 Swift. And, according to some with seventeen stars in their eyes, this ultravelocity was supposed to make it a much better varmint cartridge than either the .22-250 or the Swift.

The fact is that while velocity of the factory load with 25 gr. bullet is listed at 4020 fps, it clocked only 3958 fps in my Rem. M-700 test rifle with 24″ barrel. A .22-250 loaded to maximum will do about as well with a bullet twice that heavy, and the Swift will beat it by quite a margin. I loaded that same Remington Power-Lokt 25 gr. bullet, as well as the Hornady 25 gr. HP, with a great variety of powders to all they would stand for a trouble-free maximum varmint load, and very few powders will deliver more than 4000 fps. I did succeed in driving 20 and 22 gr. bullets at over 4300 fps, but on varmints of any kind from magpies to big chucks they were not as good as the various 25 gr. bullets.

A lot of time was spent experimenting with that rifle, and a great many varmints of many kinds and sizes were shot with it at ranges out to near 300 yards, and some pretty solid data was piled up. Average groups with Remington factory ammunition using the 25 gr. Power-Lokt bullet ran 1 1/8″ for five shots at 100 yards. This seemed about average for most bullets and with the better powders and charges, but some of the best loads stayed under 1″.

As far as being easy to hit with because of the 4000 fps muzzle velocity, remember that the 25 gr. .17 bullet has a ballistic coefficient of only .190 for the well-shaped Hornady HP, while the spire point–soft point .224 45 gr. Hornady bullet shows .202, and the 50 gr. spire point goes .223. Start them all at similar velocity and whatever advantage there is lies in favor of the larger caliber. The same thing applies to wind drift. I've heard some anti-seventeen shooters say they were very poor in the wind. My testing did not bear this out, but, as stated above, they are no better and not much worse than the .22 bullets.

The varmint hunter using the .17 for the first time may well draw some erroneous conclusions. If, for example, many varmints of various shapes and sizes are shot at ranges that do not exceed 150 yards, the hunter will surely come to the conclusion that the tiny bullets do indeed have some mystic power. Ground squirrels will disappear in a haze of red mist, magpies and crows go up in a cloud of feathers, and the whole offside of a big chuck may be torn away: the kind of action one expects and gets from a .22-250 or Swift with light, highly explosive bullets.

But stretch the range by even a few yards, and a drastic change occurs. The fact is, it may occur at any range beyond 125 yards. What it amounts to is erratic bullet performance. One bullet may blow a chuck completely to shreds, while the next may punch a bullet-size hole in one side and out the other. And a .17 caliber hole is pretty small. The effect may also be anything in between. I remember shooting one large chuck on the far side of a canyon that was at about 275 yards with the 25 gr. Remington Power-Lokt bullet backed by 24 gr. of H4895 that started at 4054 fps. I knew how these bullets performed by that time and was lucky enough to place it through both shoulders. The chuck moved a few inches, flopped his tail a couple of times, and lay still. When I looked him over later, I at first had the impression that he had either died of fright or had a natural heart attack. Finally, after much looking, I found tiny entrance and exit holes with a single drop of blood concealed by hair on each side! Only the fact that the shot landed in a vital area and broke both shoulders and spine kept him from wandering off before he knew he was dead. Some that were not hit so well did make it into rock piles and were dug out with hits through the lungs.

This bullet action occurred with Remington Power-Lokt and Hornady HP 25 gr. bullets starting at around 4000 fps, and Lee 22 gr. and Baker 20 gr. HP bullets at 4300 fps. The probable cause of this is the very small cavity in the bullet's point. Hollow point bullets depend on trapped air, moisture, or other substance to expand them, and these cavities are so small that this function does not always take place. This results in erratic expansion, from explosive to none. As long as velocity is high, expansion is quite reliable, but as range increases and velocity drops, as it does quite rapidly with this light bullet, expansion is no longer reliable. A soft point bullet might change this situation, but I know of no one who produces a soft point bullet in .17 caliber.

What this all simmers down to is that the .17 Remington is about on a par with the .22-250 for ease of hitting the target out to near the 300 yard mark. After that, the .22-250 has a decided edge. But when it comes to killing power beyond 150 yards for consistently sure kills, the .17 doesn't even approach the .22-250 or the Swift. Personally, I prefer either the .222 Remington or the somewhat more powerful .223 and .222 Magnum. I have heard rumors that some .17 bullets have been improved recently and no longer show this erratic performance, but I have no firsthand proof that this is so.

.22 Caliber Cartridges Are Not for Big Game

There always has been a great deal of controversy over whether the .22 varmint cartridges are adequate for hunting big game in the antelope-deer class. As far as this writer is concerned, that argument could be settled with one word: *no.* But there is much more to it than that. The main issue is not whether these cartridges will kill deer-size game but whether they will do it reliably under all hunting conditions. Just because it can be done does not prove that it is sound advice to try to do it.

I've known of a deer or two—one a big mule deer buck—being killed with a .22 Short rimfire, and when I was growing up and didn't worry much about such things as quick, certain kills, I'll admit to killing a few muleys with the .22 Long Rifle cartridge, but when I lost one I wised up pretty fast. The .22 varmint cartridges in all dimensions have accounted for great numbers of deer and other game of similar size, and some a good deal larger, but they have also wounded uncounted numbers. A high velocity .22 caliber bullet placed broadside in the lungs of a deer often gives a spectacularly instantaneous kill. A hunter who sees this happen once or twice often comes to the conclusion that these cartridges are completely reliable. The truth is that they do not always do this even on the ideal broadside lung shot, and usually fail miserably under hunting conditions where the shot must be fired at an angle that causes impact somewhere other than the thin rib cage. If the explosive little bullet must be driven in at an angle that requires penetration, or if it strikes bone heavier than a rib, it usually stops there, causing a large, shallow wound that will kill the animal only after many hours or days of suffering, if it kills it at all.

Some advocates of big game hunting with .22 caliber bullets have said that bullet performance was the reason why the light, small caliber bullets failed to kill, and that if a bullet of heavier weight and controlled expansion were used it would be entirely adequate. They seem to forget a couple of points: First, the spectacular kills that sometimes come from the .22 varmint cartridges on deer-size animals are caused by high velocity and explosive bullet action in the lung-heart area. A great deal of vital tissue is destroyed and a terrific amount of hydrostatic shock transmitted, and the outcome is an instantaneous kill *if* it gets inside. But slow the little bullet down by adding weight, and eliminate the explosive effect by controlling expansion, and you also eliminate spectacularly quick kills.

If the expansion of the .22 bullet is controlled so even the heaviest bullets like the Speer 70 gr. will penetrate the heavy muscle and bone necessary to reach the vitals of a mature buck deer on angle, front, or rear shots, it will leave a very small wound channel, and be very poor medicine for broadside lung shots. Yes, the .22 varmint cartridges will kill deer-size game, but that doesn't mean they are adequate or should be used for that kind of hunting. There are dozens of cartridges that are a whole lot better, so what is there to be gained in using a varmint cartridge for big game hunting? I firmly believe that any hunter who can lay claim to being called a sportsman owes it to the game he hunts to make every effort to kill it quickly and humanely, with the least chance of wounding or loss. I do not feel he is justified in using any cartridge for hunting big game just to prove it can be done.

One last reason for using the .22 caliber varmint cartridges for hunting varmints is economy. Varmint hunters burn more powder than any other shooters except competition target shooters. Whether you buy factory ammunition or load your own, the saving is very real over using larger caliber cartridges. The smaller .22 caliber cases are considerably cheaper than the 6mm's, .25s, or what have you, and the larger .22 hulls are no more expensive. Powder charges are lighter, which means quite a lot at today's powder prices, but the big saving comes in bullets. Any way you cut it, you can shoot a lot more for the same cost.

How to Use Charts and Load Tables

Before the reader uses the load tables that follow, either for reference or for actual loading, a few words of explanation, caution, and advice are in order. Reloaders in general are inclined to pick up a reloading manual and turn to the load data section without ever reading anything about how to use the loads listed therein. Not only that, it seems to be normal procedure to start with a maximum load instead of a milder load and work up to it. It seems very difficult to impress most reloaders with the fact that every rifle is an individual, and that what proves to be a maximum load in one may be quite mild in another, or vice versa. And of equal importance, any change in components may change pressure a great deal. It is hoped that readers will take careful note of what is said in the next few pages and apply it in using the loads listed here as well as those from any reloading manual.

First, an explanation of the term *maximum* as it is used here: when we refer to a maximum load we do not mean a load that develops all the pressure the case will stand without blowing, or locking the action; what we mean is a load that has been carefully checked in the test rifle and found to give trouble-free, safe performance for hunting use. Bolt lift in the test rifle was free in all instances and primer pockets did not expand. Case life also proved to be good. However, *this does not mean that the same load will prove safe in your rifle,* or even desirable. Any load listed here should be approached from at least 5% below. We use the 5% load reduction rather than listing starting loads because it is simpler and of equal value. Starting loads with attendant velocities could be given, but the velocity of that load might vary so much in other rifles as to be of little value.

All the loads listed in the charts are near maximum for the test rifle used unless otherwise stated. They were arrived at by increasing the charge until excessive pressure signs appeared, then backed off enough to give trouble-free hunting performance. They are not necessarily intended for use in other rifles or with other components, but are given more to show what kind of load and velocity can be expected from similar rifles and components.

As for the use of components other than those listed, any change may make a good deal of difference in pressure and/or velocity, and a change in the combination of components can and usually does increase that variation.

Do not have more than one can of powder, one box of bullets, and one box of primers in the work area of the loading bench while loading ammunition. This will avert the possibility of using the wrong powder, the wrong bullet, or the wrong primer.

Starting with the case, a slight difference in case weight affects capacity but little, but brands that are considerably heavier than others can and do cause some pressure/velocity change. Changing makes and types of primers also causes velocity to go up or down to some extent. All bullets of the same weight and caliber are not exactly alike either, and will cause more variation in velocity and pressure. But by far the greatest source of velocity/pressure variation is with various lots of the same powder number. I have chronographed different lots of the same powder that showed as much as 100 fps difference with all other components being identical. It is obvious what can happen if it was changed in the wrong direction.

Neither has the accuracy of the loads been listed, because the same powder and charge, or the same bullet style, weight, and make, that proved exceptionally accurate in the test rifle may be sour in another.

For these reasons as well for as several others, the powder charges shown here often will not coincide with those given in the various reloading manuals, and neither will the velocities that go with them. Perhaps the rifles used were of even more importance than was the difference of the components used in testing in the various manuals and those used by me. Some manuals were compiled from results taken from pressure barrels that were mostly of 26″ length, whereas sporting rifles chambered for the same cartridges have 22″ and 24″ tubes. This, of course, sometimes makes considerable velocity difference, but of even more importance is the chambering, and possibly the bore diameter, of these test pressure barrels.

These test barrels are normally held to minimum allowable dimensions in chamber size as well as bore, while production sporting rifles are chambered to accommodate any cartridge and bullet that is likely to be encountered. The smaller a chamber and/or bore is, the smaller the charge of a given powder will be to develop a certain pressure—for example, we'll say 50,000 per square inch (psi). It has often been said that if one barrel takes less powder to attain a certain pressure, the velocity of that barrel will be equal to another chambered for the same cartridge and using the same components except for the heavier powder charge. My own experience in working with many rifles chambered for the same cartridges by different makers, and sometimes by the same maker, is that the one that takes the largest powder charge will almost always deliver the highest velocity, sometimes by quite a margin.

There is also the fact that many cartridges have at some time been chambered in actions of doubtful strength. Therefore, most reloading manuals hold the loads down below any possibility of pressure problems. Other cartridges are or have been chambered in lever, slide, or autoloading actions that are neither as strong as a good bolt action nor function well with high pressure loads. Some examples of this are the 7×57 Mauser, the .280 Remington, and even the .30-06. Using good, modern, bolt actions, these cartridges and many others will stand more pressure and develop considerably more velocity than most manual loads show, which is all as it should be.

I know of one reloading manual where the loads listed were worked up and checked for pressure in a pressure gun, then fired for velocity in standard sporting arms. Velocities were, of course, far below those expected from the cartridges used, and the charges below those normally used in the same sporting arms.

In working up the loads used in the charts in this book, only the rifles listed were used if not otherwise stated. This does not mean that another identical rifle from the same maker will accept the same load, or that it will give the same velocity if it does, but it will be much nearer than if the chart load had been taken from a pressure barrel.

Again, let me emphasize, *none of the loads listed in this book should be used without starting from at least 5% below and working up gradually!* These loads were all worked up and clocked at about 70°F., which is considered normal; they will show somewhat less pressure at lower temperatures and a bit more at high temperatures, but they were perfectly safe under all normal temperatures found in hunting. If the reloader starts 5% below these charges and works up, he should do so at temperatures of 65°F. or over. *Never* work up to a maximum load at low temperatures, because a load that is very near the maximum allowable working pressure that was developed at 40°F. could give plenty of trouble at 100°F. However, if the load is developed at 90°F. it will be safe at all hunting temperatures, but on the mild side at low temperatures.

The bullet drop figures that are incorporated in the load charts will be found to depart greatly from normal bullet drop tables where bullet drop is given for a rifle sighted at from 100 yards to, say, 300 or 500 yards, or for the mid-range trajectory (distance of bullet above line of bore at mid-range between rifle muzzle and sighting distance). Rather, we give a standard sighting of 1″ high at 100 yards for varmint loads, and 3″ high at 100 yards for big game loads. This sighting is designed to take advantage of the trajectory of the cartridge to give an average of the longest practical sighting range the rifle can be sighted at with no danger of going over the vital area on the smaller species of varmints and big game at the high point of the trajectory curve, which is normally somewhat beyond mid-range.

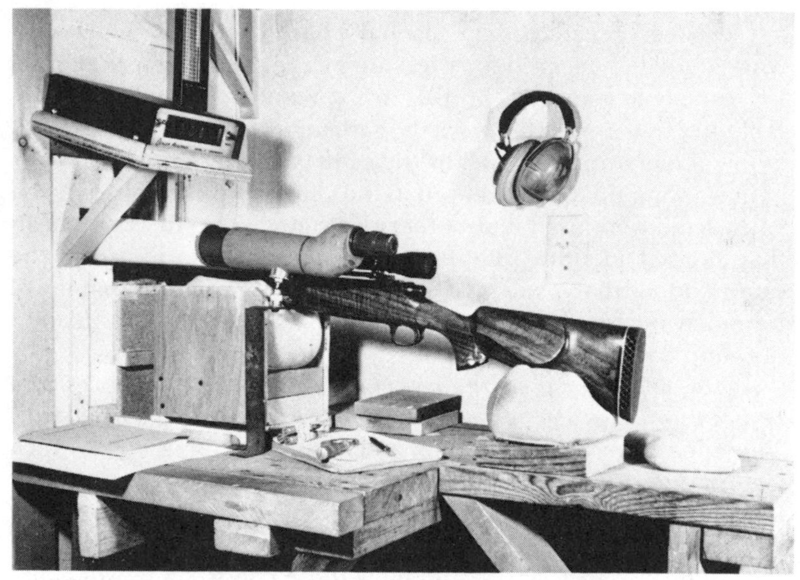

Velocity and accuracy of loads listed in charts were taken from tests made in indoor chronograph room under controlled conditions.

The drop figures used were not necessarily taken from the specific bullet used in the powder charge/velocity end of the chart, but mostly from an average of bullets of the same weight and shape. In many instances there will be many points' variation in the ballistic coefficient between different makes of bullets of the same caliber, weight, and shape. It will be noted that all drop figures were held to the nearest even inch except in some instances at the 200 yard range where a full inch would cause the drop at longer ranges to be out of perspective. As far as hunting is concerned, especially big game hunting, this is of little consequence. While these figures were calculated by the use of the drop of bullets having a ballistic coefficient that averaged out for a bullet of that weight and shape, we do not say they will be completely correct for all bullets or all atmospheric conditions and altitudes. Many of the figures were checked out by actual shooting at the various ranges at altitudes of 4,000 to 5,000 feet, and were very close in all cases. In fact, in most instances, actual bullet drop proved to be just slightly less than those given.

The best advice I can give any varmint or big game hunter is to take his rifle and the load he will use, which will include the *same bullet used to hunt with,* and check out the actual drop at various ranges out to 400 yards if he thinks he may shoot at game that far away. But when he does that he must remember that if he wants to know where the bullet will land at those ranges, the rifle will have to be sighted *exactly 1″* or *3″* high at exactly 100 yards, and with all ranges thereafter measured off and not guessed at. Also, enough shots must be fired at each range to establish an accurate point of impact according to the accuracy of the load.

No effective range has been given for any varmint load, because the size and shape of varmints vary too much to make hard figures of any value whatever. A feeding ground squirrel allows no more than 1″ below or above point of aim for a sure kill, but if he stands up the bullet can be 4″ or so above or below the center and still be effective.

The vital hit area on big game has been arrived at by measurement of average mature male animals. It will serve all practical hunting purposes on standing animals where the depth of the body can be seen. The hunter will have to make allowances for smaller animals of the same species.

SUPPLEMENTARY INFORMATION

Norma 205 powder is no longer available and has been replaced by Norma Magnum Rifle Powder (MRP). Burning characteristics are so similar that charges listed for N205 will give velocities and pressures close enough to avoid trouble, but all loads listed for either N205 or MRP should be approached from at least 5% below with either powder.

The spherical powders 748 BR, 760 BR, and 780 BR, all made by Olin (Winchester-Western), were replaced by 748, 760, and 785. Charges are similar but not necessarily the same.

.17 Remington, Remington Model 700 24″ bbl. 1-9 twist
R-P cases weight 94.5 gr.
Remington no. 7 1/2 primers
Temp. 75° F.

BULLET	POWDER	CHARGE	MV fps
25 gr. Hornady HP	BL-C2	23.5	3967
	4320	24.5	4067
	3031	22.5	4019
	H4895	24	4054
	748	24	4000
Remington factory load with 25 gr. PL	—	—	3958

All the above loads were near maximum in test rifle and should be approached from 1.5 gr. below.

ABBREVIATIONS USED IN CHARTS

Rem.—Remington	HP—hollow point	bbl.—barrel
Win.—Winchester	Ptd.—pointed	CCI—Cascade Cartridge Company
R-P—Remington-Peters	BT—boattail	CCI BR—Cascade Cartridge Company Benchrest primers
W-W—Winchester-Western	FB—flat base	CCB—Colorado Custom Bullets
Wby.—Weatherby	PL—Power-Lokt	BC—ballistic coefficient
H—Hodgdon	gr.—grain	
N—Norma	MV—muzzle velocity	
SP—soft point	fps—feet per second	
RP—round point	psi—pounds per square inch	

BULLET IMPACT WHEN SIGHTED 1″ HIGH AT 100 YARDS

100 YARDS	200 YARDS	300 YARDS
+1″	+0.5″	−4″
Bullet drop will be approximately the same for all loads listed.		
+1″	0	−5″ Difference in bullet drop due mostly to poorer ballistic coefficient of Power-Lokt bullet.

.222 Remington, Remington Model 700 Varmint Special 24″ bbl.
R-P cases weight 94 gr.
Remington no. 7 1/2 primers
Temp. 70° F.

BULLET	POWDER	CHARGE	MV FPS
60 gr. Hornady HP	BL-C2	25.5	3146
	H335	25.5	3193
	3031	23.5	3128
55 gr. Nosler SP	BL-C2	26	3266
	H335	26	3292
	H4198	20.5	3090
52 gr. Rem. Bench Rest HP	BL-C2	26	3332
	H335	26	3311
	Rl-7	21	3227
	H4198	21	3212
50 gr. Nosler SP	BL-C2	26.5	3392
	Rl-7	21.5	3353
	H4198	21.5	3326
	H322	23	3288
45 gr. Hornady SP	BL-C2	27	3484
	Rl-7	22	3474
	H4891	22	3350
40 gr. Speer SP	BL-C2	27.5	3587
	Rl-7	22.5	3598
	H4198	22.5	3574
Remington factory load with 50 gr. PL	—	—	3022

All loads were near maximum in test rifle and should be approached from 1–2 gr. below.

BULLET IMPACT WHEN SIGHTED 1″ HIGH AT 100 YARDS		
100 YARDS	200 YARDS	250 YARDS
+1″	−1.5″	−4″
Bullet drop will be similar for all loads.		
+1″	−1.5″	−4″
+1″	−1.5″	−4″
+1″	−2″	−5″
+1″	−1.5″	−4″
+1″	−2″	−5″
+1″	−1.5″	−4″
Approximately same drop.		
+1″	−2″	−5″
+1″	−1.5″	−4″
Approximately same drop.		
+1″	−2″	−5″
+1″	−1.5″	−6″
Bullet drop will be similar for all loads.		
+1″	−3″	−7″

.223 Remington, Remington Model 788 24″ bbl.
R-P cases weight 95 gr.
Remington no. 7 1/2 primers
Temp. 70° F.

BULLET	POWDER	CHARGE	MV FPS
60 gr. Hornady SP	4320	27	3209
	H4895	26.5	3210
	748	28	3307
	3031	25	3202
55 gr. Nosler SP	H335	27.5	3365
	3031	25.5	3311
	748	28.5	3355
	BL-C2	26.5	3320
52 gr. Rem. Bench Rest HP	H335	28	3519
	748	29	3494
	BL-C2	27	3497
50 gr. Sierra SP Ptd.	H335	28.5	3500
	748	29.5	3529
	BL-C2	27.5	3473
	H4198	23	3436
45 gr. Hornady SP	H335	28.5	3605
	748	30	3672
	BL-C2	28	3674
40 gr. Speer SP	H335	29	3800
	748	30.5	3846
	BL-C2	28.5	3832
	H322	26.5	3811
R-P 55 gr. factory load	—	—	3147

These loads were developed for bolt action rifles and were near maximum in the test rifle. They should be approached from 1–2 gr. below. They are not recommended for use in semiautoloading rifles.

BULLET IMPACT WHEN SIGHTED 1″ HIGH AT 100 YARDS

100 YARDS	200 YARDS	250 YARDS
+1″	−1.5″	−3.5″
+1″	−1.5″	−3.5″
+1″	−1.5″	−3″
+1″	−1.5″	−3.5″
+1″	−1.5″	−3.5″
Bullet drop will be similar for all loads.		
+1″	−1.5″	−3″
Bullet drop will be similar for all loads.		
+1″	−1.5″	−3″
Bullet drop will be similar for all loads.		
+1″	−1.5″	−3″
Bullet drop will be similar for all loads.		
+1″	−1.5″	−3.5″
Bullet drop will be similar for all loads.		
+1″	−2″	−4.5″

.22-250 Remington, Remington Model 700 24″ bbl.
R-P cases weight 166 gr.
CCI BR primers
Temp. 70° F.

BULLET	POWDER	CHARGE	MV FPS
70 gr. Speer SP	MRP	41	3317
	H205	39	3322
	IMR4831	40	3353
	N204	39	3378
63 gr. Sierra SP	MRP	42	3466
	4350	40	3465
	760	41	3532
	N203	37	3588
55 gr. Hornady SP	N203	38	3735
	H4895	36	3701
	760	43	3783
	H414	41	3615
52 gr. Winchester HP BT	N203	38	3775
	H4895	36	3799
	760	43	3857
50 gr. Sierra SP	N203	38	3781
	H4895	36	3773
	760	43	3808
45 gr. Speer SP	N203	39	3947
	H4895	38	4087
	748	37	3808

These loads were all near maximum in the test rifle and should be approached from about 2 gr. below.

BULLET IMPACT WHEN SIGHTED 1″ HIGH AT 100 YARDS

100 YARDS	200 YARDS	300 YARDS
+1″	0.0″	−8″
Bullet drop will be similar for all loads.		
+1″	+1″	−4″
+1″	+1″	−4″
+1″	+1″	−3″
+1″	+1″	−3″
+1″	+1″	−4″
+1″	+1″	−4″
+1″	+1″	−4″
+1″	0.0″	−5″
+1″	+1″	−3″
Bullet drop will be similar for all loads.		
+1″	+1″	−4″
Bullet drop will be similar for all loads.		
+1″	+1.5″	−3″
+1″	+1.5″	−3″
+1″	+1″	−4″

.220 Swift Ruger, Model 77 26″ bbl.
W-W cases weight 164 gr.
CCI no. 200 primers
Temp. 70° F.

BULLET	POWDER	CHARGE	MV FPS
70 gr. Speer SP	N205	43	3493
	H4831	44	3465
	4350	41	3476
	N204	41	3431
63 gr. Sierra SP	N205	44	3583
	4350	42	3545
	4064	38	3610
	N203	39	3660
55 gr. Sierra SP	4064	40	3930
	N203	40	3909
	760	45	3958
	H4895	38	3784
52 gr. Speer HP	4064	40	4011
	760	45	4014
	H4895	40	3983
	N203	40	3960
50 gr. Hornady	4064	41	4109
	H4895	40	4006
	3031	38	4000
Win. factory 48 gr. load	—	—	4029

These loads were near maximum in the test rifle and should be approached from 1–2 gr. below. Where Norma 205 is shown, the same charge of Norma MRP that replaced it will give similar pressure and velocity.

BULLET IMPACT WHEN SIGHTED 1″ HIGH AT 100 YARDS		
100 YARDS	200 YARDS	300 YARDS
+1″	0.0″	−7″
Bullet drop will be similar for all loads.		
+1″	+1″	−3″
Bullet drop will be similar for all loads.		
+1″	+1.5″	−3″
+1″	+1.5″	−3″
+1″	+1.5″	−3″
+1″	+1″	−4″
+1″	+1″	−3″
Bullet drop will be similar for all loads.		
+1″	+1.5″	−3″
Bullet drop will be similar for all loads.		
+1″	+1″	−3.5″

3

Varmint/Big Game Cartridges on Varmints

For any cartridge to be classified as a true varmint/big game cartridge it must meet certain criteria that other cartridges do not meet. That is, it must have certain qualities and capabilities that make it ideal for both kinds of shooting under most hunting conditions. As mentioned in chapter 2, there are some very unlikely cartridges used for varmint hunting, and this is also true of cartridges used on big game. I know of one fellow who insists on shooting mule deer with a .222, and another who uses a .25-20 for all big game hunting. I also had some correspondence with a joker who claimed he dearly loved shooting chucks with a .378 Weatherby! None of these cartridges are ideal or even practical for the use they are put to, and they certainly can't be classified as combination varmint/big game cartridges. Also, nearly any big game cartridge can be used for varmint shooting. But, while this makes for ideal practice for shooting the big game rifle during the off-season, few of these cartridges fit snugly into the varmint/big game class.

To completely and successfully fill the combination varmint/big game notch in the cartridge line, a cartridge must be of small bore, probably not more than 6.5mm (.264), to be ideal for a varmint cartridge, while being no smaller than 6mm (.243) to be adequate for the smaller species of big game in the antelope-deer class. To be successful for varmint shooting it must shoot the lighter weight bullets of that caliber at high velocity so that drop is minimized at the longest varmint shooting ranges. And to help its flat shooting capabilities along, bullets must be available that have good long range shape. Those same bullets must also be designed to expand on very small targets that have very little resistance; not only expand, but blow up even after velocity has dropped off at long range.

On the other hand, the same cartridge, when used for big game shooting, will need bullets of heavy weight for the bore to ensure the sectional density required for adequate penetration, on even the smaller species of big game, to reach the vitals from all angles. Those heavy bullets should also have good shape so that when coupled with good sectional density they have the high ballistic coefficient to not only shoot flat on the far side of a wide canyon or sage flat, but also retain a punch when they get there. And while this may seem simple, it is a rather large order. In a straight varmint cartridge like the .22-250, you don't expect it to do anything except be an efficient varmint cartridge. When using a cartridge like the .30-06, you are interested in how well it performs on big game, with no thought whatever of shooting ground squirrels with it.

This lineup covers the commercial cartridges that can be considered ideal combination varmint/big game numbers. Many others are used, but are not really ideal. *From left:* .243 Win.; 6mm Rem.; .240 Wby.; .250-3000; .257 Rem. Roberts; .25-06; .257 Wby.

We have just mentioned the fact that high ballistic coefficient and good sectional density are of great importance in a big game bullet. These terms will be used repeatedly throughout this book, so for those who are not familiar with the meaning, we'll explain in practical terms.

First, it must be understood that a bullet can have very high sectional density while at the same time showing rather poor ballistic coefficient. However, if ballistic coefficient is high, sectional density is usually good. As an example, the Hornady 180 gr. .30 caliber spire point (pointed) bullet has a sectional density of only .271 and a ballistic coefficient of .482, and the Hornady 220 gr. round nose shows a sectional density of .331 and a ballistic coefficient of only .290.

To understand this, let's take a look at sectional density first: Technically, the definition is "the ratio of a bullet's weight in pounds to the square of its diameter in inches." In practical terms, this means the relationship of the bullet's length to its diameter if it were perfectly flat on both ends. That is, if two bullets of the same shape in the same caliber are of two different weights, the heavier bullet will have the higher sectional density.

Ballistic coefficient is not as easy to define in practical terms. Mathematically, it is the ratio of the bullet's weight to the product of the square of its diameter and its form factor. In practical terms that are of interest to the target shooter and the hunter, it is the ability of the bullet to overcome air resistance. To put it another way, if you gave the 220 gr. Hornady round point bullet the same spire point of the 180 gr., it would have a much higher ballistic coefficient than the 180 gr. As an example of how much the point shape influences ballistic coefficient in bullets of the same weight, the Speer 180 gr. spitzer has a ballistic coefficient of .474, while the round nose is only .321.

The higher a bullet's ballistic coefficient, then, the better is its ability to overcome air resistance, and the more it therefore retains of its original velocity and energy at long range, which also means it shoots flatter and delivers more punch out where the game is.

The reason why sectional density is important to the hunter, aside from the fact that it is an important part of ballistic coefficient, is that it is an aid to penetration. One example is that if you have two bullets in the same caliber in solid form that do not expand, and you fire them into the same substance at the same velocity, the one that has the higher sectional density will penetrate deeper. Another way of looking at it, which is even more revealing, is that if a bullet in a large caliber is heavier than one in a smaller caliber, but the smaller caliber bullet has the greatest sectional density, it will give more penetration than the large caliber bullet. Take the 220 gr. .30 caliber bullet with an SD of .331, and the 300 gr. .375 at .305, and the 220 gr. will give the deeper penetration if both strike at the same velocity.

In the case of expanding bullets, it isn't quite that simple, because expansion performance must be *identical* for this to always hold true, and it seldom is. Generally speaking, though, if you load two Nosler bullets of the same shape to the same velocity and fire them into the same medium, the one with the greatest sectional density will give the deeper penetration. We'll dig deeper into the aspect of sectional density and bullet performance later on.

Simmered down, this all comes down to two calibers as being about ideal, and these two are the .243s and the .25s. If this seems like a pretty slim choice, this is a lot more than we had even thirty years ago. Back when I was growing up, and up until the advent of the .243 Winchester and the .244 Remington, the choice in this class of cartridge centered almost entirely around the .25 caliber.

Apparently the old .32-40 got a little play as a varmint/big game cartridge, mostly because it gave outstanding accuracy for that day, but it was far too slow for a varmint cartridge by today's standards, and it did not pack enough wallop to be a good deer cartridge at anything except very close ranges, and even then it was marginal.

Probably the most popular combination cartridges of that day were the two .25-20s, the Single Shot and the Repeater; and the .32-20, from which the .25-20 Repeater (WCF) was formed, was also quite popular. These cartridges were small enough to be reasonably economical for varmint shooting, either in factory form or reloaded, but they were limited as to the effective range, because of high trajectory curves and poor bullet expansion on small animals at anything but close range. Great numbers of deer were killed with them, and even some heavier game, but the great numbers that were wounded and lost were somehow overlooked by those who used them and told tales of their great performance.

The old 6mm Lee Navy cartridge would have made an excellent varmint/big game cartridge if light bullets had been made for it that were well shaped and of the right jacket construction to give the explosive effect necessary for long range shooting of varmint-size game. It was used almost exclusively as a big game cartridge and was not overly successful. At least some of this was due to the bullets used in factory loads. I never used the cartridge because both rifles and ammunition were very scarce by the time I started hunting big game. My father did own a Lee Straight Pull rifle by Winchester, and he told me that if the 112 gr. round nose bullet expanded it did a good job on deer. However, if ranges were on the long side, the bullets usually failed to expand and exited leaving a bullet-size hole—and a 6mm bullet hole is pretty small. It follows that most of those animals ran off, leaving no blood trail to follow, and were seldom recovered.

First Successful Varmint/Big Game Cartridges

Perhaps the first really successful commercial varmint/big game cartridge to come along was the .250-3000 Savage. This Newton-developed cartridge appeared in 1915 and, strangely, we have not improved on it a great deal as a varmint/deer cartridge even today. It had, of course, been preceded by such .25s as the .25-35 Winchester, the .25-36 Marlin, and the .25 Remington, but none of these cartridges had the right bullets for varmint shooting, and they were short in the velocity department for both varmint and big game hunting.

In spite of the fact that around 1920 A. O. Niedner, and probably several others, worked with the .30-06 case necked to .25 caliber as a varmint/big game cartridge, there was not to be another commercial .25 until the wildcat .257 Roberts was adopted by Remington in 1934. As we'll see later, this was to become, and still is, a great cartridge in this class. However, its life was to be rather short, because of the advent of the .243 Winchester and the .244 Remington in 1955. These cartridges in 6mm caliber, especially the .243 and the 6mm Remington that is identical with the .244 Remington that it replaced, emerged as the classic varmint/big game combination cartridges of all time. Whether these cartridges deserve this honor is largely a matter of opinion, so we'll air the pros and cons in covering the points that serve to create a top-flight varmint/big game cartridge.

The give-and-take regarding how these cartridges really fit into the varmint and big game hunting scene also strongly influenced the success of the .243 and .244 cartridges, as least as far as sales went. Winchester apparently felt that the .243 was a big game/varmint cartridge, while Remington took the attitude that the .244 best fit the varmint/big game classification. By this we mean that the folks at W-W felt their new creation was at its best for taking deer-size game, but Remington placed their cartridge in the class of a super long range varmint plinker with big game as a secondary consideration. With Winchester leaning toward the big game angle, they initially brought out factory ammunition loaded with a 100 gr. bullet on the heavy end, and an 80 gr. on the light end. The R-P offering in original factory ammo was with a 90 gr. heavy bullet and a 75 gr. light bullet.

It is doubtful if this alone would have made a great deal of difference in sales appeal to the hunter using either cartridge as a combination number, but another fly dropped into the chowder that did make potential buyers take a second look. And this came about by the fact that the Winchester rifles were rifled with a 1-10 twist, while Remington cut their barrels with a twist of 1 turn for every 12". How much effect this had on stabilizing 100 gr. bullets, or whether the 10 gr. spread between the 90 gr. R-P and the 100 gr. W-W bullet was especially critical in taking deer-size game, is still a moot question, but some gun writers apparently thought it bad and spread the word. These tales ran to the effect that the 90 gr. bullets were entirely inadequate for killing anything but rockchucks, while the 100 gr. was hell on wheels for clobbering deer. To further complicate matters, it was stated that the 1-12 twist would not stabilize pointed 100 gr. bullets, so they could not be used in the .244 caliber Remington rifles. As a result, and whether these stories were founded on fact or not, the sale of .244 cartridges and rifles dropped far behind the .243. I have never tested a .244 rifle with the 1-12 twist thoroughly enough to say that they will completely stabilize 100 gr. pointed bullets at all hunting ranges, but I know fellows who load them regularly in the .244 Rem. M-722 rifles and get good accuracy. In fact, they even use Remington factory ammunition in 6mm Remington caliber with 100 gr. pointed Core-Lokt bullets.

As far as bullet weight is concerned for deer and other game of similar size, difference in performance is due much more to construction than to 5–10 gr. of weight. I have used bullets of many weights and styles for shooting deer and other animals of similar size with the 6mm Remington, but my favorite is the Nosler 95 gr. spitzer bullet.

To pin things down as to the effectiveness of the 6mm's and the .25s as varmint cartridges, there is no doubt that they are very good, but how good depends entirely on the bullet used in them. Let's take the .243 and the 6mm Remington first.

There isn't actually a great deal of difference in performance between the two cartridges, but what there is lies in favor of the 6mm. This is reflected in factory ballistic data and also shows up in handloads held to about the same pressure levels. To satisfy my own curiosity regarding the velocity differential between the two cartridges, if any, I procured a pair of Remington M-700 BDL rifles new from Remington and ran extensive load tests to as nearly the same pressure levels as possible. Both rifles had 22" barrels, which is normal for today's sporters. All cases were from once-fired R-P ammunition. Primers were CCI BR 2 from the same carton, and bullets were from the same boxes for tests in both cartridges. Chronographing was usually done with both rifles with a given bullet weight at the same session. It would be hard to make more-uniform tests unless the same barrel were to be rechambered from one cartridge to the other, and this is not possible with these two cartridges without cutting off and rethreading the rear of the barrel, because of the difference in chamber dimensions.

These carefully executed tests showed that the 6mm Remington will deliver around 100 fps more velocity with most bullet weights than will the .243 Winchester. This isn't an awful lot, and, generally speaking, the .243 will do about anything the 6mm will, but the 6mm will do it a little better.

Varmint Bullets for Varmint/Big Game Cartridges

There are a great many good varmint bullets made in .243 caliber, starting with the 60 gr. and running up to about 85 gr. My personal experience has been that bullets of over 85 gr. generally do not have jackets that are thin enough to be good varmint bullets when ranges start to stretch out. It is even more critical that bullets of

.243 caliber and larger blow up completely at all reasonable hunting ranges than it is with .224 varmint bullets. The heavier the bullet and the larger the caliber, the more danger of a ricochet after striking the ground or passing through a small animal and then striking the ground. It must also be remembered that to be thoroughly effective as a varmint bullet on the smallest varmints, the larger caliber bullets must have the same explosive effect as the .22 caliber. Just because a bullet is large in caliber and heavy in weight does not mean it will kill a chuck quickly unless it expands violently.

I've seen this lack of varmint killing ability illustrated many times on various kinds of varmints. Several years ago I spent a day hunting jackrabbits with a friend using his custom-built .243 and ammunition loaded with 100 gr. big game bullets of a brand I no longer remember. They were handloads and loaded reasonably hot. The first rabbit I shot was at about 125 yards and we were both sitting. At the shot the bunny took off through the sage. I sat there with my mouth open, wondering how in hell I'd managed to miss him. When he came into an opening I was about to speed him on his way with another one, when he made a tight little circle, lay down, kicked a couple of times, and gave up the ghost. I found that the bullet had gone through the lungs broadside and had left about an inch exit hole as it started to expand, but the bullet lacked the explosive effect it takes to kill a jack instantly, as any good varmint bullet does with anything that resembles a solid hit. A dozen or so rabbits later I found that if I shot one either coming or going at ranges out to 150 yards, the bullets met enough resistance to expand sufficiently to disintegrate the far end of the big bunny, but on broadside shots they nearly always ran several yards before piling up.

On another occasion, there were some surplus 160 gr. loads for a .285 OKH to burn up. These were Western Tool & Copper Works cavity point bullets that have long since been discontinued. At least half of the rabbits shot ran some distance before they seemed to realize they'd had it. Some of those bullets failed to expand at all at ranges of under 100 yards, and they were starting at about 2900 fps ahead of 56 gr. of 4350.

This shooting was done in winter, with snow on the ground, no stock on the range, and hills in the background to stop the bouncing slugs. It is not suggested as the way to hunt varmints, but it shows why you should not hunt them with big game bullets regardless of which cartridge you use.

As far as the varmint bullets go in .243 caliber, there are about as many in hollow point form as in soft point. My experience has been that the hollow point design is just as reliable at all varmint shooting ranges as the soft point. I suspect the reason they are more effective and explosive at all ranges than some of the HP bullets in .224 caliber is that the larger bullet diameter allows for a larger diameter cavity while still retaining good form. Another advantage offered by hollow point bullets for calibers from .243 up is that the points are not battered and flattened in the magazine under the recoil of the larger cartridges.

As to the question of what is the best bullet weight for shooting varmint-size animals with .243 caliber bullets, it actually doesn't make as much difference as most hunters believe. It is mostly a matter of which weight gives the tightest groups in your rifle. As regards trajectory and killing ability on varmints up to chucks and even coyotes, there isn't a dime's worth of difference in any of them with similar form factor from 60 gr. to 85–87 gr. I know this statement will raise some eyebrows, but any good ballistic chart will bear this out. I know that many writers have for years told us how the heavier bullets in any given caliber with a given cartridge soon outdistance the light bullet in the same cartridge because of the better ballistic coefficient. This would be completely true if they were started at the same velocity, but, having an equal form factor, the lighter bullet can be driven at enough higher velocity that the heavy one never catches up within reasonable varmint hunting ranges, which we'll stretch out to a full 500 yards! Fact is, if you want to get technical, the Sierra 85 gr. HP pointed boattail bullet that has a ballistic coefficient of .401, when started at 3300 fps in a 6mm rifle, does not catch up with the 60 gr. Sierra HP pointed bullet started at 3700 fps that has a ballistic coefficient of only .270, even at 600 yards; it still drops a total of nearly 3″ more than the lighter bullet at that range! And there are damn few jackrabbits and chucks shot at an honest 600 yards.

These two bullets can be started somewhat faster than the velocities mentioned in either a .243 or a 6mm, but bullet drop difference between the two weights will remain quite constant. The same situation, varied only slightly, will apply to the other varmint weight .243 bullets that fall between these two weights: the 70, 75, and 80 gr. bullets, provided they all have similar form factor and are loaded with the best powders to the full velocity potential of the bullet weight. This same situation applies to the .25 caliber and, in fact, right on up the line, provided bullet weight is kept within reasonable limits.

And this isn't all of the tale. There are many varmint hunters who swear by the .243 and .25 cartridges, and even the 6.5s and the .270, for long range varmint shooting. They tell you that the heavier bullets in varmint weights will far outrange the .224 bullets because they retain velocity so much better that they soon catch up and pass the smaller, lighter bullets to shoot flatter at long range. This might prove true at ranges of half a mile or more, but how many chucks are shot at that range? The truth is that the very efficient 85 gr. pointed BT Sierra bullet has a total drop of nearly 8″ more at 500 yards when started at 3300 fps than does the 55 gr. spitzer .224 bullet that is started at 3800 fps. True, the 6mm 85 gr. bullet packs a lot more wallop at that range than does the 55 gr., but for an animal the size of a chuck or John bunny, energy isn't very important—explosive effect is what counts, and the .224 bullet has about as much of that as the larger bullets, often more.

If there is a wind blowing, the story is somewhat different. Started at 3300 fps, the 85 gr. .243 BT bullet is deflected about 38″ by a 20 mph wind blowing at a 90° angle to the line of fire at 500 yards. The 55 gr. .22 bullet is drifted around 10″ more to about 48″ under the same conditions. But at more realistic varmint shooting ranges, the 300 yard drift of the 55 gr. .22 bullet is not quite 3″ greater than that of the 85 gr. 6mm. However, no matter how you cut it, the advantage lies with the 6mm, .25s, and even larger calibers, when shooting varmints in windy country. At 200 yards, which takes in about 90% of the varmint shooting, there is only slightly over 1″ less drift with the 85 gr. 6mm than with the 55 gr. .224 bullet.

As regards the effectiveness of various weights of .243 varmint bullets on varmints of all sizes, there is one disadvantage found with the 60 gr. bullet, and that is that not every rifle will shoot it with the same accuracy that it will give somewhat heavier bullets. Also, I suspect that even though it proves to give sufficient accuracy in your rifle on the 100 yard target, it may not do very well out at 400 yards or so. I have never used it at over about 250 yards, and it performed very well at that range from rifles that shot it well.

One of the best 6mm bullets I have ever used for varmint shooting in the 6mm caliber rifles, from the .243 Winchester to the .240 Weatherby, is the 75 gr. Hornady HP. This bullet has good ballistic coefficient and is highly explosive at all reasonable ranges on the smallest varmints at velocities delivered by cartridges from the .243 Win. up. The various 70 gr. bullets in both HP and SP form are also fine varmint bullets. And an equally effective bullet is the Remington Power-Lokt 80 gr. with its shallow cavity point. This bullet is very accurate in most rifles and is highly explosive. I have had lots of R-P factory ammunition loaded with this bullet, which gave a level of accuracy that I was hard pressed to duplicate with my best handloads. If I had to use factory ammunition in either the .243 Win. or the 6mm Rem., this is the load I would select for varmint shooting.

It has always seemed to me that in using varmint bullets of 80–87 gr. in .243 caliber, they were more effective in the .240 Weatherby or some similarly potent wildcat than in the smaller cases. The extra 150 fps or so that the .240 Weatherby will push its bullets over the 6mm Remington, with barrels of the same length, makes it better suited to the heavier weight varmint bullets.

Most of the things we've said about the varmint weight bullets in .243 caliber also fit the varmint bullets made in .25 caliber. One disadvantage where the .25 is concerned as a varmint cartridge, regardless of case capacity and consequent velocity, is that there are fewer weights and styles than in .243 caliber. I have never received overly good accuracy with 60 gr. bullets in any rifle I've used them in, certainly not varmint class accuracy. Also, the ballistic coefficient of the 60 gr. .25 is pretty sad. There are 70, 75, and 87 gr., and Sierra makes an excellent 90 gr. HP BT bullet in .25 caliber. This variety is really quite enough, but some of these are made only by one company, which can be somewhat of a disadvantage if your rifle will not give varmint accuracy with that brand in that particular weight. As an example, only Nosler makes a 70 gr. in their excellent HP solid base bullet, and Sierra makes the only 90 gr. offering in their HP BT varmint bullet. These bullets both give top-flight varmint performance, but they may or may not give the best accuracy in every rifle. It is also wise to check out results of explosive effect on small varmints at long range with 87 gr. bullets before loading very many at one time, especially in the smaller cartridges like the .250-3000, because the 87 gr. bullet was always considered a deer bullet for that cartridge and some brands are not designed with explosive effect in mind.

As far as drop is concerned between the .243 and .25 caliber varmint bullets of the same weight, the .243 has a slight advantage if weight, form factor, and velocity are the same, due to the better ballistic coefficient of the smaller diameter .243 bullet. However, if the cartridge case has the same powder capacity, as with the 6mm Remington and the .257 Remington Roberts, bullets of the same weight can be driven at higher velocity in the larger .25 caliber. This will just about offset any advantage of sectional density and ballistic coefficient offered by the smaller caliber, and drop will be almost identical—close enough that the same sighting will let you use the same hold with both cartridges at all practical ranges.

While this fits the .257 Roberts as a varmint cartridge, it does not fit either the .250 Savage or the .25-06 Remington. My own testing with the two cartridges shows that with a good bolt action rifle the .250 will start the 75 gr. Hornady at around 3400 fps from the M-77 Ruger with a 22″ barrel with full-throttle loads and the best powders. The .257 Roberts fired in the same model rifle, with the same 22″ barrel, gave the same bullet over 3650 fps with the best powders. However, the spread isn't that great with most powders, but more like 100–150 fps. Even then, the .257 does hold advantages both in ease of hitting and in effectiveness at the longer varmint ranges.

One thing that must be remembered is that these .250-3000 loads were developed in a strong, modern bolt action. They will not blow the action of the Savage Model 99 lever action if fired in a new case, but lever drop will probably be decidedly sticky. If the same load is fired more than once or twice in the same case, a complete head separation is inevitable.

The reason for this is that this type of lever action is locked at the rear of the bolt instead of at the front like a bolt action. This allows the bolt to compress a very small amount, and the receiver may also stretch a little under high pressure loads. This lets the case stretch between head and shoulder. To rechamber the case, the shoulder must be set back in full length resizing; in fact, the case must fit quite loosely in the chamber, because the lever action does not have the camming power for either chambering or extracting that the bolt action has. The next time the case is fired, it lengthens again and a stretch ring or groove starts to appear just forward of the solid head portion on the inside of the case. This ring grows each time the case is fired and resized, and the case soon cracks and separates so only the head portion is extracted—which can leave you in one hell of a predicament out in the brush. . . .

If you use the conventional rear end bolt lockup lever action for the .250-3000 or any other cartridge, the .243 and the .308 Win. included, you'll have to load accordingly if you don't want trouble with head separations. What this means is that your velocity will be lower, bullet effectiveness less, and drop greater than with most loads listed for the cartridges. Even when taking loads from any loading manual you'd better check this angle if you don't want problems.

Going the other way in the line of .25 caliber cartridges, the .25-06 compares quite closely with the performance of the .240 Weatherby as a varmint cartridge. There is very little difference in the velocity delivered to bullets of the same weight by either cartridge. Therefore, bullet form and structure being similar, results are almost identical. Probably the biggest, most noticeable difference to the average varmint hunter will be in the recoil department. Here the .25-06 kicks a bit harder, but this is mostly with the heaviest bullets that are heavier for the .25 than for the .243 caliber.

For those who must have the most in velocity and what they expect to be greatly increased range in a varmint/big game cartridge in .25 caliber, the .257 Weatherby is the only answer in a commercial cartridge. This cartridge will boost the 75 gr. bullets along at 3900 fps and the 87–90 gr. bullets at well over 3700 fps. These bullets, of course, have a very flat trajectory over the longest varmint ranges, and carry the explosive effect so necessary for varmint shooting to farther than you are likely to hit them. As with the .224 and .243 cartridges, and the smaller .25s, there is little difference in drop with the various varmint bullets of 75–90 gr. And this means that if you sight 1″ high at 100 yards, the bullet will be about on the nose at 225 yards, only about 3″ low at 300, and down about a foot at 400 yards! This is, of course, with well-shaped varmint bullets.

Regardless of this long range hitting and killing ability, I can't see the .257 Weatherby as a varmint cartridge. It is expensive to shoot in the quantities a varmint hunter burns, it sets back pretty hard on the rear end, which is not conducive to long range varmint hits, and it makes a lot of noise and kicks up a lot of muzzle blast. Further, the barrel heats very fast, and, if you shoot it in long strings, as is often done in varmint shooting, you are very likely to burn the throat out in a couple of varmint shooting sessions. Frankly, few sporters chambered for the cartridge have the kind of accuracy it takes to consistently hit chucks at 500 yards, or even 400. Last, but not least, it shoots no flatter at these ranges than a .220 Swift, and may or may not kill varmint-size animals any better, depending on bullet action. It does hold a definite advantage in windy country, but I question whether this offsets the disadvantages.

What applies to the .257 Weatherby also applies to the .264 Winchester with varmint weight bullets. A choice as good as either in a cartridge that is definitely a big game cartridge but boasts some varmint weight bullets is the .270 Winchester. There are 90, 100, and 110 gr. bullets made in that caliber that are very effective. These bullets buck the breeze very well and shoot about as flat as the varmint weight bullets in the 6mm Remington. However, the .270 certainly holds no advantage over the 6mm's as a varmint cartridge.

Sighting and Effectiveness of Varmint Bullets in .243 and .25 Cartridges

To get back to the two calibers that we feel are the two true varmint/big game combination cartridges, the .243s and .25s, and to sum up a little on the varmint shooting end, probably the best sighting for small varmints—ground squirrels, crows, chucks, and jackrabbits—is 1″ high at 100 yards. Some varmint hunters sight 1 1/2″ up at that range, but, considering target size, this sighting will cause many misses at around 150 yards, which is usually about average range in most areas. With the 1″ high sighting with most varmint bullets fired from a .243 Win., a 6mm Rem., or a .257 Roberts, zero will be right on at 200 yards and down about 6″ at 300. At 400 yards you'll have to hold nearly a foot and a half over, a bit too much for consistent hits. With the same 1″-plus sighting at 100 yards, the .250-3000 and the 6mm International, a popular wildcat on the same case, the bullet will be on at around 180 yards, and down about 8″ at the 300 yard mark. This drop for the .250 Savage would be for full power loads in a good bolt action rifle, but somewhat more for lever action loads.

If the same sighting is used for the .240 Weatherby and the .25-06, most varmint bullets will be about on at 220 yards, down about 5″ at 300, and near 16″ at 400 yards. These figures are only average, and the specific bullet used, the exact velocity your load develops, atmospheric conditions, and elevations will all serve to change actual bullet drop. However, the main point that is brought home here is that the larger cartridges do not provide a great deal of advantage in range on varmints.

As the drop figures indicate, the larger calibers hold no advantage whatever over the .22 calibers in what we might term the magnum class as far as long range hits are concerned. They do drift less in a stiff breeze, which does make hitting easier where wind is a problem. They also have the advantage of showing where the heavier bullets land at long range, so that a miss can be corrected by adjusting your hold by the spurt of dust. But this is useful only on targets that stay in one place, like prairie dogs and chucks; it is of little help on targets that continually move around or perch on a limb.

On the debit side, the larger caliber cartridges make more noise, have more muzzle blast, and kick harder. They are also a good deal more expensive to shoot in the quantities used by varmint hunters. If you intend to use varmint bullets to shoot fur-bearing animals like foxes and coyotes, there is no way to eliminate tearing a large exit hole in the hide. Some big game bullets will do less damage, but you can't depend on it. As with the .224s, solid bullets are likely to expand at ranges where velocity is still high and leave a large exit hole, and if they don't expand there is little killing effect and no blood trail, so many hides will be lost entirely.

It follows, then, that the big advantage in this class of cartridge lies not in its desirability as a straight varmint round but in its ability to handle both varmint- and deer-size game effectively. For the fellow who feels he cannot afford to own more than one rifle but wishes to shoot it a lot both on varmints and on the smaller big game, these cartridges are indeed a good choice. We've looked at them from the varmint shooting angle, so let's see how they stack up as big game cartridges.

.243 Winchester, Remington Model 700 22″ bbl.
R-P cases weight 176 gr.
CCI Benchrest primers
Temp. 70° F.

BULLET	POWDER	CHARGE	MV FPS
100 gr. R-P factory load	—	—	2831
105 gr. Speer SP Ptd.	H4831	46	2941
	N205	46	3000
	IMR4831	45	2998
	4350	44	2991
100 gr. Sierra Ptd.	H4831	46	2976
	N205	45	3080
	4350	44	3011
95 gr. Nosler Ptd.	H4831	47	3059
	N205	47	3180
	4350	45	3121
85 gr. Sierra HP BT	N205	47	3287
	4350	47	3295
	760	46	3295
	4320	40	3200
75 gr. Hornady HP	N205	49	3447
	4350	47.5	3387
	4320	42	3341
80 gr. R-P factory load	—	—	3037

These loads were near maximum in the test rifle and should be approached from 2 gr. below. Where Norma 205 is shown, the same charge of Norma MRP that replaced it will give similar velocity.

See pp. 44–45 for note with supplementary information, and for explanation of abbreviations used in charts.

BULLET DROP SIGHTED 3″ HIGH AT 100 YARDS FOR BIG GAME SHOOTING

100 YARDS	200 YARDS	300 YARDS	400 YARDS	VITAL HIT WITH CENTER HOLD
+3″	+2.5	−5″	−17″	Antelope 300 yards Deer 320 yards
+3″	+4″	−2″	−12″	Antelope 310 yards Deer 325 yards
All loads similar drop.				
+3″	+3.5″	−2″	−12″	Roughly same as above
+3″	+3.5″	−1″	−11″	
+3″	+3.5″	−2″	−12″	
+3″	+3.5″	−2″	−12″	Roughly same as above
+3″	+3.5″	−1″	−10″	
+3″	+3.5″	−2″	−11″	Antelope 325 yards Deer 340 yards
Bullet drop sighted 1″ high for varmint shooting.				
+1″	−0.5″	−4″		
+1″	−0.5″	−4″		
+1″	−0.5″	−4″		
+1″	−1″	−5″		
+1″	−0.5″	−4″		
+1″	−0.5″	−4″		
+1″	−1″	−5″		
+1″	−2″	−8″		

6mm Remington, Remington Model 700 22″ bbl.
R-P cases weight 183 gr.
CCI Benchrest primers
Temp. 70° F.

BULLET	POWDER	CHARGE	MV FPS
100 gr. R-P factory load	—	—	3089
105 gr. Speer Ptd.	H4831	47	3038
	N205	47	3098
	IMR4831	47	3093
	4350	46	3085
100 gr. Sierra Ptd.	H4831	47	3034
	N205	47	3146
	IMR4831	47	3120
	4350	46	3131
95 gr. Nosler	H4831	49	3192
	N205	48.5	3240
	4350	47	3235
	H450	49	3207
85 gr. Sierra HP BT	N205	49.5	3420
	4350	48	3380
	760	48	3457
	4320	42.5	3387
75 gr. Hornady HP	N205	51	3593
	4320	45	3584
	4350	49	3478
90 gr. R-P factory load	—	—	3027

These loads were near maximum in the test rifle and should be approached from 2 gr. below.

BULLET DROP SIGHTED 3″ HIGH AT 100 YARDS FOR BIG GAME SHOOTING

100 YARDS	200 YARDS	300 YARDS	400 YARDS	VITAL HIT WITH CENTER HOLD
+3″	+4″	−2″	−12″	Antelope 310 yards Deer 325 yards Approximate for all loads
+3″	+4″″	−2″	−11″	
All loads similar drop.				
+3″	+4″	−2″	−11″	Antelope 310, deer 325 yards
+3″	+4″	−1″	−10″	
+3″	+4″	−1″	−10″	
+3″	+4″	−1″	−10″	
+3″	+4″	−2″	−9″	Antelope 325 yards Deer 340 yards Same all loads
Bullet drop sighted 1″ high at 100 yards for varmint shooting.				
+1″	+1″	−3″		
Bullet drop will be similar for all loads.				
+1″	+0.5″	−4″		
+1″	+0.5″	−4″		
+1″	0.0″	−5″		
+1″	−1.5″	−7″		

Where Norma 205 is shown, the same charge of Norma MRP that replaced it will give similar velocity.

.240 Weatherby Mark V 24″ bbl.
Weatherby cases weight 181 gr.
Norma no. 210 primers
Temp. 70° F.

BULLET	POWDER	CHARGE	MV FPS
105 gr. Speer SP	H4831	54	3262
	N205	54	3241
100 gr. Hornady	H4831	55	3377
	N205	55	3354
	780 BR	56	3354
95 gr. Nosler SP	H4831	55	3400
	N205	55	3382
	4350	51	3277
80 gr. Rem. PL	N205	58	3676
	4350	54	3556
70 gr. Hornady	N205	60	3900
	4350	57	3834

These loads were near maximum in the test rifle and should be approached from 2 gr. below. Where Norma 205 is shown, the same charge of Norma MRP that replaced it will give similar velocity.

BULLET DROP SIGHTED 3″ HIGH AT 100 YARDS FOR BIG GAME SHOOTING				
100 YARDS	200 YARDS	300 YARDS	400 YARDS	VITAL HIT WITH CENTER HOLD
+3″	+4.5″	+1″	−7″	Antelope 350 yards
+3″	+4.5″	+1″	−7″	Deer 375 yards
+3″	+4.5″	+1″	−7″	Antelope 350 yards
All loads similar drop.				Deer 375 yards
+3″	+4.5″	+1″	−7″	Antelope 350 yards
+3″	+4.5″	+1″	−7″	Deer 375 yards
+3″	+4″	0.0″	−8″	Same
				Antelope 350 yards
Bullet drop sighted 1″ high at 100 yards for varmint shooting.				Deer 375 yards
+1″	+1″	−3″		
+1″	+1″	−4″		
+1″	+1″	−3″		
Similar drop.				

.250-3000 Savage, Ruger Model 77 22″ bbl.
W-W cases weight 153 gr.
CCI no. 200 primers
Temp. 70° F.

BULLET	POWDER	CHARGE	MV FPS
120 gr. Hornady HP	N205	42	2803
	4350	39	2706
	4320	35	2797
100 gr. Speer SP	N205	44	3043
	4350	41	2935
	4320	36	2930
	4064	37	2960
87 gr. Speer SP	N205	46	3235
	4320	39	3214
	4064	39	3240
	3031	37	3273
75 gr. Hornady HP	4320	40	3412
	4064	40	3416
	3031	37	3413

These loads were all near maximum in the test rifle and should be approached from 2 gr. below. They were developed for the strong Ruger M–77 bolt action rifle and should be cut by about 3 gr. for use in the Savage M–99 lever action rifle for good case life. Velocity will be 100–125 fps lower.

BULLET DROP SIGHTED 3" HIGH AT 100 YARDS FOR BIG GAME SHOOTING

100 YARDS	200 YARDS	300 YARDS	400 YARDS	VITAL HIT WITH CENTER HOLD
+3"	+3.5"	−6"	−17"	Antelope 250
+3"	+3.5"	−7"	−19"	yards
+3"	+3.5"	−6"	−17"	Deer 275 yards
+3"	+4"	−4"	−15"	Antelope 250
+3"	+4"	−4"	−16"	yards
+3"	+4"	−4"	−16"	Deer 275 yards
+3"	+4"	−4"	−16"	
+3"	+4"	−3"	−13"	Antelope 300
				yards
				Deer 325 yards

Bullet drop sighted 1" high at 100 yards for varmint shooting.

+1"	−1"	−5"

All loads similar drop.

Where Norma 205 is shown, the same charge of Norma MRP will give similar pressure and velocity.

.25-06 Remington, Remington Model 700 24″ bbl.
R-P cases weight 202 gr.
CCI no. 200 primers
Temp. 70° F.

BULLET	POWDER	CHARGE	MV FPS
120 gr. Speer SP	H4831	54	3190
	N205	54	3184
	4350	52	3175
115 gr. Nosler SP	H4831	56	3294
	N205	56	3315
	4350	53	3225
100 gr. Speer SP	H4831	57	3382
	N205	57	3395
	4350	55	3325
87 gr. Speer SP	H4831	59	3587
	4350	56	3543
	H4895	47	3428
75 gr. Hornady HP	4350	57	3665
	H4895	50	3639

These loads were all near maximum in the test rifle and should be approached from 3 gr. below. Where Norma 205 is shown, the same charge of Norma MRP that replaced it will give similar velocity.

BULLET DROP SIGHTED 3″ HIGH AT 100 YARDS FOR BIG GAME SHOOTING

100 YARDS	200 YARDS	300 YARDS	400 YARDS	VITAL HIT WITH CENTER HOLD
+3″	+4.5	+1″	−8″	Antelope 350 yards Deer 375 yards All loads with 100–120 gr. bullet
All loads similar drop.				
+3″	+4.5″	+1″	−7″	
+3″	+4.5″	+1″	−7″	
+3″	+4.5″	+1″	−8″	
+3″	+4.5″	+1″	−7″	
All loads similar drop.				
Bullet drop sighted 1″ high at 100 yards for varmint shooting.				
+1″	+1″	−3″	−13″	
+1″	+1″	−3″	−13″	
+1″	0.0″	−4″	−16″	
+1″	0.0″	−4″	−16″	

4

Varmint/Big Game Cartridges on Big Game

Perhaps the most important point for the hunter to consider in using one of the varmint/big game combination cartridges for hunting big game is that there are many bullets designed specifically for varmint shooting. This is true of factory ammunition in nearly all brands and calibers, and the bullet companies produce an even wider range of bullets made for no other purpose. We've just covered these bullets for varmint shooting and explained how they perform on varmint-size game, and why they perform that way, but it seems that these things are often overlooked by many hunters who use these cartridges for both varmint and big game shooting. They seem to think that if a certain bullet gives spectacularly quick, sure kills on a chuck, it will do the same thing on an antelope or a deer.

The truth is that the best advice anyone can give the hunter using any of these cartridges on deer-size game is: *never* use a varmint bullet unless it's an absolute emergency, and then some second thoughts would be in order. I'll be the first to admit that if one of these varmint bullets lands in the ribs of an antelope or a deer, and sometimes on even larger animals, from broadside, it will probably get far enough into the lungs before it blows up completely to tear a fearful hole and cause a very spectacular "drop in his tracks" kill. The action is similar to that of the high velocity .22 cartridges, for the same reason, and usually about as erratic.

The point to consider is that these bullets are made to expand to the point of complete blowup on an animal with as little resistance as a ground squirrel or a sod poodle that is only 2″–3″ in diameter, and if these bullets meet more resistance than the thin rib cage, they are unlikely to get into the vitals. Many animals that appear to be broadside are quartering a good deal one way or the other, and the bullet intended to hit in the center of the lung area will land either too far back and smash into the forward part of the paunch, or too far forward and strike the shoulder. Either way, it meets a lot of resistance, in the latter case probably some heavy bone, and never even gets inside where the vital machinery is. When this happens, and especially if it lands in the shoulder, there will usually be a huge surface wound where the bullet disintegrates, but unless the animal bleeds to death, the chance of recovering it is very small.

There are probably as many shots fired at running deer and antelope as are taken at standing game, and I don't recall ever knowing any hunter who could consistently place his shots in the lung area without now and then slopping one too far forward or too far to the rear. Worse, damn few animals run around you in a circle, continually presenting a broadside shot. Most of them are hell-bent on putting a lot of country between themselves and you, and you see a lot more tails than heads to shoot at. And speaking of heads, I've been told that if you refused to take a shot at anything but the head or neck, it didn't matter too much what kind of bullet you used. While in some instances it may work on some kinds of game, there are a lot of holes in that line of thought, and I've seen a little too much game killed, with everything from the .22 Long Rifle cartridge up, to buy it. On antelope it might work part of the time if you hit the brain end of the head right, or if you center the neck with a varmint bullet, because an antelope is pretty small and has a fragile neck and head. A big buck deer, either muley or whitetail, and especially if he has a rut-swelled neck, is something else. In that case there is more than an even chance that the bullet will never reach the bone, let alone break it. So the buck hits the deck, then gets up and leaves, and that's the last you see of him. If you hit him in the head and don't place it exactly in the brain area, there isn't one chance in five that you'll kill him. But this situation will be covered in more detail later on. For now we are just trying to impress the hunter with the fact that varmint bullets are not suited for shooting any kind of big game under the vast majority of circumstances found in hunting. And this applies not only to the cartridges considered as varmint/big game combination numbers, but to any cartridge in a caliber for which varmint bullets are made, which includes everything up through the .30 caliber.

As far as big game cartridges are concerned, the .243 and .25 cartridges are some of the most controversial, especially the former. I can remember when I was a kid listening to tales of hunting and hunting guns told by old-timers who had hunted everything from plains buffalo and grizzly bears down, and with everything from the old Sharps rifles to those that were ultramodern at that time, and they would argue the pros and cons of the .250-3000 cartridge with its 87 gr. bullets at a reputed 3000 fps. And I can tell you that some of those arguments got pretty hot, and at times it seemed that some of the participants would have liked to prove their point by trying their choice big bore or the pipsqueak .250 Savage on the other fellow to see if it would shut him off.

By the time the .257 Roberts came along, people had kinda been conditioned to the idea of small bore high velocity cartridges and didn't get quite so excited about it one way or the other. For my part, I had killed, and seen killed, a good many deer with the .250 Savage, as well as with the much less potent .25-35. I'd also seen a few run off with pretty solid hits. I wasn't guessing at how solid some of these hits were, because in some instances the deer were tracked down and recovered. Of course, the .25-35 with its flat point 117 gr. bullet that started at only about 2200 fps was not nearly as effective as the .250-3000 with its 87 gr. bullet at 3000 fps. However, some hunters were pretty hard to convince that this was true, because the 87 gr. bullet quite often came apart at that velocity at close range and did not give as much penetration as did the slower traveling 117 gr. The 100 gr., when it was introduced for the .250-3000, normally gave a lot better penetration, partly because it was heavier and partly because it traveled slower, at around 2800 fps. Some bullets in 100 gr. weight were probably also of better jacket construction for big game shooting.

The .257 Roberts didn't boost the factory ballistics of the .250-3000 by so very much, but the cartridge was underloaded by the factories for some reason and could be improved on a great deal with good handloads. Its ability to produce velocities of about 2900 fps with 117–120 gr. bullets made it a better choice for big game than the .250 Savage. It did gain a fair amount of popularity, but did not set any sales records, and when the .243 Winchester and the .244 Remington appeared on the scene, it was immediately swept so far into a back corner that even Remington soon discontinued chambering rifles for it. It has only recently been somewhat revived in the Model 77 Ruger, a good rifle but one that is needlessly heavy for this cartridge.

Bullet Performance on Deer-size Game in .243 Caliber Cartridges

As with many other cartridges, when the .243 and .244 appeared in 1955, a lot of gun writers, and consequently a lot of hunters, got carried away in telling stories about the accomplishments of these 6mm cartridges. Some pretty giddy prose was written about them, and, according to some of the most effluent lines of corral dust, the hunter who used one was equipped to handle anything from mice to moose, with a few Alaskan brown bears thrown in to add a little spice. As it turned out, they are good cartridges, but not nearly that good, and if you use them enough you find that they are, like the .25s, at their best on game no larger than mule deer, black bears, and possibly caribou under the open country hunting conditions in which they are usually hunted.

I've killed a number of deer-size animals with a 6mm Remington, and a few more with the .240 Weatherby, which is just a little more of the same thing, and in nearly all instances performance was good, but I picked my shots pretty carefully, and, more important, I picked the right bullet for the job.

As with any other cartridge, large or small, bullet selection is the secret of success, but picking the right one for the game it is to be used on is not as simple as it sounds. I had never used either the .243 or .244 for big game shooting, but had seen some game killed with them, which is the same thing if you make the same careful observations, until the 6mm Remington replaced the .244. When that happened, I received one of the first Remington M-700 test rifles that had a stubby 20" barrel. Along with the rifle were 100 rounds of the new Remington Core-Lokt 100 gr. ammunition. As this was before I acquired my first chronograph, I don't know what velocity the 20" barrel gave from that first lot of 100 gr. ammunition, but tests with later lots in other rifles indicate that it probably churned up somewhat under 3000 fps instead of the 3190 fps listed in factory velocity data. Be that as it may, the 100 gr. Core-Lokt bullet proved very effective on deer-size game. It not only expanded very well at ranges out to at least 300 yards, which is as far as I ever recall shooting a deer with it, it held together well and retained enough of its initial weight to give adequate penetration for game of that size from any angle.

The 100 gr. pointed Core-Lokt bullets performed so well on mule deer that I decided to use the light little rifle with the same ammunition on an Idaho goat hunt that took place in early December when the goat country was blanketed with snow. Under those conditions there was little chance of running into serious trouble if the little bullets didn't perform as well on goats as they had on deer. Goats are considered to be extremely tough for their size, and very hard to anchor to the spot where they are shot. However, they are not large animals and do not require a great deal of bullet penetration to reach the vitals if any kind of care is taken in placing the shot. And in goat hunting there is usually time to pick your shot well if you know anything about the rather peculiar anatomy of these unique cliff climbers.

My old hunting partner Ben Banks was packing a .300 H&H Magnum, but it was decided that if we were together when he found a goat he wanted, and if conditions were right, he would shoot it with the 6mm Remington. If we were both lucky, it would let us check the action of the 100 gr. Core-Lokt bullets on two billies.

Locating a good billy in a small band on a ridge on the far side of a wide canyon, we finished the stalk just after they dropped over the far side, and when we eased out on top of the rock backbone of the ridge, they were at the bottom, no more than 35 yards almost straight down. In fact, the angle was so steep that Ben had to brace himself against the ledge at his back and shoot literally between his boot toes. The billy was standing quartering away, and the little bullet took him at the edge of the spine and ranged down through the lungs to the off shoulder. He dropped at the shot and slid 50 yards down the hill on the frozen snow. He may have kicked a couple of times, but that was all. This was excellent performance, but, due to the placement near the spine and on through the lungs, it was about what might be expected.

A few days later we got a second chance to see how well the 6mm load performed on goats when I took another billy of about the same size. This billy was 100 yards below me on a steep slope but out of the cliffs. The bullet took him through the lungs from broadside, leaving an exit hole an inch or so in diameter in the hide, and a wound channel in the lung tissue more than twice that size. This billy performed in typical goat fashion. At the shot he showed no sign whatever of having been hit. He just stood and continued to stare at me for a few seconds, then slowly turned around and walked straight down the steep, snow-covered slide for 50 yards. There he stopped and sat down on his fanny like a big dog. It seemed he sat there staring out over the canyon for at least a minute, then he tipped over and died without even a feeble kick.

This is written not to prove that the 6mm cartridges are ideal for hunting Rocky Mountain goats, but to show that they will do quite well even on these tough mountaineers with the right bullets placed in the right spot.

Since that time I have killed a number of deer with the 6mm Remington and the .240 Weatherby, as well as a couple of good-sized black bears. Most of these have been killed with either 100 or 95 gr. Nosler bullets, and results have been even better than with the Core-Lokt R-P factory load. My personal preference is the 95 gr. for all game for which the 6mm caliber is suited, because its pointed form gives it a higher ballistic coefficient than the 100 gr. This, coupled with the fact that it can be loaded to give somewhat higher velocity, gives it a little flatter trajectory for less calculation in putting it where you want it to go at long range. It also retains velocity and energy better at long range, and it is for that kind of shooting that these cartridges are usually chosen in the first place. The only possible reason for choosing the 100 gr. Nosler over the 95 gr. would be for use in timbered areas where ranges are not likely to be overly long. And after using both bullets a good deal under a variety of hunting conditions in and out of the timber, I question if there is any advantage offered by the 100 gr. even then.

Most black bears are killed in the course of hunting other game, especially deer, and with deer cartridges. This one fell to .240 Weatherby Mark V and 95 gr. Nosler with 55/N205 at 3382 fps.

Nearly everyone who makes bullets in .243 caliber makes a good 100 gr. bullet that will do quite well on deer-size game, and some will normally give a bit faster kills with lung shots than the Nosler because they expand to a greater extent and tear up a bit more tissue. If shots must be taken from front or rear angles, or if you insist on using them for heavier game, they will not penetrate as well. As mentioned earlier, there are also some 90 gr. bullets designed with big game in mind, and Nosler also makes an 85 gr. partition jacket bullet. There is little doubt that the 85 gr. Nosler bullet will give deeper penetration than the 90 gr. bullets of other makes, but it is of semi-spitzer form with rather poor ballistic coefficient for long range shooting.

Effectiveness of .25 Caliber Bullets and Cartridges on Big Game

As mentioned earlier, when the 6mm cartridges came along, the .25s took a back seat. For some reason that no one who has ever done much hunting or knows anything whatever about ballistics will ever know, the 6mm's somehow got the reputation of being a lot more potent on big game than the .25s. This is far from true. Whatever advantage there is lies with the .25 caliber, both from the standpoint of bullet diameter and from that of sectional density of the heaviest weight bullets for both calibers. While the .25 shows no advantage over the .243 as far as varmint killing ability goes, this is mostly because whatever extra power it has is wasted, but when it's used for big game shooting it is a different story. Actually, it isn't so much a matter of power, because any difference in the velocity increase with bullets of the same weight in the .25 over the 6mm, from cases of the same powder capacity, is offset by less sectional density. But the fact that much heavier bullets are made for the .25 does make a difference when shooting even deer under all conditions. There are a number of 120 gr. bullets made in .257 diameter that have a sectional density of .260, as compared to .242 for the 100 gr. .243. To further boost the all-around effectiveness of the .25 caliber 120 gr. bullet, in pointed form it has a ballistic coefficient of .410–.450, depending on who makes it, as compared to an average of about .375 for the 100 gr. .243.

As the 117 gr. bullet was the heavyweight bullet used in the .25 caliber cartridges for a number of years, and as the short throats and magazines of most .257 Roberts rifles, along with the very short .250 Savage cartridge, were not suited to long bullets, there are a number of 117 gr. bullets that are made in round nose form. These bullets are a very poor choice for any of the .25s for most hunting situations, because of excessive drop at all longer ranges. A better choice for the .250-3000 would be a good pointed 100 gr. and the 120 gr. pointed bullets for the larger cartridges. There is an exception to the 120 gr. heavy bullet rule, in the form of the

115 gr. Nosler pointed Partition Jacket bullet. This is perhaps the best choice for general big game hunting with all the larger .25 cartridges, and maybe the smaller ones. This bullet has a ballistic coefficient that is nearly identical with the pointed 117 and 120 gr. bullets, and sectional density is only slightly less. With its partition jacket it will give deeper penetration than any other .25 caliber expanding bullet I know of, with the possible exception of the Nosler 117 gr., and it is to be preferred over that bullet for 98% of hunting situations.

While some of the bullets with conventional style jackets will do a reasonably good job on quite heavy game in 120 gr. weight in the .25-06, they are almost certain to come apart at the seams when fired from the .257 Weatherby. For that cartridge, the two heavy Nosler bullets are a near must, especially if ranges are under 250 yards or so. This is particularly true if hunting in timbered areas where the game is likely to be on the run or will be shot at various angles with no chance to wait for a broadside shot. There is also the sad fact that if you use bullets with jacket construction that allows them to come apart, the pieces of that bullet will spray through a very large area to ruin many pounds of good meat. This is a certainty if the bullet finds a shoulder either coming or going.

There is no doubt whatever that the various .25 caliber cartridges from the .257 Roberts up will do a better job on game larger than deer than will the 6mm's when good heavy bullets are used. Even so, they are not exactly ideal for shooting heavier game under any circumstances, and this includes the .25-06, the .257 Weatherby, and all wildcats of .25 caliber. One exception to this would be for caribou hunting, but there are several reasons for this. First, even the largest bull caribou is not as heavy as many mature cow elk; they are not hard to kill, and they are nearly always shot in open areas where shots can be picked on stationary or slowly moving animals. And if the first shot doesn't prove effective, it is next to impossible for the animal to escape without giving the hunter plenty of chances to finish him off.

They will also do a good job on elk and moose in open country if the hunter knows where the bullet should land, has the shooting skill to put it there, and is cool enough to wait for the right opportunity to present itself, and to pass up the shot if it doesn't. But with these animals this is more often impossible than possible, and in spite of what a lot of hunters write and tell you, few of them will pass up an opportunity at a trophy animal. As we'll see later, there are many reasons why a number of other cartridges will do a lot better job on species much larger than deer.

.257 Weatherby Mark V 24" bbl.
Weatherby cases weight 214 gr.
CCI no. 250 primers
Temp. 70° F.

BULLET	POWDER	CHARGE	MV FPS
120 gr. Hornady HP	H870	82	3324
	H4831	70	3332
	MRP	69	3377
	IMR4831	68	3375
115 gr. Nosler SP	MRP	69	3410
	IMR4831	68	3407
100 gr. Sierra FB	H870	85	3615
	H4831	73	3596
	MRP	72	3544
	IMR4831	70	3579
100 gr. factory load	—	—	3467
87 gr. Speer	H4831	74	3721
	MRP	73	3697
	IMR4831	72	3788
	4350	70	3717
87 gr. factory load	—	—	3633
75 gr. Hornady HP	H4831	75	3815
	785	75	3822
	MRP	75	3871
	4350	72	3948

These loads were all near maximum in the test rifle and should be approached from 4 gr. below.

See pp. 44–45 for note with supplementary information, and for explanation of abbreviations used in charts.

BULLET DROP SIGHTED 3″ HIGH AT 100 YARDS FOR BIG GAME SHOOTING

100 YARDS	200 YARDS	300 YARDS	400 YARDS	VITAL HIT WITH CENTER HOLD
+3″	+4.5″	+1	−7″	Antelope 360 yards Deer 385 yards
All loads similar drop.				
+3″	+4.5″	+1″	−7″	Antelope 360 yards Deer 385 yards
+3″	+4.5″	+1″	−7″	
+3″	+5″	+2″	−6″	Antelope 360 yards Deer 385 yards
All loads similar drop.				
+3″	+4″	0.0″	−8″	
Bullet drop sighted 1″ high at 100 yards for varmint shooting.				
+1″	+1.5″	−3″	−13″	
All loads similar drop.				
+1″	0.0″	−5″	−14″	
+1″	+1.5″	−3″	−13″	
+1″	+1.5″	−3″	−13″	
+1″	+1.5″	−3″	−13″	
+1″	+1.5″	−2″	−10″	

.264 Winchester, Winchester Model 70 24″ bbl.
W-W cases weight 246 gr.
Federal no. 215 primers
Temp. 70° F.

BULLET	POWDER	CHARGE	MV FPS
160 gr. Hornady SP RN	H870	74	2947
	H570	69	2931
	H4831	59	2808
140 gr. Nosler	H870	78	3139
	H570	74	3184
	H4831	65	3163
	N205	64	3113
W-W 140 gr. factory load	—	—	3035
125 gr. Nosler	H870	80	3285
	H570	77	3370
	H4831	67	3329
100 gr. Speer HP	H4831	70	3455
	N205	68	3492
	4350	65	3525
Sierra 85 gr. HP	H4831	72	3780
	N205	72	3760
	4350	68	3809

These loads were all near maximum in the test rifle and should be approached from 4 gr. below.

BULLET DROP SIGHTED 3″ HIGH AT 100 YARDS FOR BIG GAME SHOOTING				
100 YARDS	200 YARDS	300 YARDS	400 YARDS	VITAL HIT WITH CENTER HOLD
+3″	+3.5″	−4″	−21″	Antelope 275 yards
+3″	+3.5″	−4″	−21″	Deer 300 yards
+3″	+3″	−5″	−23″	Elk 335 yards Moose 360 yards
+3″	+4.5″	0.0″	−9″	Antelope 350 yards
All loads similar drop.				Deer 375 yards Elk 410 yards Moose 440 yards
+3″	+3.5″	−2″	−11″	Approximately same range as handloads
+3″	+4.5″	+1″	−7″	Antelope 360 yards Deer 385 yards Caribou 400 yards
Bullet drop sighted 1″ high at 100 yards for varmint shooting.				
+1″	+1.5″	−4″	−14″	
All loads similar drop.				
+1″	+1.5″	−3″	−12″	
All loads similar drop.				

.270 Winchester, Sako Finnbear 24″ bbl.
W-W cases weight 190 gr.
CCI no. 200 primers
Temp. 70° F.

BULLET	POWDER	CHARGE	MV FPS
160 gr. Nosler Partition	H4831	58	2877
	N205	56	2910
	4350	54	2889
150 gr. Speer SP Ptd.	H4831	58	2906
	N205	57	2932
	4350	54	2890
130 gr. Hornady SP	H4831	60	3149
	N205	59	3134
	IMR4831	59	3147
	4350	57	3084
100 gr. Speer HP	N205	63	3457
	4350	61	3464
	4064	54	3400

These loads were all near maximum in test rifle and should be approached from 3 gr. below. Where Norma 205 is shown, the same charge of Norma MRP that replaced it will give similar velocity.

BULLET DROP SIGHTED 3″ HIGH AT 100 YARDS FOR BIG GAME SHOOTING				
100 YARDS	200 YARDS	300 YARDS	400 YARDS	VITAL HIT WITH CENTER HOLD
+3″	+4″	−2″	−14″	Antelope 310 yards Deer 335 yards Elk 375 yards Moose 400 yards
All loads similar drop.				
+3″	+4″	−2″	−13″	Same as for 160 gr. Nosler
All loads similar drop.				
+3″	+4.5″	−1″	−10″	Antelope 325 yards Deer 350 yards Elk 400 yards Moose 435 yards
All loads similar drop.				
Bullet drop sighted 1″ high at 100 yards for varmint shooting.				
+1″	0.0″	−5″	−17″	
All loads similar drop.				

.270 Weatherby Mark V 24″ bbl.
Weatherby cases weight 212 gr.
CCI no. 250 primers
Temp. 70° F.

BULLET	POWDER	CHARGE	MV FPS
170 gr. Speer SP RN	H870	80	3010
	H4831	69	2848
	MRP	69	2884
	IMR4831	68	2891
160 gr. Nosler	H870	82	3156
	H4831	71	3140
	MRP	71	3081
	IMR4831	70	3113
150 gr. Sierra BT	H870	83	3208
	MRP	72	3150
	IMR4831	70	3158
	785	72	3153
130 gr. Hornady	H870	85	3342
	IMR4831	72	3304
	MRP	74	3291
	4350	71	3325
Weatherby 130 gr. factory load	—	—	3230

These loads were near maximum in the test rifle and should be approached from 4 gr. below.

BULLET DROP SIGHTED 3″ HIGH AT 100 YARDS FOR BIG GAME SHOOTING

100 YARDS	200 YARDS	300 YARDS	400 YARDS	VITAL HIT WITH CENTER HOLD
+3″	+4″	−3″	−19″	Antelope 275 yards
+3″	+3.5″	−4″	−22″	Deer 300 yards
+3″	+3.5″	−4″	−22″	Elk 330 yards
+3″	+3.5″	−4″	−22″	Moose 360 yards
+3	+4.5″	0.0″	−10″	Antelope 325 yards
All loads similar drop.				Deer 350 yards
				Elk 400 yards
				Moose 435 yards
+3″	+4.5″	0.0″	−8″	Antelope 350 yards
All loads similar drop.				Deer 375 yards
				Elk 425 yards
				Moose 460 yards
+3″	+4″	−1″	−8″	Antelope 350 yards
				Deer 375 yards
				Elk 425 yards
				Moose 460 yards

Slightly more drop than for 130 gr. handloads.

7×57 Mauser, Ruger Model 77 22″ bbl.
W-W cases weight 170 gr.
CCI no. 200 primers
Temp. 70° F.

BULLET	POWDER	CHARGE	MV FPS
175 gr. Speer SP Ptd.	N205	52	2695
	H4831	53	2599
	H450	53	2673
	4350	49	2572
160 gr. Nosler Partition Jacket	N205	54	2832
	4350	52	2816
	N204	52	2814
150 gr. Nosler Partition Jacket	N205	55	2910
	H450	55	2864
	N204	54	2939
	4350	53	2880
139 gr. Hornady	N205	57	3014
	N204	55	2981
	4350	53	2904

These loads were all near maximum in the test rifle and should be approached from 3 gr. below. It will be noted that powder charges are heavier and velocities higher than shown in any of the reloading manuals. The reason is that the manual

BULLET DROP SIGHTED 3″ HIGH AT 100 YARDS FOR BIG GAME SHOOTING

100 YARDS	200 YARDS	300 YARDS	400 YARDS	VITAL HIT WITH CENTER HOLD
+3″ +3″	+3.5″ +3″	−5″ −6″	−20″ −21″	Antelope 290 yards Deer 310 yards Elk 340 yards Moose 370 yards
+3″ All loads similar drop.	+4″	−3″	−16″	Antelope 310 yards Deer 335 yards Elk 360 yards Moose 385 yards
+3″	+4″	−2″	−14″	Approximately the same as for 160 gr.
+3″	+4″	−1″	−12″	Antelope 325 yards Deer 350 yards

loads are held to low pressures for older rifles with actions of doubtful strength, while the Ruger M-77 is a modern, strong action. These loads *should not* be used in any of these old actions of doubtful strength.

.280 Remington, Remington Model 725 22″ bbl.
R-P cases weight 206 gr.
Federal no. 210 primers
Temp. 70° F.

BULLET	POWDER	CHARGE	MV FPS
175 gr. Nosler Partition Jacket	H4831	56	2718
	N205	54	2700
	4350	53	2722
160 gr. Nosler Partition Jacket	H4831	58	2904
	N205	56	2898
	4350	54	2862
139 gr. Hornady SP	H4831	61	3002
	N205	59	3027
	4350	57	3000
130 gr. Speer SP	H4831	63	3151
	N205	61	3207
	4350	59	3156

These loads were near maximum in the test rifle and should be approached from 3 gr. below. Rifles with 24″ barrels will give slightly higher velocities, and some

BULLET DROP SIGHTED 3″ HIGH AT 100 YARDS FOR BIG GAME SHOOTING

100 YARDS	200 YARDS	300 YARDS	400 YARDS	VITAL HIT WITH CENTER HOLD
+3″	+3.5″	−4″	−19″	Antelope 300 yards Deer 325 yards Elk 340 yards Moose 370 yards
All loads similar drop.				
+3″	+4″	−2″	−13″	Antelope 325 yards Deer 350 yards Elk 375 yards Moose 400 yards
All loads similar drop.				
+3″	+4″	−1″	−12″	Antelope 325 yards Deer 350 yards
All loads similar drop.				
+3″	+4.5″	0.0″	−11″	Antelope 335 yards Deer 360 yards

other rifles will give higher velocities at same pressure levels. Same charges of Norma MRP will give pressure and velocity similar to that of N205.

5

Long Range Shooting of Deer-size Game

It will be noted that there was no mention of bullet drop or sighting of the varmint/big game cartridges with big game bullets. Since there are so many other cartridges that are used for shooting deer-size game that have bullets of similar ballistic coefficient and are fired at the same velocity levels, thus giving about the same drop figures for all hunting ranges, it seems wise to cover that point for all these cartridges at one time in this chapter. There are so many other factors of equal importance to be considered in a discussion of long range shooting of animals in this weight class that bullet drop and sighting are only a small part of the overall picture.

Perhaps the term *weight class* isn't completely correct when referring to game that range in weight all the way from an average mature buck antelope at around 100 pounds, up through the various members of the deer family to include big buck muleys that may go well over 300 on the hoof, to mountain goats and sheep, which are just as heavy. And as mentioned in discussing the merits of the 6mm and the .25 cartridges on big game, we might well include the various subspecies of caribou, even though a big mountain or barren ground bull from some areas will probably weigh nearer 500 pounds when summer-fat just prior to the rut. However, while there is a good deal of difference in how well some cartridges and bullets handle these animals at long range, there isn't enough difference in how the rifle should be sighted for hunting them in open flat or mountain country to matter much. The main point is that you don't use a .30-30 for long range shooting, nor do you use a round nose bullet by choice no matter how fast the cartridge will start it.

Of all the animals mentioned, more antelope are killed at long range than any others. And if your rifle is sighted to get the most from the load being used on long range antelope, it will do equally well on the other game as far as certain hits are concerned. What this boils down to is that the rifle should be sighted so that the full potential of the load is realized. To put it another way, it does little good to buy a rifle chambered for one of the hot magnum car-

Antelope like this Wyoming buck require more long range shooting than does any other American game animal. The flattest shooting loads available are highly desirable with bullets designed to expand at the longest practical hunting ranges.

tridges from the .257 Weatherby up through the big .30s, or even a .270 Winchester, for that matter, then sight it dead on at 100 yards and take it out to shoot antelope that may let you approach no nearer than 400 yards.

All cartridges and loads are not going to shoot to the same point of impact with the same sighting even though they fit into the long range cartridge line, so there are some things you'll have to learn about your cartridge and load by experimenting at various ranges if you want to know exactly where the bullet will land. But, like most of the other big game hunters who have hunted a lot of different kinds of game in a lot of different kinds of country, I find that if the long range load is sighted to impact 3″ high at 100 yards, it will give the full potential of most long range cartridges on deer-size game.

Sighting to Bring Out the Full Long Range Potential of the Cartridge

In order to understand why this sighting works best for this kind of shooting, the hunter must first realize that the drop of the bullet and the size of the *vital* area of the animal must be the first consideration in where the rifle is sighted so that the bullet will land within that vital area with the least amount of guesswork and calculation on the part of the hunter. To do this, the rifle should be sighted so that if the hold is on the center of the ribs on a broadside animal, the bullet will land within the vital area at all ranges from the muzzle to where the bullet drops below that area, without ever being out of it on the high side. It is obvious that if it is sighted correctly for antelope it will also work well on larger-bodied game in the deer class, and the 3″ high 100 yard sighting is about as close to the ideal as you can come.

First, let's consider the size of an average antelope buck. What you see when you look at him broadside will measure 15″–16″ for a good-sized buck, with a small buck or doe 2″–3″ less. Remember that this includes hair and some flesh and bone that *are not* within the vital area. Figuring the vital area from the spine to the bottom of the lungs or the heart, the height is only about 11″ for the big

Photo and diagram showing approximate points of impact at various ranges from 100 yards to limit of sure hit range in vital area of mature buck antelope with 160 gr. 7mm pointed bullet starting at 3100 fps with rifle sighted 3″ high at 100 yards.

1: Depth of vital area 10″
2: Depth from hairline to hairline 15″–16″
3: Bullet impact at 350 yards, limit of sure hit range in vital area
4: Point of aim and bullet impact at 300 yards
5: Bullet impact at 100 yards
6: Bullet impact at 200 yards

---

buck. If you hold for the center of what you are looking at, the bullet can hit no more than 5″ or so high, or that much low, and give a clean kill.

To convert the sighting of plus 3″ at 100 yards to sure killing range on the vital area of a buck antelope, let's see where a 7mm magnum will land the 160 gr. pointed bullet of normal ballistic coefficient at various ranges when started at about 3100 fps, which is about a normal full-power handload. That bullet will be around 4″ high at 200 yards, which will be about as far as it will ever get above the line of sight; it will be approximately on the nose at the 300 yard mark, and around 9″ low at 400 yards. Assuming a dead center hold on the buck, the bullet can't drop more than about 5″ and give a sure kill, and it will stay within that limit out to about 350 yards. What this all simmers down to is that you can forget about range and hold halfway up the ribs of that antelope and get a vital hit right out to 350 yards. No guessing, no holdover.

The .264 Winchester with the 140 gr. bullet, the .257 Weatherby with a 120 gr., and the .270 Weatherby with the 150 gr., all in pointed form, will give almost identical results. The .240 Weatherby with 100 gr. bullets, the .25-06 with 120 gr., as well as the .270 Winchester with the 130 gr. and the .30 magnums with 180 gr. bullets, all spitzers and starting at around 3100 fps, will stay within the high impact limit at 200 yards, but will drop below the allowable drop limit at over 320–325 yards, and will be down 10″–12″ at 400 yards.

It will be noted that we have not given drop beyond the 100 yard sighting in exact figures right down to the last 1/10″ or in some cases even to the exact inch. To do so would just be influencing the reader into believing figures that exist only on paper, because too many factors enter into the actual drop of a bullet from any load. Unless you chronograph *your load in your rifle,* you are only guessing at the velocity. Bullets of different brands in the same weight and style vary greatly in ballistic coefficient. Altitude and atmospheric conditions change drop figures even more, so trying to split hairs is meaningless and serves only to confuse the hunter. The load/drop charts give figures that are nearer for most hunting conditions with various bullets at velocities that vary somewhat from those mentioned above.

The vital area–sure hit range can be extended a little in some cartridges by loading a little hotter, or by loading lighter bullets with good ballistic coefficient to higher velocity. An example would be the 140 gr. 7mm bullet loaded to give 3300–3400 fps in most magnum cartridges, or the 150 gr. loaded to around 3400 fps in a big .30. These loads would add nearly 25 yards of sure hitting range on the far end without impacting too high at the 175–200 yard mid-range.

Of course, the hunter who uses factory ammunition will have to remember that the loads he uses are probably giving him something like 100 fps less velocity from his hunting rifle than is listed in factory velocity sheets. The .270 Winchester 130 gr. factory load is listed at 3140 fps, but I have never chronographed a factory load that came nearer than 100 fps of that figure, some a lot less. About the same velocity discrepancy exists between factory-quoted velocity and actual velocity in hunting rifles for the 7mm Remington Magnum and the .300 Winchester Magnum. This difference between quoted and actual velocity in your rifle will not make any meaningful difference in mid-range bullet height, but it will cut the sure vital hit range by at least 25 yards with the 3″ high 100 yard sighting. But in any event, it is still the best way to sight to realize the full range potential of a long range cartridge.

About now someone is sure to ask: why not sight your rifle for 200 or 300 yards and use the drop figures as listed in some factory and reloading manual drop charts? Certainly you can do this and know about where your bullet will land at the various ranges listed on the chart, but that sighting will not always give you the best your cartridge and load has to offer for sure vital hits at the longest possible range while holding dead on the animal. A close look at these charts will show that for most long range cartridges the 200 yard zero will raise the bullet only 1″–2″ above the line of sight at the 100 yard mid-range, and it can stand to go a lot higher than that and still stay well within the vital area of even a small antelope or deer. Some of the flattest shooting cartridges will be just about right with a 300 yard zero, but only a few. The big problem here is that very few hunters have a place where they can sight in for 300 yards. However, if you sight in at 3″ high at 100 yards, which is always available on any range or other area where sighting can be done, you'll know by the velocity of your load and the bullet you use if it will be near zero at 300 yards or some other range.

And while we are on sighting and how to sight at very short

ranges if longer ranges are not available, don't be misled into sighting at 25 yards and thinking your bullet will be right on at some given range, and that you are ready to head for the hills and a shot at a record buck. Sighting at 25 yards will put you fairly close as far as windage adjustment is concerned, but you can't depend on elevation being anywhere near close enough. There are a number of reasons why this won't work, but mostly it is because the bullet that is off 2″ at 200 yards, and 4″ at 400 yards, will be off only 1/4″ on the 25 yard target. Few hunters will try to sight closer than that at 25 yards, and it is damn near impossible to set most hunting scope adjustments that close anyway. It is fine to "rough sight" at 25 yards or so, but finish the job by sighting in *exactly* where you want the bullet to go at 100 yards. (Complete directions for sighting will be found in chapter 12.)

When I started hunting big game there were few really long range cartridges available, and long range bullet designs were about as scarce, so everybody sighted their hunting rifles to zero at 100 yards, and that idea still persists today in the minds of many hunters. Why the 100 yard range was picked is hard to say, but today it is largely a matter of tradition. To dispel this notion, let's take a look at what happens to the 7mm magnum that will land a good long range 150–160 gr. bullet in the vital area of an antelope right out to 350 yards with the 3″ high 100 yard sighting. Zeroed at 100 yards, the bullet will be down nearly 3″ at 200 yards, over 10″ at 300 yards, and more than 2 feet at 400 yards. This translates into a sure hit range of no more than 225 yards, or about 125 yards less than the 3″-plus 100 yard sighting will give!

To be complete, and because what we are considering here in terms of bullet drop and sighting will apply to all cartridges and long range shooting at all game, the round point bullet should also be considered to show why it is not adapted to long range work.

Using the .300 magnums as an example, what happens to the 325 yard vital hit range of the pointed 180 gr. bullet if it is replaced by a round point started at the same 3100 fps and sighted 3″ high at 100 yards? The round nose bullet that is 3″ up at 100 yards will be right on at around 250 yards, and will drop below the vital area of an antelope buck at just over 300 yards. At 400 yards it will be down something like 20″. Sighted to zero at 100 yards, the sure

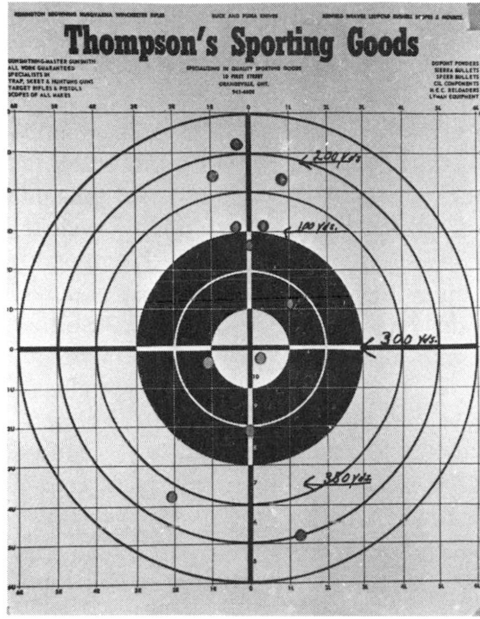

This target shows approximately where bullets will land at ranges out to 350 yards—sure hit range on pronghorn—with 7mm magnum and 160 gr. pointed bullet starting at 3100–3150 fps with center hold. Squares subtend 1″.

hit range would be reduced to just over 200 yards with a center-of-the-ribs hold.

Logically, if you know that you are going to be shooting at big buck mule deer, or trophy-size rams or billy goats, you could sight in so the bullet impacted at least 3 1/2″ high at 100 yards, but you don't always get a broadside shot; and if the mid-range height of the bullet is much over 4″ above point of aim, it can go too high even on a big buck deer if the cross hair isn't placed just right. But even with the same 3″-plus 100 yard sighting, the vital hit range will be increased by a few yards, because the vital area of buck, ram, or billy will run about 14″ deep, which will allow a couple of inches more drop while still giving a clean kill.

The main reason for stretching the sure hit range of the cartridge to the limit is so that the hunter doesn't have to try to estimate the range and where to hold at what should be considered near the long range–game killing ranges for most of us. Very few once-a-year hunters have even the haziest notion whether a buck on the far side of a mountain canyon is 200 yards away or 400. And this also goes for many of those who live in the country and see it every day, as well as over 50% of the guides and outfitters. Regardless of what a lot of both novice and veteran hunters tell you about knocking off bucks at 600 yards on every trip, 300–350 honest yards is long range, for many reasons. If your rifle is sighted so that a flat shooting cartridge will put its bullet in the vital area out to that range without guessing either how far away the buck is or where to hold to put the bullet in the right spot, you'll miss a lot less game and, more important, wound fewer animals.

Using Size of Animal to Judge Hold at Long Range

If for some reason you find you have to shoot at ranges beyond where the bullet will land in the vital area with a center hold, you'll have to know something about the size of the animal you are shooting at to know where to hold to drop it into that area. Remember that we are not talking about vital area now, but the distance from the bottom of the chest to the top of the back, including the hair. As already mentioned, a big buck antelope will measure 15″–16″, hairline to hairline. Deer are usually listed as 18″, but this is in error for either a big buck mule deer or whitetails from some sections. What you see is more likely to be 20″–22″. Most trophy-size rams, with the exception of the desert sheep, will span about the same. Mountain goats vary a great deal, but any trophy billy will push 2 feet top to bottom because of the heavy mane hair. It follows that if you hold on the back line, the bullet can drop half the width of the body and give a center hit. For most deer-size game this means about 10″–11″. With most of the long range cartridges, from the .270 with the pointed 130 gr. up, this means that with the 3″ high 100 yard sighting, a back line hold will land the bullet in the vital area at 375 to 400 yards. At 500 yards the same bullet will drop 30″ or so, which means the reticle will have to be held one body depth or 20″–22″ over a big buck's back to make a hit in the center of the ribs, assuming you have the range pegged right, and that is a bit too complicated for consistent hits even for the best of us, let alone the average hunter.

To further complicate shooting at much over the range where the sighting of the rifle will send the bullet into the vital area of the animal being hunted, there are the times when it is lying down with maybe only half of the total body height showing. It may also be partially concealed by some object. If the range and sighting are such that the bullet will be within 3″–4″ of point of aim, it is a lot more likely to find the vital area than if you start guessing where to hold to slop it into that spot.

Bullet Performance on Light Game at Long Range

While placing the bullet in the right spot at long range may be the most important point, it is by no means all there is to long range shooting even of deer-size game. If the bullet doesn't perform right after it finds the target, you may be a lot worse off than if it had missed. In order for a bullet to do a good job on any big game animal hunted in North America, it has to expand and tear up enough nerves and other vital tissue to ensure a quick kill. But there are times when it must also penetrate a lot of bone and heavy muscle to get inside where the machinery that keeps the animal running is located. Jacket design must be right so expansion starts as soon as the bullet starts to penetrate. This is because if the bullet lands broadside in the rib cage of any of the smaller big game animals, there is little resistance to start expansion, and it should be complete before it penetrates more than halfway to ensure a large wound channel and to destroy enough lung tissue to cause massive internal hemorrhage. On the other hand, if the animal is quartering so that the bullet must penetrate a lot of bone, muscle, or paunch material to get inside, it has to hold together and retain much of its original weight. That is why the thin-skinned explosive varmint bullet won't work for most situations. On the perfect broadside shot it may, but for angle shots it will almost certainly fail.

Using the heavier bullets that are designed for deeper penetration on heavier animals can also create problems in the other direction. Some of these bullets may expand too slowly to create a sufficiently large wound before passing on through the lungs of antelope and deer. They work fine on heavier game, and do well on quartering shots on deer, but may fail on lung shots. This failure of the heavier bullets to expand properly almost never shows up until velocity has dropped off beyond the 300 yard mark, and nearly all of them will expand very well out to nearly 400 yards. This is another good reason for not shooting at big game at much beyond the vital hit range of a rifle sighted to impact 3″ high at 100 yards. Remember that as the muzzle velocity and ballistic coefficient drops, the vital hit range is also reduced, and as that range goes down so does the sure expansion range of the bullet.

This is a product not only of bullet design but of retained velocity. Just as important, and a part of the retained velocity picture, is retained energy at long range. This is where the heavier big game bullets show up over the lighter, faster bullets. They may start out with about the same energy, but by the time they reach 400–500 yards the heavier bullet packs a lot more energy, with bullet form being equal and both loaded to full velocity in the same cartridge.

While I am a strong believer in strong jacket construction for nearly all big game hunting that will give deep penetration when it is needed, these bullets are not a must for long range shooting of deer-size game. Nearly any of the bullets designed for big game and not for varmint shooting will do very well. In fact, the bullets that expand quite rapidly without coming completely apart will normally give more spectacularly quick kills than will controlled expansion types on game of this size. Most of the factory loads do quite well as far as bullet performance is concerned, but the normally lower velocity that good handloads develop does cut the sure hit range somewhat.

It may appear up to this point that only the small bore high velocity numbers from the 6mm's up, along with the larger caliber magnums, are suitable for long range shooting of the smaller big game animals. This, of course, is not correct. Cartridges like the 7×57 Mauser, the .30-06, and the .308 Winchester, to mention a few, will do quite well with the right load, but few if any factory loads can be classed as ideal or even suitable long range loads. This is especially true of the 7×57, which is badly underloaded. The point is that most factory loads do not produce enough velocity to be effective at long range in hunting rifles. You can load these cases with fairly light bullets to full-throttle and make them into reasonably good long range–light game cartridges, but even then they will not produce the results of the faster stepping numbers. Of course, the 7×57 pushing a 140 gr. bullet to nearly 3000 fps from a good handload like 57 gr. of N205, or the .30-06 kicking a 150 gr. a bit faster, will show up quite well and have a vital hit range of nearly 350 yards with the 3″-plus sighting. The .308, even with the 150 gr. loaded to the hilt, will give only about a 300 yard sure hit range with a center hold.

If I've created the impression that I'm conservative in long range shooting of deer-size game, as compared to some writings and advertising, I am. First, few hunters have the ability to judge range accurately, and when they start guesstimating the range and how much to hold over at the same time, they are asking for trouble. Not just the possibility of a miss, but, worse yet, a wounded animal. If the hunter stays within the range where the cartridge will land its bullet within the vital area without holding out of that area, he will eliminate most of the range problem. Even then it may not be as easy as it sounds to land a bullet inside a 12″ square at 325–350 yards from the shooting positions you must usually use in hunting country. If we always remember that any shot that misses is more likely to wound, we won't take so many long-odds chances. Also remember that if you are good enough to hit the vital area, if the range is beyond the efficient performance level of the load, it may also wound the animal. It is better to pass up the shot that you are not sure of than to muff it.

Fallacies of Shooting at Extremely Long Ranges

I've done my share of long range shooting here and there at game of all sizes from antelope to moose, but I consider 400–500 yards to be the limit with the best cartridges, rifles, and scopes under ideal shooting conditions. It seems, however, that all too many hunters feel they have to try to impress others with tales of knocking off rams, billy goats, and pronghorn bucks at 1,000 yards or so, sometimes on the run. They do impress some of us who have been around the hunting country here and there, but they would not feel complimented if they knew the kind of impressions those yarns create. I've even seen a number of testimonials in bullet and ammunition advertising telling about the glory of such feats. Any experienced big game hunter knows that the tale-teller is either plain lying, doesn't have the faintest idea how far 1,000 yards is, or has had one of the great accidents of all time. But the big trouble is that a lot of hunters just starting out will believe it and think they have to duplicate it to make their mark in the hunting world.

If we take a hard look at facts and figures, it immediately becomes obvious how small the chance would be of hitting a ram at that range under hunting conditions with hunting rifles and sights, while shooting from hunting positions. If an average 180 gr. pointed .30 caliber bullet is started at around 3100 fps, it will have a total drop of about 30 feet at 1,000 yards. Sure, your sighting will take care of some of that huge amount, but you will still have to figure out how much that is at that range, and when you find out that the bullet will still land somewhere around 20 feet low, give or take a couple of feet, you'll find it pretty hard to know how much to hold over the ram to drop the bullet into the vital area. This, of course, assuming that the range is an exact 1,000 yards. And even if you dope the bullet drop to the exact inch for 1,000 yards, if you misjudge the range by 25 yards you'll miss.

To complicate a hit even more, a mild 10-mile-per-hour breeze will drift the bullet off more than the full length of the ram if it is at a right angle to the bullet's flight path. And if there is a wind, it may vary a great deal in velocity and direction between you and the ram, and it may not even be blowing in the same direction.

That bullet that started out at 3100 fps will be just trotting along at a bit over 1400 fps when it reaches 1,000 yards, and the 3840 foot-pounds of muzzle energy has lost more than 3000 fp. If the bullet that was designed to expand at velocities of no less than 2200 fps—and probably not with any certainty even then—expands at all, it will have to hit a very large bone, and even if it does it is extremely doubtful that it will upset enough to do any damage.

Another point that is often overlooked is time of flight. It will take that bullet about 1 1/4 seconds to get there, and if the ram decides to move just when you touch it off, he may be over the ridge before the bullet kicks up the dirt where he *was*.

6

Deer in the Brush

When we talk of hunting deer in the brush or heavy timber, we also refer to any other game of similar size, but it is quite unusual to hunt any other North American game animal of deer size where most or all of the hunting will be done in heavy cover, with the exception of black bears. In spite of what a lot of hunters believe, any cartridge that works well on deer will also do about as well on black bears. Except for a few very large and very fat specimens, the black bear is no heavier than a big buck muley or a whitetail. The only difference as far as a good black bear load is concerned is that the black bear is more compact, with his weight more concentrated. His flesh and bone structure also give greater resistance to bullet penetration than those of a deer, so penetration is of greater importance. A bullet that will go on through from most angles is desirable, because an exit hole that leaves a good blood trail is often important. With a heavy layer of fat, a long coat of thick hair, and a spongy thick hide, the black bear will leave little or no blood from the entrance hole of even a large caliber bullet, so a large exit hole is a big help. This is much more important on bears than on deer, because a bear leaves little sign to follow in the way of tracks, whereas a deer kicks up a lot of dirt and forest litter when he takes off.

As most black bears that are killed during the fall in heavy timber are incidental to deer hunting, they will nearly always be shot with whatever bullet the hunter is using for deer. The only advice I have to offer is that the hunter who thinks he may see a black bear while

Cartridges like the .30-30 and .35 Remington are great whitetail numbers when you hunt them in the thick stuff, but when out in the open like this, a cartridge that has more sure hit range is a better bet. It will also do just as well in the timber at close range.

hunting deer should use a bullet designed for deep penetration. I know of no factory load that offers a better bullet for either deer or black bear in the brush than the Remington Core-Lokt. And for close timber hunting the round point is as good as or better than the pointed style if made in that caliber. This doesn't mean that many other factory loads with other makes and styles of bullets will not do a good job on deer in the brush, but for that kind of hunting, where a shot at over 100 yards is the exception rather than the rule, a flat shooting bullet is of little importance. For this reason, it is better to use one of the heavier weight bullets made for the caliber you are using rather than a light one. It is not quite as important that a bullet exit from a deer in the thick stuff as it is for a black bear, but it is a big help if there is plenty of blood to follow if the animal gets out of sight. Most once-a-year hunters can't expect to follow a track 50 yards in the deep woods without the aid of a large helping of blood, and more deer will travel at least that far after a vital hit than will drop where hit. Also, any bullet should go through a deer and make exit on a broadside shot if it is to give sufficient penetration on the north end of a deer rapidly disappearing to the south.

Another reason for the need for deeper penetration on deer in the brush, as opposed to deer in open country, is that it is next to impossible to know exactly which way the deer is standing. There are far more times that it will be quartering to or away from the gun than standing broadside. This is even more likely on running shots. The buck may also be standing in a twist, so the bullet that appears to be headed for the vitals may actually be pointed away from them.

Yet another reason why a bullet should be capable of reaching the boiler room from any angle is the fact that you are often forced to slip it through a very small hole in the brush. While you may be fairly certain of what part of the animal you are shooting at, you are often wrong as to the angle at which the bullet will travel after it lands. You may also be sighting at some other part of the animal than you think you are looking at.

It is for these reasons that many deer hunters, especially whitetail hunters, use the heaviest weight bullets in whatever cartridge they use to shoot for deer. If they use any of the 7mm's, they pick the 175 gr., and if it is the .30-06 they use a 200 or 220 gr., either in factory loads or handloads. They don't require flat trajectory, but they like a bullet that exits and leaves a good blood trail, and they have found that the heavier, slower bullet ruins a lot less meat than does the light one at high velocity. Of course, part of the reason for less meat spoilage from the heavy bullet is that it is designed to give deep penetration on large animals and does not expand as much or as fast as the light one.

These are also some of the reasons why many deer hunters who find their deer in the thick stuff prefer some of the larger calibers from .30 to .45. In some areas the old .35 Remington, the more modern .348 Winchester, and the .358 Winchester are all popular deer cartridges, and there are good, experienced deer hunters who like the .444 Marlin and the die-hard .45-70 for heavy-cover hunting.

Brush Bullets

Of course, the reason why a lot of hunters prefer the big, slow traveling bullets over the faster, lighter, smaller caliber bullets for brush hunting is that they think they "buck the brush" better. They believe that if they use the .45-70 they can mow down a half acre of bushes and saplings and drive the slug through the heart of a buck on the far side. I've heard these tales about the "brush-bucking bullets" all my life, and before I knew any better I tried it now and then, until I found out "there ain't any such thing."

One of the first experiences I remember came about when I shot a fork-horn muley buck that was behind a sapling I didn't even see when looking over the iron sights of an old Krag rifle. The bullet was a round nose–soft point 180 gr. that probably didn't start at more than 2400 fps. The sapling was about 35 yards from the muzzle, and the little buck only 10 or 15 feet beyond. He ran off a few yards and piled up but wasn't completely over the hill when I reached him. The bullet had come apart as it exited the sapling and had sprayed the deer from shoulder to hip in four separate pieces of jacket and core. One piece had, luckily, penetrated a lung and caused him to collapse. If that hadn't happened he could easily have escaped, because the other pieces had penetrated only a couple of inches.

Another time I shot at what I thought was a cow elk in heavy brush with a .35 Winchester and a 250 gr. factory load that started at 2200 fps. There was a small opening over the shoulder with plenty of room to put a bullet through. But there was also a wrist-size limb in the middle of it, which I couldn't see through the

When anyone talks or writes about brush-bucking bullets that will mow down an acre of this kind of stuff and still give good performance on a deer *somewhere* on the far side, he not only doesn't know what he's talking about, he is advising the beginning hunter to try it. Advertising brush-bucking cartridges is just as bad. A great deal of game is wounded and lost each year by this kind of shooting, and it doesn't do anything good for the hunter's image!

peep sight in the dim light. The elk ran off about 50 yards and lay down to be dispatched with a bullet in the brain. But when I got to it I found the cow had shrunk down to calf size, and the bullet passing through the limb had landed in the paunch, already expanded, and penetrated only a few inches. I was only 50 yards from the elk and it was no more than 20 feet beyond the limb. Had it been a big bull instead of a calf, my chances of ever seeing it again in that tangle would have been pretty thin. That about broke me of shooting through the brush if I wasn't sure of a clear hole, and I also began having doubts about brush cartridges and bullets—the .35 Winchester was considered among the best. . . .

A few years ago, after reading a great deal about some of the great brush-bucking bullets and cartridges, and the effectiveness of the big bores in driving through while leaving the bullet in nearly original form to hit the point of aim, I decided to do some experimenting under conditions where I could tell what happened. There had been some work done along this line by others, but it seemed that everyone who had run tests had put the target only a few feet beyond the obstacle course the bullet passed through—wooden dowels, brush, or what have you. In most instances the target had been placed within 4–5 feet of the last obstruction the bullet might hit. Also, most of the material used was under 1" in diameter. My experience had shown that in timber shooting, especially at running game, the bullet not only clipped twigs and branches along the way, it often tore hunks out of trees and penetrated saplings as large as it could get through. In looking back at the cases where I'd checked what had happened when game was killed after the bullet got tangled up with brush or trees, it was also found that the animal hit was nearly always within a few feet of the intervening object, and if it was farther away it was either unhit or wounded. On running game, the bullet-deflecting twigs, saplings, or trees may be anywhere between the gun and the animal, often as much as 50 yards from the target. In cases where the hunter tries to drive a bullet through the brush at an animal dimly seen somewhere on the far side, the animal may be a lot farther beyond the thick stuff than it seems to be. If it is more than a few feet beyond, the result will almost certainly be a miss or a wounded animal.

To prove or disprove these findings under controlled conditions, a target consisting of a cardboard box 13″ × 19″ was set up on a snow-covered slope 35 feet from a clump of birch that the bullet would have to pass through to reach it. Firing position was some 30 feet from the intervening brush, making a total distance of about 22 yards. With this setup I could place all bullets of various weights and calibers in a birch stem of the same size to assure equal resistance to the bullets. Impact of bullets or pieces could also be found in the snow if they missed the box. As pointed bullets are supposed to be much less effective in the bushes than round point bullets, the 180 gr. Nosler was used in the .30-06 loaded to about 2800 fps, as opposed to the round nose 220 gr. Hornady at 2585 fps. For the big bore heavy bullet at low velocity —the real brush cutter according to some sources—the .45-70 with Remington factory 405 gr. load that clocked just over 1200 fps in the '73 Trap Door Springfield was used.

By changing position slightly, a long enough section of a 3″ birch could be lined up with the center of the box, and several bullets fired through it so that all would have equal resistance. None ever reached the box, which was only 30 feet beyond! Pieces of core or jacket clipped off limbs and twigs in a wide arc starting within 2 feet of the stem penetrated, and pieces and what remained of the bullet shank landed around the box in the snow, but none was nearer than a couple of feet. If there was much difference in the performance of any of these bullets as far as hitting and killing a deer was concerned, the several fired from each load did not show it. The 405 gr. .45-70 with its flat nose gave no better results than the spitzer 180 gr. .30 caliber. And remember that these bullets only passed through a single 3″ stem hit in the center, while many bullets fired at a deer in the brush may make contact with several.

We are not saying that a 100 gr. 6mm bullet fired at high velocity is just as effective as a 500 gr. from a .45 caliber; what we are saying is that *none* of them will plow through much brush and reliably reach the vital area of an animal even 20 feet beyond! There just isn't a bullet made that can be considered a good brush bullet. If you want sure hits and no wounded game crawling off to die when hunting in the brush, don't hit any. I know that on running game it is often impossible to avoid it, but don't think any cartridge or bullet will automatically let you mow down a bushel of brush and assure a clean kill on the buck on the far side.

To clarify the position of those who claim that a pointed bullet, especially at high velocity, is more easily deflected than a round nose form, it is believed that the pointed nose tends to "glance" off twigs, brush, and trees easier than a round nose. There may be some small substance to this *if* the bullet just touches the edge of the object with its point, but this is a pretty thin chance. The biggest problem is expansion when the bullet contacts the obstruction, which leads to deflection or breakup, and not just deflection. The flat point would be the best of all from that angle, and we've seen what happened to the .45-70 flat pointed slug.

Others who believe that point shape has little to do with bullet breakup or deflection claim that the faster twist of most of the small bore–high velocity cartridges causes the bullet to remain stabilized by the faster rotation even after striking the limbs and twigs. This theory doesn't hold much water either, for at least two reasons: First, when the bullet contacts the limb or whatever, it expands and either breaks up or is badly distorted. Either way, the rotation will simply throw it off balance and cause it to drift. Second, they forget the heavy, slow bullet theory where the bullet may be turning only once in 20″ or more.

The straight fact is that a hunting bullet is made to expand when it strikes something, and after it expands it is very unlikely to continue on its original course, and it matters not if it is traveling fast or slow, or is fat or slim.

Reloading Not Desirable for Some Rifles

No discussion of cartridges, loads, and bullets would be complete without some mention of what has long been considered the most popular and reliable of all short range deer cartridges, the .30-30 Winchester, along with the .32 Winchester Special and .30 and .32 Remington rimless counterparts. There is little doubt that these cartridges, with bullets of around 170 gr. traveling at under 2200 fps from most hunting rifles, have accounted for a fantastic number of kills of deer, black bears, and heavier game. There is also little doubt that they do a good job on deer-size game at close ranges in the woods. Reasonably well controlled expansion is no problem at the velocity these cartridges develop at ranges up to 150–200 yards, which is as far as they should be used.

Most of the rifles chambered for them are short, light, and fast to handle in the thick stuff, and they kill deer well, with a minimum of meat ruined if the bullet is well placed. They are not, however, the answer to the handloader's prayer. If you have ideas about improving on factory loads to improve either the punch or the trajectory very much, you are kidding yourself.

In the first place, most of the lever, slide, or autoloading rifles they are chambered in are not well adapted to handling pressures much higher than those developed by factory ammunition. You can normally increase the velocity somewhat if you intend to use the case for only a couple of reloads, but if pressures are much greater than factory ammunition develops, continued use of the load will cause a head separation of the case—something that is not exactly desirable while hunting. Second, I doubt that any of the bullets from the various bullet makers perform any better than factory bullets in these cartridges. And since they are not used for varmint shooting or target work, few rounds are used per year by most hunters, so economy offers little incentive for loading your own. The average deer hunter is probably better off to stick with factory ammunition than to reload.

Sighting for Timber Shooting

Last, but not necessarily least, for short range timber shooting of deer, or game of any other size for that matter, is the sighting of the rifle. This is especially true for the fellow who hunts entirely in heavy cover, as is done in many whitetail areas. The 3″ high 100 yard sighting is not ideal for close woods shooting, for several reasons. To begin with, shots are not likely to be more than 100 yards away, so flat trajectory is of little consequence. Being sighted to hit a very small target at ranges up to 100 yards or so is of consequence, so if the rifle is zeroed at around 100 yards, fewer misses will be made. If the whole animal is visible, the 3″ high sighting makes no difference whatever, but there are many times when only the neck or the head is visible, or there is a very small hole in the brush to shoot through. In these cases, the 3″ high sighting may cause a miss or only a shallow wound if you don't remember to hold that much below where the bullet must land. If sighted dead on at 100 yards, most loads will be within about 1″ of point of aim from 25 yards to nearly 130 yards—close enough to give a clean kill if you do your part.

This doesn't mean you should resight your rifle if you have it sighted 3″ up at 100 yards and go into the timber for a day's hunting. If you just remember where it is sighted and hold accordingly for the close shots, you'll have no problem. I never change my sighting from the 3″ 100 yard high bullet impact, but I have used it so long that I know where to hold on small spots at close range without even being conscious of it.

When we add up all the points that make a cartridge, bullet, or the rifle that shoots it either desirable or undesirable for shooting deer-size game in the timber, we find that it really isn't so very different from what is required for other types of hunting for game of the same size. I've found that if I use the same cartridge, load, and rifle when I go into the heavy stuff that I use on deer elsewhere, I get along about as well with it there as anywhere else. Just remember that you can't drive a bullet through a thicket and expect to reach a deer on the far side. And the scope on your open-country rifle, if it doesn't have too much power, will let you see brush in line with the deer which would be completely invisible with iron sights. Also, the high velocity of the 6mm's, the .270, the 7mm's, and the fast .30s will do in a buck in the brush just as well as a slow bullet. It may ruin a bit more meat, but if you use a controlled expansion bullet like the Nosler, it may not even do that.

If you don't have a rifle for every purpose, don't hesitate to hunt in heavy cover with the rifle you use elsewhere. In many sections of the country you may hunt deer in the morning and evening where shots are long when they come into the open to feed, then go into some pretty hairy jungles after them in the middle of the day. It should be obvious that the long range load will do the job under both conditions, but the slow load will not.

I hunted whitetails a few years ago in an area where the river breaks were pretty rough, with very heavy cover on the north-facing canyon sides and open grass country and small patches of thorn brush on the south faces. Many of the big bucks fed the open country during the moonlit nights and bedded in the thorn thickets in the daytime, but some also stayed in the heavy cover. Part of the time we hunted in the open, part in extremely heavy brush, ferns, and timber. When I finally shot a buck after several days' hunting, one of my hunting partners kicked it out of a thorn thicket on an open hillside on the other side of the canyon from where I was hunting. Seeing it moving along, I found an opening, sat down, wrapped up in the sling, and when it stopped to look for my partner, I put a 100 gr. Nosler bullet, backed by 46 gr. of H4831 that started at 2946 fps from the 20″ barrel, into its lungs from a 6mm Remington at about 275 yards. Had I been using a .30-30, I wouldn't even have considered the shot; with the 6mm I knew the buck was dead before I squeezed the trigger. He would have been equally dead if I'd shot him at 25 yards in the brush.

Another angle the hunter of deer-size game may wish to consider, which is an option that only the handloader has, is loading a big cartridge down to lower than normal velocity for shooting in heavy timber where he *knows* the range will be short, say under 100 yards. As an example, we'll say he is using a 7mm magnum or a .300 belted cartridge; it is the only rifle he has, and he feels that it is more powerful than necessary for deer, or that it will likely ruin too much meat. In that case he can take any of the bullets of conventional jacket design, either round or pointed, and from any of the ammunition companies or bullet makers, and of medium to heavy weight, and load it to about the same velocity as the 7×57 Mauser or the .30-06 will give. To do this he will have to pick a faster burning powder than used in full-power loads, powders like 4895, 4064, or 4320. (Do not use the slow powders normally recommended for large capacity cartridges, because there is the possibility of a rifle-wrecking detonation.) While the loads in the charts in this book do not give reduced loads for most cartridges, nearly all the reloading manuals do. Pick a manual that gives the velocity you want.

There is, however, the chance that a fly may fall into the soup here—not all reduced loads give top accuracy in big cases. You may find that you have to juggle powders and charges to obtain reasonably good accuracy. Another point to keep in mind is that you will have to resight your rifle for these low velocity loads.

As will be noted elsewhere in this book, I do *not* recommend loads reduced much below normal for any other type of hunting, and not for heavy game even if you know the range will be close.

I strongly suggest that if you own more than one rifle you pick a cartridge suited to short range shooting of deer-size game rather than loading a big cartridge to low velocity. You'll find it more reliable, and the rifle you use it in is usually much better suited to hunting in heavy cover, because it is smaller and lighter.

Whitetail buck shot across canyon at 250 yards with 6mm Remington and Nosler 100/47/H4831 at 2986 fps. The same rifle and load would work as well at 50 feet in the brush, but the Winchester M-94 .30-30 (shown in left background) with iron sights would be far from ideal for the long shots this country offered.

7

Cartridges and Loads for Shooting Heavy Game at Long Range

When we refer to heavy North American game, very few species are included. Caribou are included, not because they are very large or hard to kill but because they are considerably heavier than deer, and because they are hunted in the same areas and often at the same time as moose and grizzly. In discussing caribou hunting I am not thinking of the people native to the land of the caribou, who often hunt them at times and in places where no other game will be seen or killed. These hunters can and do use some cartridges that would be inadequate for mixed bag hunting, or for hunters of less experience, and especially for trophy hunters, where the success or failure of the whole trip may depend on a single shot.

No Long Range Shooting of Big Bears

Going on up above the size of caribou, there are only elk, moose, and the big bears of the grizzly family. There is little use in considering polar bears, because they are off limits in most areas where they are found, and any load that is effective on Alaskan brown bears will be equally effective on the white bears. Also, as far as this section is considering cartridges, loads, and bullets for heavy game at medium to long ranges, it does not apply to shooting the big bears anyway, except in an emergency. And why doesn't it apply to hunting the big bears? Simply because the author does not feel that *anyone* is ever justified in shooting either a mountain grizzly or an Alaskan brown bear, or a polar bear for that matter, at what would be considered long range for elk and moose. The only exception to this is that if the animal is wounded and shows up at long range, the hunter should try to dispatch him—if he wounds him with such a "desperation" shot, nothing is lost, and it may kill him or at least slow him down even more so that he may be approached and finished off. But to shoot at a grizzly at 350–400 yards to start with is simply asking for trouble, even with the best long range cartridge and load.

While some of these points will be covered in more detail later, remember that the energy of any bullet has fallen off badly by the time it arrives at that range. Even a big grizzly or brown does not offer nearly as large a vital area as either a bull elk or moose. And putting the bullet in exactly the right spot within the vital area of a grizzly is much more critical than it is with either elk or moose, for several reasons. But the main one is that if you wound him and have to follow him into the brush, you may have to *try* to stop him at a range that is far closer than you'd like it to be!

These are a few of the cartridges that give the best results for shooting various species of American big game at long range. The cartridge picked should be suited to the kind of game to be hunted, and bullets should be of pointed design and high ballistic coefficient like those shown. *From left:* .264 Win.; .270 Wby.; 7mm Wby.; .300 Win.; .338 Win.; .340 Wby.

Back in the early '60s I made a couple of hunts along the east slope of the Alaska Range above the Tanana River with guide Johnny Porter. This was some of the finest grizzly country left anywhere at that time, and we saw them nearly every day. The first thing Porter usually told his hunters was never to shoot at a grizzly closer than 50 yards or farther than 150 yards. The moral of this is that if the bear was more than 150 yards away, the average hunter probably wouldn't put the bullet close enough to the right spot and would only wound the bear; if the bear was less than 50 yards from the hunter and he muffed the shot, the grizzly could be eating on him before it could be stopped. While I might add another 50–100 yards on the long end, and cut the close range a little for a good and very cool rifleman using a potent cartridge with the right bullet, it is sage advice. After seeing a number of both mountain grizzlies and Alaskan browns killed with various cartridges and bullets, I do not believe even the best riflemen should ever shoot at one at more than 250 yards or so.

Sighting and Vital Measurements of Heavy American Game

So for true long range shooting of the heavier North American big game, this leaves the hoofed varieties, caribou, elk, and moose. Even though all these animals afford much larger targets than the deer-size animals, the long range sighting should remain the same —that is, 3″ high at 100 yards—for a number of reasons. The first and most important reason is that in the great majority of cases the same rifle used for the larger game will be used for shooting some of the deer-size game on the same hunt. Second, we come back to the situation where only part of the animal may be seen at anything from a few yards to the longest range; and under these conditions, if the rifle is sighted to place its bullets much over 3″ high at 100 yards, you can miss a moose just as easily as a ram.

As an example, a bull elk is lying behind a log at anywhere from 100 yards to 200 or so, and only 8″ or so of his back and parts of his head and neck are showing through the brush. If your rifle is sighted to land its bullets 3″ high at 100 yards, you know the bullet will be from 3″ to no more than about 4″ high where the elk is with most loads in the 2900–3100 fps range. If you hold tight against the log, the bullet will break the animal's spine. If you aim for the head or neck, you know the bullet will only hit about 3″ above the point of actual aim, which isn't too hard to figure. Logically, a rifle could be sighted as much as 5″ high at 100 yards for elk and moose on shots where the full depth of the body can be seen, and still land within the vital area at 200–250 yards, and the sure hit range would be extended considerably; but for the shots like that mentioned above, where only a small part of the animal can be seen, the 8″ or so that the bullet will be high at mid-range will cause a miss, because you can't judge how much to hold under.

Photo and diagram showing approximate points of impact at various ranges from 100 yards to limit of sure hit range in vital area of mature six-point bull elk with pointed 180 gr. .30 caliber bullet starting at 3100 fps with rifle sighted 3″ high at 100 yards.

1: Depth of vital area 22″
2: Depth from hairline to hairline 32″–34″
3: Bullet impact at 375 yards, limit of sure hit range in vital area
4: Point of aim and bullet impact at 280 yards
5: Bullet impact at 100 yards
6: Bullet impact at 200 yards

But even with the same 3″ high 100 yard sighting used on deer, the sure hit range for a mature bull elk can be increased from about 325 yards for a center hold on a deer to about 360 yards for the bull with a .300 magnum 180 gr. spitzer bullet starting at 3100 fps. On a big bull moose the range at which the bullet will land in the vital area will be boosted to around 400 yards. For caribou it will be increased very little above the sure hit range for deer—not more than 20 yards or so. (It is in long range shooting of heavy game that good handloads really show their worth. Not only does factory ammunition usually fall below the velocity given, but trajectory will also be correspondingly higher. Also, factory bullets are a compromise for various kinds of game and shooting, but in a handload you can use the bullet best suited to the situation. You can also load it to the highest velocity your rifle will stand with safety, trouble-free operation and acceptable accuracy, which will increase the sure hit range somewhat. Information on the best bullets to use for long range shooting of big game will be found in chapter 11.)

To fully understand how we arrived at these figures, the hunter will need to know something about the size of the animals. While there is some variation in size among animals of the same species found in different localities, and some individuals are larger or smaller than normal, we are thinking here of mature animals of average size or above. Young animals, even though they may have reasonably good hardware on their heads, often do not have their full growth. Also, females will run a great deal smaller than the figures used here.

Starting with caribou, I have measured a number of Alaskan caribou from both the interior and the Alaska Peninsula, and the big bulls varied little in size. I am told that those from the Arctic herds are somewhat smaller, but I have not measured one to find out. Anyway, the big bulls I have measured stand about 52″ at the shoulder, and tape 24″ average from back to bottom of rib cage, hairline to hairline. The vital area will run nearly 16″ in height.

Mature bull elk in most sections of the Mountain West will stand 62″–66″ at the shoulders, and will average about 32″ from back to brisket. I say average because many bulls that have full six-point antlers are not fully mature and will measure no more than 30″, and I have measured big old bulls that were a full 36″ top to bottom, of what you could see. The vital area will run from a low of at least 22″ to about 26″.

Moose vary even more than elk because there are three subspecies recognized, with the Shiras (Wyoming) being the smallest, the Alaska-Yukon being the largest, and the Canadian holding the middle ground. The Wyoming moose will normally stand no more than 6 1/2 feet at the shoulder and be a maximum of no more than 3 feet deep through the body, which leaves a vital area very little larger than that of a big bull elk. On the other hand, I killed one Alaskan bull that taped an even 7 feet at the shoulder, heel to hump, and spanned 45″ from hump to belly line. That bull had a vital area of well over 30″! However, I have measured other Alaskan bulls that carried larger racks that were 3″–4″ less in all measurements.

The reason we go into these height measurements here is to give the hunter something to go by not only in knowing how large the vital area is on the various animals, but also to help some in judging range and overall bullet drop if he finds for some reason he has to shoot at ranges that are beyond the sure hit range of his load with a center-of-the-ribs hold. As with deer-size game, and with even greater emphasis, we do not suggest or approve of shooting at heavy game at ranges where you find you have to hold over the animal with any good long range cartridge unless it is wounded and escaping.

There are some other exceptions to this, where the hunter is using some big bore cartridge that shoots a large caliber heavy bullet at rather low velocity, we'll say 2400–2700 fps, but that packs a lot of punch at fairly long range. Of course, even then the range will be no longer than the range of the flatter shooting cartridges where no holdover is required, but with the big bore number you will have to either hold well up on the animal or over his back. Examples of these cartridges and loads would be the .338 Winchester with 300 gr. round nose bullet, the .358 Norma with 250–300 gr. round nose bullets, the .375 H&H Magnum with 300 gr. bullets and many 270 gr., and the .458 Winchester that will kill fairly well out to 300 yards or so but has excessive bullet drop at that range. This will, of course, also apply to all wildcats in the same class. To be justified in shooting at ranges where the cartridge and load requires holding above the animal's back even with the larger calibers, the hunter must have a thorough knowledge of exactly where the bullet will land at those ranges if he estimates them correctly, and he should be a damn good judge of distance. He should also be reasonably certain that the bullet will expand, because even though the large caliber bullet punches a fairly large hole through the animal, if it doesn't expand, there will be little shock and no tearing up of the vital tissue it takes to make a sure, clean kill.

This brings us around to some of the other requirements of shooting the heavier species of American game at long range besides being able to hit them. It doesn't take much experience or thought to know that the bigger they are the easier they are to hit, but that same bulk does present some problems that a lot of hunters either don't consider or don't know about.

Limitations of Small Bore Cartridges for Heavy Game at Long Range

To start at the beginning, we can go back to the varmint/big game cartridges like the 6mm's and .25s. It is no trick to put one of their 100–120 gr. bullets in the ribs of a bull elk up to 400 yards with the sighting we've just discussed, but what happens when it gets there? With an antelope or deer, you try to stick it in the lungs and you know that everything will work out fine if it lands there. And even if it misses the lungs and lands in the shoulders or the back of the diaphragm instead, the deer will probably be killed fairly quickly anyway. Or if the animal you thought was broadside turns out to be quartering to or from the gun so that the bullet must penetrate shoulder or front of paunch to find the vital lung area, the little bullet of proper design will get through on a deer, but an elk or moose is a different story. And the farther away the game is, the harder it is to be certain of exact position, and the better the chance the bullet will wander a bit from the intended landing point.

The thing to remember is that the small caliber light bullet is marginal for game of this size when placed exactly right, and no matter how well it is placed on angle shots, it will lack the penetration it must have to plow through the bone, muscle, or paunch material between the entrance hole and the vital organs. The second point to keep in mind is that its ability to leave the large wound channel that is required for shock and tissue destruction vital to quick kills on large animals is minimal at close range, and drops rapidly as range lengthens. While there is little argument regarding the oft-quoted fact that energy figures don't kill big game (a solid bullet gives the same energy figures as an expanding bullet), shock and the ability of the bullet to tear things up are directly related to it. Energy is an outgrowth of velocity and bullet weight, and when velocity drops off as range increases, so does the energy. It follows that bullet efficiency is also reduced even if expansion did remain consistent, which it does not. It's like the difference between a 180 gr. bullet fired from a .308 Winchester at 200 yards and the same bullet fired from the .300 Weatherby. There is one hell of a lot of difference in the wallop they pack!

What this amounts to is that just because you can hit an elk with a .243 at 400 yards doesn't mean it will kill him without a liberal helping of luck. At 100 yards the .243 bullet that starts at 3100 fps packs about 1790 foot-pounds (fp) of energy and the wound-creating ability that goes with it; at 400 yards it has dropped to a bit over 1,000 fp of energy, or only about 100 fp more than the .222 Remington has with the 50 gr. bullet at 100 yards. Now compare this with a .30 caliber 180 gr. spitzer bullet starting at the same 3100 fps that arrives at 400 yards with 2160 fp of energy, which is about 25 fp more than the .243 100 gr. had at the muzzle. The much larger frontal area of the expanded .30 caliber bullet and its greater retained weight also cause a more severe wound and a lot deeper penetration.

Considering all this, it is obvious that even if an elk or a moose is broadside and the .243 or .25 bullet hits dead center of the lung area in the thin rib section where little penetration is needed to reach the center of the lungs, it has lost enough velocity and energy to reduce the shock and the wound channel to a minimum for killing game of that size quickly. There is just no way that anyone is justified in using these cartridges and loads for shooting heavy game at long range. The only exception I can think of is a .25 like the .257 Weatherby with a bullet like the 115 gr. Nosler started at the highest possible velocity, and then used only when conditions are exactly right—otherwise, don't shoot.

This brings us up to the .270 Winchester with the 130 gr. bullet and the .264 Winchester Magnum with the 140 gr., both in spitzer form. Both of these loads give better penetration, a larger wound channel, and greater shock at long range than the .243 and .25 cartridges. The .264 has the edge on the .270 Winchester at long range both in retained energy, which adds up to shock and tissue destruction, and in penetration, due to greater sectional density, if both bullets are identical in construction. In the energy department, the .270 130 gr. bullet and the .264 with a 140 gr., both started at 3100 fps, churn up about 1350 and 1600 foot-pounds of energy at 400 yards respectively. Loaded full-throttle in some barrels, either cartridge will beat this velocity by 50 fps or more, but these are fairly hot loads with either cartridge in most sporters with 24″ barrels.

These figures do not necessarily give the .264 Win. Mag. as much advantage over the .270 Win. on heavy game at long range as it may appear. While the 130 gr. bullet in the .270 cartridge is a little flatter at 400 yards when started at 3100 fps than is the 150 gr. at 2900 fps when both have about the same form, it does not retain as much energy at that range. Using Nosler bullets, which to me are a near must in the .270 for heavy game, the new *Nosler Reloading Manual* shows that the 130 gr. packs 1381 fp of energy at 400 yards when started at 3100 fps, and the 150 gr. that has an MV of 2900 fps at about the same pressure still has 1549 fp at the same range. When you consider that the 130 gr. has a sectional density of .242, and the 150 gr. has .280, it is quite obvious that with identical bullet design the 150 gr. will penetrate heavy bone and other tough pieces of animal anatomy a lot better.

For those who think the 130 gr. shoots a great deal flatter than the 150 gr. at long range, at the respective velocities given above, there is only about 1″ difference in point of impact in favor of the 130 gr. at the 400 yard mark. Give this some thought the next time you load ammunition for hunting game heavier than deer with your .270.

To get back to the long range comparison with the .264 Win. Mag., the 140 gr. bullet that starts at 3100 fps has only a little over 100 fp more energy at 400 yards than the 150 gr. from the .270 Win., and penetration of identical bullet design will be equal because sectional density is within .003 point for the two bullets. True, there are a few 160 gr. bullets made for the 6.5mm's, but all

I know of are of round point design, and even at the 2900 fps possible in the .264 Winchester, drop at 400 yards is excessive. Also, if these bullets expand well at that range, it is extremely doubtful if they will penetrate as deeply as the 140 gr. Nosler.

Everything considered, my feeling after seeing many, many head of game of various sizes, and at various ranges, killed with the .270 Winchester, and some with the .264, is that they are marginal for heavy game for really long range shooting at 400 yards or more. This is not to say they won't do the job if you are a good shot, pick your spot well, and make sure the animal is in the right position when you shoot. I think Jack O'Connor has proved that point many times, but Jack has had a bit more experience than the average hunter, knows big game anatomy, is a good game shot, and also knows when to hold his fire.

For long shots at heavy game the .270 Weatherby is a better choice than either the .270 Winchester or the .264. The .270 Weatherby Magnum will start a 150 gr. bullet just as fast as the .270 Winchester starts the 130 gr. if you use the right powder in both. In fact, there are several of the slower powders that will give the 150 gr. over 3150 fps from a 24" barrel and the very slow H-870 spherical powder will send it along at 3200 fps without excessive pressures. The 160 gr. Nosler also sprints along at plus 3100 fps with the best powders suited to this heavy semi-spitzer bullet. The 150 gr. spitzer bullet retains velocity and energy better than the semi-spitzer 160 gr., so it is just a tad flatter at 400–500 yards, also delivers more energy than the 160 gr., but the heavier bullet has it outclassed in sectional density to assure deep penetration. In fact, due to the high velocity attained with the .270 Weatherby with all bullet weights, anything except bullets with full expansion control like Nosler should not be used for shooting heavy game at any range, because of the likelihood of bullet breakup. The .270 Weatherby load chart will show which powders do the best job with the various bullet weights, as well as the long range potential of the cartridge.

The Efficient 7mm Magnums

The various 7mm magnums have won an enviable reputation as very effective long range cartridges for all classes of North American big game from antelope to moose, and my own experience has proved that this reputation is well founded. Due to the wide range of bullet weights and styles, there is literally a bullet for every use, and for long range shooting of heavy game the very high ballistic coefficient of spitzer bullets in 150–175 gr., which is coupled with good sectional density in the 160 gr., and the outstanding SD of .310 for the 175 gr.

To backtrack and reminisce a little, the 7mm magnum originated as the .275 Holland & Holland in 1912–1913, an offshoot of the famed .375 H&H. It gained a reputation as a good killer within a few years, but was badly underloaded by today's standards. It was at one time loaded by the old Western Cartridge Co. in this country, but no commercial rifles were ever made for it by American manufacturers. For that reason, it never gained any popularity here, and except for a few wildcats, no interest was shown in 7mm magnums until Roy Weatherby brought out the 7mm Weatherby Magnum in about 1944, which eventually wound up as a commercial number. Even that cartridge did not get much play until much later. The 7×61 Sharpe & Hart made some stir in the 7mm magnum market when it appeared in 1953 in a commercial cartridge and rifle. The big problem here was that both rifle and ammunition were of foreign manufacture, and distribution was none too good.

About that time Warren Page, then Shooting Editor of *Field & Stream,* got interested in the 7mm Mashburn Super Magnum, hunted with one all over the world with great success, and wrote reams of material on its performance. Even then, it wasn't until 1962 that Remington finally saw the light and necked the .264 Winchester case up to take a .284 caliber bullet and called it the 7mm Remington Magnum—a cartridge that was shortly to become one of the most famous big game cartridges of all time, rooting out a seat beside the venerable .30-06 and .375 H&H.

Warren Page had always used the 175 gr. bullet for all his big game shooting, regardless of the size of the game or the range at which it was shot, feeling that if you were going to use a magnum seven for about everything, the heavy bullet was the one to use. At that time I don't believe there was a single pointed 175 gr. 7mm bullet made in this country, and the 175 gr. Nosler was in semi-pointed form. Using the same cartridge, I soon found that the 160 gr. Nosler shot a good deal flatter at long range than the 175 gr., not only because of its spitzer shape but because it could be started about 150 fps faster in that cartridge. However, when Remington unveiled the 7mm Remington Magnum, the ammunition that went with it fired a 150 gr. pointed bullet for a light offering and a 175 gr. round point as a heavy game bullet. The 175 gr. round nose proved to be a very poor choice for a cartridge with the long range potential of the 7mm magnum. What Remington engineers seemed to forget was that the 150 gr. .284 bullet was just a little on the short side in both sectional density and ballistic coefficient to be the optimum for long range shooting of heavy game in the big case, and that the round nose 175 gr. was very poor indeed; actually much less effective than the 150 gr., because it had lost most of what it started with by the time it reached an elk on the far side of a mountain canyon.

Even so, the 150 gr. Remington factory load with the pointed Core-Lokt bullet did very well at long range on game of all sizes, even though in hunting rifles it fell far short of the 3260 fps muzzle velocity quoted in factory ballistic sheets. Most of the hunters who became addicted to the 7mm magnum cartridges soon started handloading for it anyway, and used the better 160 gr. bullets, and the pointed 175 gr. that soon appeared from the various bullet makers as well as in Remington ammunition boxes. (See load charts for various 7mm cartridges, and also chapter 11.)

As we've seen earlier, few cartridges will shoot flatter over long game ranges than a 7mm magnum (using the 7mm Remington Magnum as a standard) when loaded with a 160 gr. spitzer bullet, and very few retain as much energy. A look at the figures on Nosler bullets shows that the 160 gr. spitzer starting at 3100 fps arrives at 400 yards with just under a ton of energy, and the 175 gr., even with its poorer semi-spitzer form, that takes off at 3000 fps lands at 400 yards with almost the identical energy of the 160 gr. There is, according to Nosler figures, only a couple of inches more drop with the 175 gr. than with the 160 gr. at that range—not enough to matter too much on the side of a bull elk.

Even the best of calculations do not always agree, but when we look at Sierra figures on their excellent long range–boattail bullets, we find that the 160 gr. with an MV of 3100 fps delivers over 2100

Record-book caribou from Alaska Range shot with 7mm Mashburn Super Magnum and Nosler 160 gr. backed by 74 gr. H4831 at 3240 fps. This bull was shot at a paced 400 yards because there was no way to get closer on open tundra. He was already moving out. It was very comforting to be using that rifle that day!

fp of energy at 400 yards, and the new 175 gr. spitzer BT bullet with its amazing BC of .654 arrives at that range packing 2317 fp of energy when started at 3000 fps. Bullets of other makes in similar styles will give figures in the same general area. This, of course, doesn't mean they will all perform with equal efficiency, but the potential is there if jacket design is right.

The Best .30 Caliber Bullets for Long Range on Heavy Game

Here in the U.S. the .30 caliber has long been the bullet diameter by which all other calibers were judged in performance on big game. I don't say this is the way it should be, but that's the way it is with many big game hunters. I suppose this all started back in the days when the .30-40, .30-30, and .30-06 far outstripped all others in popularity for use in hunting American game. And make no mistake, the .30 caliber is top-flight for hunting *any* North American big game at any range, but the cartridges mentioned above are not the best choice for long range shooting of heavy game, because they do not shoot flat enough or pack enough wallop at long range—yes, this does include the great old .30-06 unless the most potent handloads are used. Certainly factory ammunition does not have either the flatness of trajectory or the retained energy to be considered ideal for long range shooting of heavy game.

This pretty well eliminates all the .30 caliber cartridges as ideal for shooting large animals at over about 350 yards, except the various .300 magnums, and they are some of the best. The first true .30 magnum cartridge actually originated here in the form of the .30 Newton in about 1913. It was followed by the .300 H&H that appeared in England in 1920, but ammunition for it was not loaded commercially in this country by Western Cartridge Co. until about 1925. Newton rifles were chambered for the .30 Newton sometime before 1920, but those rifles were discontinued within a few years, and Western discontinued loading ammunition for it during the late '30s. Except for a few wildcat .30s and custom rifles for the .30 Newton and .300 H&H, no rifles were made for a magnum .30 in this country between the demise of the Newton rifle and the chambering of the Winchester Model 70 for the .300 H&H in 1937.

Both of these cartridges were good long range numbers, but were not especially potent as compared to the more modern big .30s, mostly because of a lack of suitable powders at the time of their introduction. But they did lead up to the .300 magnums of today, with the .300 Weatherby as the first of the modern line to be loaded commercially in about 1948. There was a long gap then until the .308 Norma Magnum ammunition was imported into this country in about 1961, even though an American-made commercial rifle has never been chambered for it in quantity production. Shortly thereafter, Winchester came out with the .300 Winchester Magnum, which was to become the most popular .30 magnum of all time.

In considering the .300 magnums for long range shooting of heavy game and in analyzing what it takes to make reasonably certain of a sure kill under average hunting conditions, I feel that

Big Dall ram taken by the author in Alaska Range with Winchester M-70 .300 Win. loaded with 180 gr. Nosler/78/H4831 at 3150 fps. Most sheep are not shot at long range—this one, at only a bit over 100 yards. But a long range cartridge is the best choice in case you need it.

anything less than the 165 gr. bullet is inadequate. It is quite true that the 150 gr. at 3300–3400 fps shoots very flat and is easy to hit with at the longest hunting ranges, but its rather poor ballistic coefficient causes retained energy to be rather poor when it reaches the 400 yard mark, and, more important on big animals, sectional density is much less than the .270 130 gr., which eliminates its ability to penetrate heavy bone and muscle even if expansion is fully controlled as with the Nosler bullet.

This leaves three bullet weights in .30 caliber that are fully suitable for long range work on heavy game—the 165, 180, and 200 gr.—and to be most effective they should all be in pointed form. This eliminates the 220 gr. because they are all in round nose form and shed velocity too fast either for flat trajectory or for retained energy.

The 165 gr. is the least effective because even though you can start it some 100 fps faster than the 180 gr., there is so little difference in drop at 400 yards that you can't tell it. It delivers 200–400 fp less energy (depending on whose figures you look at) at that range than the 180 gr., and, of course, everything else being equal, will give somewhat less penetration. If the 165 gr. bullet is used for shooting heavy game at long range, it should certainly be of controlled expansion design, and Nosler and Bitterroot make the only bullets I know of in that weight with this feature. While controlled expansion is important with the 180 gr. bullet for heavy game at any range, it is even more important with the 165 gr. .30 caliber bullet because of its lack of sectional density—.247 for the 165 gr. as compared to .271 for the 180 gr. It is also important to load the 165 gr. to the highest practical velocity the cartridge it is used in will handle, to ensure retained long range energy.

The 180 gr. .30 caliber bullet has long been considered about optimum in the .30 caliber cases from the .30-40 Krag to the .300 Weatherby for all-around shooting of all sizes of American game at all ranges, and there is more than a little merit in this line of thinking. The reasoning behind this is that high velocity is possible, which, when coupled with the excellent ballistic coefficient of most pointed 180 gr. bullets, leads to flat trajectory. Sectional density is also sufficient to give deep penetration from a controlled expansion bullet.

If given a hard look, however, there is room for question in this assumption. A well-shaped 200 gr., especially in the magnum cases, may just be the most ideal .30 caliber bullet weight for all-around shooting of heavy game at all ranges. The big problem here is that few are made in hunting bullet design by the bullet companies, and only the 200 gr. Speer is made in spitzer form. In factory-loaded ammunition, the only .30 caliber cartridge I know of that is loaded with a 200 gr. bullet is the .308 Winchester, which certainly is not a long range load.* Assuming bullet form is equal, the 180 gr. spitzer with an MV of 3100 fps will have almost the same impact point at 400 yards as the 200 gr. at 3000 fps—less than 1" with the 3" high 100 yard sighting. The 200 gr. reaches 400 yards with about 200 fp more energy than the 180 gr. and will

*While this book was being written, Federal Cartridge Co. started loading the .30-06 with a 200 gr. spitzer SP BT bullet by Sierra. These bullets are not yet available to the handloader and I have not tried them.

give even more penetration and bone-smashing punch if jacket construction is the same.

This is one place I feel Nosler has fallen down badly in bullet design. Their 200 gr. .30 bullet is good, but it could be a lot better if made in spitzer or even semi-spitzer form like their 175 gr. 7mm bullet. Also, the smaller amount of exposed lead on the point, and the fact that the partition could probably be placed farther forward in the longer bullet, would give a little slower expansion and more retained weight for deeper penetration. I have killed many head of heavy game with the 200 gr. Nosler in various .30 magnums with fine results at both long and short ranges. I have also killed many more with the 175 gr. Nosler in 7mm magnum cartridges. My experience has been that the 175 gr. 7mm always gives deeper penetration than the 200 gr. .30 at all ranges. If Speer can make a 200 gr. spitzer and Sierra can make a 200 gr. spitzer boattail match bullet that work very well in all big .30 cases, so will a pointed 200 gr. Nosler perform well with no problems, since they eliminated the relief groove, thereby lengthening the full bearing surface so it will hold in the short neck of the .300 Winchester.

This big silvertip mountain grizzly taken in Alaska Range by the author was shot with .300 Win. Mag. and 200 gr. Nosler backed by 76 gr. of H4831 at 3000 fps. This cartridge and load is a good choice for Alaskan hunting.

While the .30 magnum bullets mentioned will not give any more penetration than 7mm bullets in their respective sectional density levels, and do not pack much more punch at long range, and do not shoot quite as flat, they are of larger caliber. When expanded equally they form a larger frontal area and, as a result, tear up a bit more tissue and deliver somewhat more shock. Which all adds up to a little more killing power than any of the smaller calibers have.

Long Range Cartridges and Bullets in Calibers Larger Than .30

The next step up the caliber ladder as long range heavy game cartridges are the .338 Winchester and the .340 Weatherby. Either of these cartridges will give better performance on heavy animals at *all* hunting ranges than will the smaller calibers, but this does not necessarily mean they are better for long range shooting. Many hunters who use either of these .338 caliber cartridges feel the 200 gr. bullet is the best medicine for anything at long range because of the 3000 fps the .338 will give it, and the 3200 fps churned up by the .340. This is not completely correct, for several reasons. First, the 200 gr. .338 bullet has far less sectional density and ballistic coefficient than the 180 gr. .30 caliber bullet. And this does not lead either to flat trajectory or to deep penetration. Second, I have yet to see any 200 gr. .338 bullet that is designed so that it will not expand too rapidly on heavy game and come apart. When the short 200 gr. expands its jacket very far, it is almost certain to lose its core, if of conventional design. When this happens, penetration soon stops. They are fine for light game but not ideal for heavy animals under anything but ideal conditions.

For the handloader there is, happily, another choice, in the form of the 210 gr. Nosler and the 225 gr. Hornady. The 210 gr. Nosler can be boosted along at about the same velocity as the 200 gr., and has a little better sectional density and ballistic coefficient. But its outstanding feature is that it does not blow up at any range even from the impact of the .340 Weatherby. I have killed a number of elk with it at various ranges, with the bulls standing in various positions, and have recovered only one bullet to show expanded form; the others made exit and may still be going.

I have no problem in starting this bullet at 3200 fps with 88 gr. of N205 from my .340, and Nosler figures show it drops less at 400 yards than the 180 gr. .30 started at 3100 fps. My own long range drop tests prove this to be true, and sighted 3″ high at 100 yards this bullet drops less than 8″ at 400 yards when fired at an altitude of 5,000 feet. It is also still packing over 2300 foot-pounds of energy when it gets there, which adds up to more than what the 180 gr. factory load for the .308 Winchester has at 100 yards, and 500 fps more than the .30-30 170 gr. factory load develops at the muzzle!

From the .338 Winchester cartridge with the same bullet at 150–200 fps less velocity, the load is not quite as efficient at long range, but it is still among the best.

The 225 gr. Hornady with its sectional density of .281, and ballistic coefficient of .452, is an ideal bullet for long range shooting in either the .338 or the .340 when boosted along at about 2900 and 3000 fps respectively. According to Hornady figures, it will have only about 1″ more drop at 400 yards when started at 3000 fps than the 200 gr. at 3200 fps. Also by Hornady figures, it retains a little more energy at a bit over 2400 fp at 400 yards. With all due respect to my old friend Joyce Hornady, this bullet does have a couple of points that could stand improvement. If ranges are over the 300 yard mark it will hold together quite well, especially at .338 Win. velocities, but at ranges below that it is very likely to come apart on big animals if heavy bone is encountered as in shoulder shots. And the extra velocity of the .340 Weatherby only serves to accentuate this point. Also, it has been my experience that not every rifle shoots it well.

As there are those who sing the praises of the 200 gr. for long range shooting, or any other kind of shooting for that matter, there are those, like Elmer Keith, who wouldn't even consider using anything less than the 250 gr. for shooting any game at any range. I'll be the first to agree that the 250 gr. is the optimum bullet weight in either cartridge for heavy game at ranges up to 300 yards or so, and it would be ideal for even longer ranges with a spitzer point, but few 250 gr. bullets have that form. Hornady's 250 gr. has a very blunt point, and Nosler is little better in the same weight. Barns (Colorado Custom) Bullets* makes a semi-spitzer that is fair for long range shape but is inclined to come apart at short to medium ranges on heavy game in its .032 jacket thickness, which is the only one they make in that weight, I believe.

By far the best 250 gr. bullet made as far as long range shape is concerned is the Sierra spitzer boattail, with its ballistic coefficient of .570. This extreme BC, coupled with the high sectional density of .313, gives it a retained energy of 2883 foot-pounds at 400 yards when started at 2900 fps from the .340 Weatherby or some big wildcat, according to Sierra figures. It is not quite as flat at any big game shooting range, however, as the 210 gr. Nosler at an MV of 3200 fps. While I have fired many rounds of handloads in both the .338 and the .340 loaded with this bullet in checking velocity and accuracy (and it is highly accurate), I have not used it on game. But after sectioning the bullet I have strong doubts that it will hold up under the velocity of the .340 on heavy bone and muscle at close-to-medium ranges. If all shots were to be taken at over 300 yards, it would be the finest long range .338 bullet of all.

More recently, I have tested the 250 gr. Sierra and 250 gr. Nosler at the same time for penetration and retained weight in my recovery box (described later) in the .340 Weatherby at an impact velocity of 2885 fps. The Sierra penetrated 18″ of the test medium and retained 107 gr. of the original 250 gr., or 42.8%. The Nosler drove in 30″ and weighed 172 gr. for a weight retention of 68.8%. Both measured .75″ across the average of the frontal area. In all fairness, the Sierra would show up better at long range where impact velocity has dropped off.

One of the best 250 gr. bullets for shooting heavy game at all ranges and in any position is the pointed hollow point Bitterroot Bonded Core. This bullet has good ballistic coefficient—listed at .508—expands well at any reasonable velocity, and gives the largest frontal area and the most retained weight of any bullet I have ever used. However, there is little reason to dwell on its performance, because it is not in production at this time, and I am told by its maker that there is no certainty if or when it will be back in

*"Barns" is the firm's original name, to which it has recently reverted, from "Colorado Custom."

production. This is indeed regrettable, because no better big game bullet has ever been made that I know of, and there are very few I have not tried at one time or another in some cartridge on some kind of game.

The round nose 250 gr. bullets of various makes, the 275 gr. Speer, and the 300 gr. Colorado Custom bullets will all kill very well at ranges out to 400 yards or more if they expand well at the reduced velocities they retain. The 250 gr. Nosler is the best of the lot, because it will expand well and will give extremely deep penetration for the heaviest game. The 275 gr. Speer has good ballistic coefficient, but even with the heaviest loads in the .340 Weatherby the velocity is not high, and by the time it reaches 400 yards it is so low that expansion is doubtful unless a heavy bone is hit—which means it may not expand at all on broadside lung shots. The same thing applies to the 300 gr. Considering this, and the greater drop of these bullets, the hunter should have second thoughts about shooting at more than about 300 yards with the latter two, especially in the .338 Winchester cartridge.

Except for a few big wildcat cartridges, there is only one .35 cartridge that can be considered for long range big game shooting, and that is the Norma .358 Magnum. There is actually little choice where bullets are concerned, because the 250 gr. is the only pointed bullet normally made in that caliber. Speer and Hornady both make pointed 250 gr. bullets in .35 caliber, and they will do fairly well on heavy game at long range when started at around 2800 fps from the .358 Norma or one of the big wildcats. The big problem with the big .35s is that no one except Bitterroot makes a controlled expansion bullet. While the pointed 250 gr. bullets mentioned do very well at the longer ranges, the fellows I have talked with who used them at short range found they were inclined to blow up on heavy game at Norma .358 velocity. Wildcat cartridges like the old .350 Griffen & Howe that boost a 250 gr. along at over 3000 fps are flat enough for long range shooting, but you only multiply the expansion problem by causing the bullet to blow up out to even longer ranges, and give less penetration at closer ranges as well. Frankly, with the .35 cartridge and the bullet situation standing the way it does today, it is not the answer to the long range rifleman's prayer.

Little needs to be said about the .375 H&H as a game killer of any thin-skinned game anywhere in the world, but considering it as a long range cartridge is something else again. There are .375 fans who maintain that it is a very good long range cartridge, but I think a close look at bullet drop will show this line of thought is not completely true. Using conventional round nose bullets in the 270 gr. at an MV of 2700 fps from the .375 H&H, you'll find that with the 3" high 100 yard sighting it will be down nearly 2 feet at 400 yards. With the 300 gr. at 2500 fps, the 400 yard drop will be just over the 2 foot mark with the same sighting. Also, energy for the 270 gr. will be down to about 1750 fp, and 1850 fp for the 300 gr. at the 400 yard mark. Of course, if these big bullets expand well at that range, killing power will be a lot more than these figures indicate. However, with these conventionally shaped bullets at these normal velocities, it brings the .375 H&H down to about 300 yards as an effective hit range without a lot of guessing that can get you in trouble. Remember that a .375 300 gr. bullet that breaks a bull elk's leg below the knee is no more effective than a .243 that does the same thing.

Hornady helps the .375 long range picture along considerably with their spire point 270 gr. that has a BC of .485. This bullet shoots very flat for a big bore, and will be down only about 18" at 400 yards with the 3"-plus 100 yard sighting. It also retains nearly 2400 fp of energy at that range at the 2700 fps normal MV. This would give a good solid hit on a bull elk out to about 350 yards with a center hold and no guesswork whatever, or a vital hit at 400 yards by holding at hairline on his back.

While this book was in the "growing" stage, the writer, along with a number of other gun bugs, was involved in the design of a 300 gr. .375 long range bullet with Sierra's Bob Hayden. After a few prototypes in both flat base and boattail, samples of the production bullet just arrived. I have not yet had time to do even bench tests, much less field testing on game or in the recovery box, but this should be the finest long range bullet ever made for the .375. According to Hayden, the new bullet has the astonishing ballistic coefficient of .577, which is the same as for the famous Sierra 200 gr. HP Matchking! Even with an MV of 2500 fps it would reach the 400 yard mark with about the same drop as the 270 gr. Hornady Spire Point. And a quick calculation shows it will retain about 2500 fp of its original muzzle energy of 4160 fp. In addition to its flat shooting capability, the new Sierra 300 gr. has a jacket that is tapered or thinned down at the point to ensure reliable expansion of the soft point at all game ranges, but the bearing surface of the bullet body behind the ogive has a very thick jacket of about .050" that should control expansion very well even at the much higher velocity delivered by the big .378 Weatherby. While the proof of the pudding is in the eating, and hunting bullet performance is proved only on big game, my own preference is for a flat base rather than a boattail because I have found that the flat base is more likely to retain its core if there is no other provision to hold it within the jacket. And once the core leaves the jacket, penetration soon comes to a halt.

For those who must have the most of everything, there is the .378 Weatherby Magnum; truly a magnum's magnum. While there is certainly little need for such a cartridge for shooting American big game, there is little doubt that it is a very potent long range cartridge. The .378 will boost both the 270 and the 300 gr. bullets along at about 400 fps higher velocity than the .375 H&H, so it is obvious that it will shoot a lot flatter. Drop figures would be nearer in line with the .340 Weatherby with 250 gr. bullets. Retained energy at long range is also higher than with the .375 H&H with bullets like the 270 and the 300 gr. Noslers, for example, and with the new Sierra 300 gr. spitzer boattail it would be a real long range heller on any thin-skinned game anywhere. The big problem here is whether you are man enough to shoot it well enough to hit anything at long range!

Some Facts About Recoil

And speaking of the recoil of the .378 Weatherby, this is one problem that all riflemen have to face up to, target shooters and hunters alike. It matters little whether you are shooting at 40 feet in the brush or 400 yards on the Alaskan tundra; the recoil is still there, and, knowing that, some hunters will bat their eyes and yank the whole rifle far out of line, causing a miss at the best, a wounded animal at the worst. The big difference between the hunter who shoots at an animal that suddenly appears in the thick stuff, and the one who stalks one and shoots from long range, is twofold. The

The author with antlers of big bull moose taken on Alaska Peninsula. Bull fell to .378 Weatherby and handload with 270 gr. Nosler backed by 116 gr. of H4831 for an MV of 3131 fps.

fellow in the brush has little time to think about anything except getting the shot off at the right spot as soon as possible while the animal is still there to shoot at. And unless he is a confirmed flincher there is little time to think about recoil. And even if he does flinch a little, the target is close and big and a few minutes of angle one way or the other isn't too critical.

It is a far different story for the fellow shooting at a muley buck or bull elk across a mountain meadow or a wide canyon. You've probably stalked him for a fairly long way and time, and you've had a lot of time to think about hits and misses before you even get within long range. Then after you get there you have a lot more time to size up the animal and the situation and get the shot off. And during this time, if you are recoil-conscious, you'll have subconscious thoughts about how hard the rifle is going to belt you. If that buck muley is 400 yards or so away, the bullet will have to land within two minutes of angle of where you know it should go, and that doesn't leave room for even a little flinch.

There are some shooters who can handle recoil extremely well. Not because they don't feel it (when some joker tells you he never feels recoil from any rifle he is either too numb to be walking around, or he is a damn liar), but because while they know it is going to belt them they can go right ahead and carefully squeeze the trigger anyway. On the other hand, there are an awful lot of hunters who are scared stiff of recoil and just plain can't help it—some admit it and some don't—but you'd just as well face up to it and either learn to whip it or shoot something you are not afraid of. It's kinda like going into the ring: you know damn well you are going to get hit, and if you don't think you can take it you'd better not crawl through the ropes in the first place.

And this recoil thing is not only a product of cartridges like the .378 Weatherby, but most of the other magnums as well, and some that aren't called by that name. How many times have you heard someone say he wouldn't think of shooting a 7mm or .300 magnum when he saw the cartridge for the first time? He didn't even have to shoot it, he just started mentally flinching when he looked at the big cartridge! With that attitude, those hunters will never find a cure for handling recoil, so they should stay away from cartridges that scare them. In fact, no matter what the reason, if you can't handle recoil, stay away from rifles that bother you, especially for long range big game shooting. If you can't hit 'em you can't kill 'em, but you may get close enough to wound them.

And one more thing, while we're on the subject of recoil. Many small people seem to think that if they were larger they could stand heavy recoil better. I've also known big guys who said they couldn't take stiff recoil because it jarred them more than it jarred the little fellow because it pushed him back easier. The plain truth is that the size of the shooter doesn't matter much. There are women around who shoot a .458 very well and don't weigh 120 pounds with a pocket full of cartridges. There are also six-foot-six, 250-pound men who do the same thing, while others just as big moan about the recoil of a .30-06. It is a lot more what you think about it than how you feel about it.

This point has been mentioned earlier, but we'll bring it up again here to drive it home: the velocity, and therefore the drop, of the bullets from factory ammunition will be found to vary considerably from those used here for the various cartridges. In chronographing the several brands of factory ammunition in standard hunting rifles, it was found that the factory-quoted velocity is almost always much higher than received. It was also found that the velocity between different lots of factory ammunition varies a good deal, just as different lots of powders will cause the velocity of handloaded ammunition to vary in the same rifle. Also, while nearly any ballistic sheet you pick up shows various brands of factory ammunition to give the same bullet weight the same velocity in the same cartridge, it is very unusual if it turns out that way. There may be as much as 150 fps difference in the velocity of a given bullet weight between brands. Generally speaking, factory ammunition will give more bullet drop than we have indicated here, because we have used normal full power handloads on which to base the figures. To project bullet drop by using factory-quoted velocity, as has been done by so many writers in the past, would only mislead the hunter. It would also be misleading to handloaders who attain much higher velocities in some cartridges than are loaded in factory ammunition.

We've done our best to give you an honest, reasonably accurate picture of where your bullets will land at various hunting ranges with various cartridges with the sighting considered the best for medium and long range big game shooting. The only way to be sure of where the bullets from *your rifle* with *your load* will land at various ranges is to shoot at those ranges. Even then, as already pointed out, you will not always be correct under all hunting conditions you'll encounter at various times and places.

8

Cartridges and Loads for Heavy Game at Close Quarters

When speaking of shooting any kind of big game at close quarters we usually visualize it as being in heavy cover. While this isn't necessarily true, it probably is the case in at least 75% of hunting situations. There are times, of course, when it is possible to stalk to within close range of game that is right out in the open; but for all practical purposes, it makes little difference as far as the load used is concerned. The main point is that at close quarters the hunter doesn't usually have much time to fool around waiting for the animal to turn to exactly the right position before firing. Any little noise, the slightest movement, or a sudden shift of air currents will alert the quarry to your presence and send it into immediate flight. And once in high gear there is certainly no chance to carefully pick the spot where the bullet will land. Even if after a jump or two the animal should stop to see what spooked it, it is very unusual for it to stand broadside. It is obvious that under these conditions a bullet that will dig in deep and reach the vital organs from nearly any angle is a must unless you intend to pass up the shot, and the truth is that few hunters will hold their fire.

It is very easy to sit in a comfortable chair in front of the fireplace and tell your hunting buddies how you never fire at an animal unless you know the bullet will land in the right place from the right angle, and it is also easy to do it on a typewriter, but when the chips are down, damn few hunters remember to do it. The plain truth is that the closer you are to the game, the more likely you are to shoot without even making sure you are shooting at the right spot, let alone from the right angle. The animal is so big and close that you are a lot more inclined to shoot at the middle of what you can see than if it is farther away, where you know you have to hold well to get the bullet in the right spot. And if you are a trophy hunter who has spent a big chunk of change on a hunt and suddenly find yourself within spitting distance of the one you've been looking for, you are even more likely to shoot first and worry about pinpoint aiming and angles afterward. Maybe this isn't the way it *should* be, but it's the way it is.

Then there is another fact of brush-hunting life that few hunters consider, because they don't know it until it is too late, and then often blame it on a bullet that for some unknown reason changed angle of flight after it landed. This does happen, but it is *damn* unusual. What really happens is that the animal is not standing in

A heavy controlled expansion bullet placed at + will drop this huge bull in his tracks. He will not die instantly but can be dispatched quickly. To reach lungs, a bullet would have to penetrate full length of paunch, and even the best may not make it. At this range it would not be difficult to place bullet in brain at base of ear, but no trophy hunter would take a chance on splitting the skull, with those great antlers scoring far up in the record book.

the position it appears to be. In the thick stuff, there are more times you don't see all of the animal than when you do. And even if you do see all of it, there are shadows and dim light to confuse the picture. There is more than an even chance that the animal that appears to be broadside is quartering one way or the other. If you can't see it too clearly, either because of light or foliage, it may be standing in a twist, so what appears to be a broadside rib shot actually lands the bullet in paunch or shoulder even though headed for the lungs.

Then there are the times when you see only part of the animal as it stands looking over its back at you, and it is easy to confuse one part of the body below the head with another. I'm reminded of an elk I once shot under these conditions, and my surprise at where the bullet landed.

I was hunting in high lodgepole pine country along the Idaho-Montana line in early October. The bulls were still bugling now and then, and would answer occasionally, but showed no inclination to come to my call. I'd had this old bull answering me every ten minutes or so while I worked up on him around the head of a canyon for nearly two miles. I was certain he had a harem with him by the way he acted, and this suited me fine because I was looking for a winter meat supply that didn't include an old rut-thin bull. I hoped to be able to slip up and pick out one of his lady friends and let the old boy go on with his lovemaking.

He had been moving slowly away from me and at last stopped on a bench just under the top of the ridge where it seemed likely they would bed for the day. After pinpointing his location with a last answer to my challenge, I eased up over the ridge and sat down to see if something could be located on the heavily timbered bench below. Shortly there was movement on the bench, and I made out part of the head of a big cow and patches of body through the hair-thick lodgepole tangle of standing and down trees. Part of the nose, one eye, and one ear were plainly visible through the 4X scope, and I could see a 10″ patch of body along the back line below the twitching ear. Looking lower, I saw a leg near the ground in direct line with the patch of body hair below the head, so it seemed obvious that the elk was looking back over its shoulder in my direction. It was only about 100 yards away and had not seen or winded me, so there was no particular hurry, but a bullet in the shoulder just under the spine was as good as any, so I settled the cross hair at the bottom of the little opening and touched it off. At the shot, elk exploded all over the bench with a crashing of timber that sounded like a logger's D-8 going through the brush, and the big cow disappeared behind the windfall.

When I came out of the brush 20 yards from where she lay, I was surprised to see her up on her front legs and trying to take off. A bullet between the eyes as she looked back put an end to that, but it was not until I stood over her that I saw where the first bullet had passed, quartering through both hips and spine. She had been looking back over her hips instead of her shoulder!

It doesn't take a great deal of experience in hunting elk to know what would likely have happened that day had I been using a light thin-skinned deer bullet of small caliber. But with the .333 OKH Belted cartridge starting a 250 gr. Barns .049" jacket bullet that

This is typical elk country at an altitude of about 8,500 feet, which may require shooting at anything from a few yards to as far as hunter and cartridge are capable of hitting and killing. A potent cartridge that shoots flat is the ideal elk medicine here.

had been hollow pointed for better expansion at 2700 fps ahead of 65 gr. of 4350, there was no problem whatever. The same shot would have taken care of a bull moose with that load just as well as the cow elk. If I made this mistake after hunting elk and guiding elk hunters to far over 100 kills, it isn't hard for the once-a-year hunter to shoot at the wrong spot even when he doesn't intend to. This is why it is a lot better to be "overgunned" for hunting heavy game in the brush, or even out of it at close quarters, than it is to be "undergunned."

Cartridges and Bullets for Close Range

As for the cartridges that do the best job at close quarters, there are a lot more of them than there are for long range shooting. One reason for this is that nearly all the long range cartridges are just as good for close-in use as they are for long range work on heavy game if you use the right bullet. This means a bullet that has complete expansion control like the Nosler, which will not blow up and cause only a shallow surface wound at the high terminal velocity of a long range cartridge at close range. And in addition to those rounds, there are many cartridges that, again with the right bullet, are ideal for short range shooting of heavy game but are near worthless at long range. These cartridges run all the way from the .348 and .358 Winchesters to the .458. We won't attempt to cover them all here, but if you'll look at any reloading manual or factory ballistic sheet, you can compare the ones that are not mentioned here with the ones that are and see how they stack up.

There are a number of cartridges that some hunters have considered good brush cartridges for heavy game but that are far from ideal because they do not pack enough punch regardless of bullet design to drive them through the heavy bone, muscle, or paunch material of big animals to reach the engine room. Two examples of this are the .30-30 Win. and the .35 Rem. Caliber makes little difference here because while the .35 Remington uses a 200 gr. bullet, and the .30-30 a 170 gr., the .30 caliber 170 gr. has a good deal more sectional density than the 200 gr. .35. The .35 Remington does pack a bit more wallop, but not enough more to be very meaningful on a bull elk or moose, and any advantage it has in energy is completely canceled out if it doesn't get inside where it counts to deliver it. I've seen a number of mule deer and elk shot with the .35 Remington and factory 200 gr. Remington Core-Lokt loads, and few went through the deer, with none making exit in even small elk shot broadside through the ribs. These bullets in that cartridge give some of the most perfect examples of mushroom you'll ever see, and retained weight is extremely good, but the cartridge just does not have enough punch to give either shock or penetration enough for big, tough animals. I hunted with a fellow who used one for a number of seasons, and it would be conservative to say that he lost two elk of every three shot, and at least one deer out of four. His trouble with deer came from trying rather long shots with iron sights, but after doing autopsies on the few elk he recovered, I want no part of the .35 Remington as an elk cartridge.

Big Bores and Heavy Bullets Not Always Reliable on Heavy Game

The same thing can be said for the .444 Marlin and the .45-70 if light bullets are used in the latter. The reason for this is that when you expand one of those short large caliber bullets, which must happen if it is to deliver any killing power, there is so little shank left that it is about like trying to drive a washer in flatwise. Also, when those short, fat bullets expand to any extent, the core almost invariably leaves the jacket and cuts penetration even further. And, believe it or not, the same thing can happen to the .458 Winchester if the bullet jacket is too thin and expands too rapidly and too much. If you don't believe this, try a .45-70 405 gr. bullet in the .458 case loaded full-power on something that is big and tough or in some good bullet expansion material.

I had an experience a few years back that illustrates this point exceedingly well. I was testing a prototype of the now defunct Sharps Model 78 modern single shot rifle chambered for the .375 H&H cartridge. The rifle gave exceedingly tight groups with the discontinued 285 gr. Speer bullet backed by 70 gr. of 4064 that gave an MV of 2745 fps from the 30″ barrel. It seemed this combination should make a good heavy game load, so I took it on a hunt for Shiras moose in eastern Idaho.

The bull I decided to take was below me and about 175 yards away, belly-deep in a big beaver pond. I figured this load should flatten the old boy (I should have known better from past experience), so when he stepped up on the edge of the beaver dam with his big nose hanging over, I held for his heart and touched it off. That bull didn't do more than shudder a little, and slowly backed out into the middle of that big ice-covered mud pie. I was sitting down with a beautiful rest over a log and knew within an inch of where that bullet had landed, so there was nothing to do but wait and pray that he'd come out of the drink before he collapsed. He made three trips backing to the center of the pond and back to the dam before he finally realized he was dead, and expired with his head hanging over the dam. The hell I had gutting him and getting him out of that mess was nothing to do with bullet action, so we'll skip it, but the shooting did prove two things: that a large caliber heavy bullet doesn't necessarily mean deep penetration, and that there is no such thing as knockdown power. The 285 gr. .375 bullet had gone exactly where intended, entering just behind the foreleg, taking the top off the heart and punching a hole in the lungs you could stick your head in, and what was left of it was lodged against the ribs on the far side. It had completely ruptured, leaving only the jacket.

Under the circumstances it had done a good job, and the fact that the moose lived a couple of minutes was not the fault of bullet action, but just moose nature. Had that bullet been placed quartering into a shoulder, it is extremely doubtful that it would ever have reached the lungs. And this was from 175 yards, where it had shed much of its original velocity; penetration would have been even less at 50 yards or so, much less.

The significance of this is that just because a bullet is of large caliber and heavy weight does not necessarily make it a good bullet for shooting heavy game at close quarters. As mentioned earlier, even large caliber combined with great sectional density does not make it ideal, because if the structure is not right, it will blow up and fail to penetrate. At the time I was doing a lot of elk hunting with the .333 OKH Belted wildcat, I tried every bullet I could lay hands on in an attempt to find one that would not come apart on the heavy bone of big bulls at close range in the brush but would drive on into the boiler room from any reasonable angle. The 300 gr. Kynoch of British manufacture seemed like a good bet with its phenomenal sectional density of .376. This bullet was to teach me a lesson that many hunters have never learned: even extreme sectional density will not make a bullet penetrate if design and structure are wrong. These bullets were not only about as long as a lodgepole pine, they had steel jackets that have been proclaimed by some to make the ideal envelope for a soft point bullet. They also had a big, round, almost flat point, with about 3/4 of the bullet diameter of soft lead exposed. To make a long story less boring, they failed miserably in the penetration department.

The first one I tried on a smallish five-point bull at about 75 yards nearly broadside through the lungs. It dropped him almost instantly, and it made an unsightly mess of his lungs, also ruining most of the off shoulder, but a 95 gr. Nosler 6mm bullet would have given more penetration. It angled forward a little from where it landed 6″ behind the near shoulder, and ended up about 4″ before reaching the hide of the off shoulder behind the bone. Only a single rib was hit on entrance. That supposedly tough steel jacket had peeled back like a banana skin clear to the heel, and the soft lead core had sprayed out like a skeet load. Sure, it did a good job, if you like blood pudding, but if it had landed in his shoulder headed back to the engine room, it would have blown up long before it got there. On the same shot a 210 gr. Nosler .338 bullet would have left a dollar-size (a pre-inflation dollar) exit hole and 75% less ruined meat. Of course, one has to take into consideration the fact that those 300 gr. Kynoch bullets were designed for the .333 Jeffery cartridge that started it at about 2100 fps in a Kynoch factory load, while I handloaded it to a muzzle velocity of over 2400 fps in the .333 OKH Belted case. (Almost identical in performance with the .338 Winchester Magnum.) That extra 300 fps, and the fact that it landed in the elk's ribs at near muzzle velocity, were more than the jacket would stand.

There are still some hunters who like some of the old large caliber cartridges for shooting heavy game in the brush that use fairly heavy bullets at rather low velocity. Their reason is that these bullets give reliable expansion without blowing up like the bullets from some of the higher velocity cartridges do. They have a point, because these old low velocity cartridges do not tear their bullets apart, but, like the .35 Remington, most of them do not penetrate very well either, because they don't have a great deal of push left after the bullet expands, and deliver no great amount of shock either. It is not a matter of the low velocity cartridge being better, but the fact that nearly any jacketed bullet will hold up under the velocity they churn up.

The plain truth of the matter is that any of the long range cartridges that are suitable for heavy game at medium to long range will perform very well on the same animals at close quarters if you use the heavier bullet weights in that caliber and they have controlled expansion. The larger calibers are to be preferred somewhat over the small bores because they make a larger, longer wound channel. And they'll break up more heavy bone if you are trying to immobilize the beast, or must drive the bullet through it to get inside. They'll also give a quicker kill, or at least slow the animal up until you can get in a second shot, than will the small bores if they don't land exactly where they should. It's about like having a little guy poke you on the button—it hurts like hell but you can still dish out a few of your own—but if a big, fast guy pokes you in the same place you'll likely wake up on the canvas.

Even so, and while my old hunting partner Elmer Keith will strongly disagree, I'd much rather go into the bushes looking for a bull elk or moose, or even an Alaskan brown bear, with a 7mm mag. with a powder charge that starts a 175 gr. Nosler at 3000 fps, than with a .358 Winchester and a 250 gr. load, either factory- or hand-brewed. Of course, if I had my druthers, I'd feel a little better, especially with a brownie, if I had my .340 Weatherby with a 250 gr. Nosler or Bitterroot. The hard fact is, and I've tried it on enough big ones to know, that the 175 gr. Nosler 7mm bullet from one of the big 7s will penetrate as deep as any expanding bullet we have in any caliber from any cartridge, the .458 included. But of course it doesn't pack the punch of the bigger bores.

Anything less potent than the .270 Winchester, or of smaller bore, is not desirable, and even with the .270 bullets like the 150 and 160 gr. Nosler, or possibly the 170 gr. Speer in handloads, or the Remington 150 gr. pointed Core-Lokt in a factory offering, are far better than the 130 gr. The venerable old .30-06 is still a good cartridge at close quarters if loaded full-throttle with well-designed 200 or 220 gr. bullets. However, as mentioned elsewhere, the .30-06 cartridge is badly underloaded in factory ammunition. As the load chart will clearly show, if the old cartridge is loaded with the right powders to its full potential, it is a pretty potent cartridge in any company. And the fact that if you handload it you can use the right bullet for the job at hand, in this case a 200 gr. Nosler or 220 gr. Hornady or Sierra, makes it even more efficient. Even the .308 Winchester will work fairly well with 200–220 gr. bullets, but when you saddle the small capacity cartridge with heavy bullets it doesn't pack any too much wallop.

The Speer 225 gr. does very well in the 8mm Mauser cartridge at close range with a stiff handload, but no domestic factory load is worth a damn for heavy game. I know of no decent bullet for heavy game in the .348 at close range being made today. I believe Hornady and Colorado Custom Bullets are the only makers of bullets in that caliber, and both Winchester and Remington load factory ammunition with the 200 gr. bullet. That bullet weight has poor sectional density, only a little more than the 150 gr. .30 caliber, so even if it held together, which it usually doesn't on anything big at close range, penetration would be poor. And with a muzzle velocity of only about 2500 fps, energy is not overly impressive. The 200 gr. Remington Core-Lokt would probably be the best bet for big animals at close range. The 250 gr. load was by far the best in this cartridge at ranges up to maybe 200 yards, but it was discontinued within a few years after its birth. It can still be handloaded with the 250 gr. CCB.

This is but a cross section of the various cartridges that are adapted to shooting heavy game at close range, and they are offered as examples to show why they work or don't. Other cartridges with similar ballistics will do as well, providing bullets are made for them that will hold up under the velocity of the cartridge when the going gets tough.

Flat trajectory is of little or no importance, and sighting should be done at about 100 yards to zero dead on. You can, of course, use the 3″ high 100 yard sighting if you take your long range or all-around rifle into the brush—just remember to hold a bit low for head, neck, and "small hole" shots. This being the case, velocity is important only because the more you have the more energy the bullet delivers when it lands. But to sum it up in a few words, if velocity is low, nearly any big, heavy bullet will do fairly well, but it won't pack too much wallop. If you do have fairly high velocity, even a long heavy bullet isn't enough for the kind of penetration needed on heavy game under adverse shooting conditions. It not only has to stay in one piece, but expansion must be controlled so there is enough weight left in the unexpanded shank to drive it through the heaviest bone and muscle, and even a big grass-and-water-filled paunch, to reach the vitals and tear them up after it gets there.

And, as was pointed out for shooting deer-size animals at close quarters, a pointed bullet will do just as well as a round nose. Fact is, I much prefer them in either pointed or semipointed form. The reason for this is that either one has less lead exposed, and if there is less exposed core with the opening in the jacket point being smaller, expansion is slower. This not only gives deeper penetration, but the greatest point of expansion takes place deeper within the animal, where it does the most good. This is probably one reason why the 175 gr. Nosler will normally give deeper penetration than the 200 gr. .30 caliber when both are started at near the same velocity and range is the same. Many hunters think the big, round, soft point bullets are the best in the brush simply because this is what they have always been told, and all the so-called brush cartridges have either flat or round point bullets. As was pointed out in hunting deer-size game, the round point bullet is little if any better for plowing through brush than the spitzer—just avoid hitting any obstruction and you'll have no problems.

Of much more importance than bullet point shape is the fact that in sharp contrast to long range shooting where velocity will always be greatly reduced from muzzle velocity, at close quarters it is always near starting speed. Because velocity is what tears bullets apart on impact, the toughest expanding bullet available is the one to use. Some form of controlled expansion is a must for close-in shooting of heavy game with high velocity cartridges, and it matters not what the bore diameter of the barrel is.

It has been suggested by some writers that for hunting in the thick stuff, where 99% of the shooting will be done at under 100 yards, the handloader can reduce the velocity and bullets will hold together better and give much deeper penetration. This is certainly correct, but remember that if velocity is cut by very much, energy also drops off, and you may find your .300 magnum delivering no more wallop than a .300 Savage. It takes a big punch to stop big animals, so you are much wiser to use a bullet that will withstand the velocity of powerful cartridges and give deep penetration, rather than to cut the velocity and energy to try to attain the same thing from a poorly constructed bullet.

.338 Winchester Magnum, Ruger Model 77 24" bbl.
W-W cases weight 240 gr.
CCI no. 250 primers
Temp. 70° F.

BULLET	POWDER	CHARGE	MV FPS
275 gr. Speer SP semipointed	MRP	74	2593
	785	78	2649
	IMR4831	73	2602
	H205	72	2606
250 gr. Nosler RP	MRP	75	2759
	785	79	2789
	IMR4831	75	2783
	H205	73	2775
W-W 250 gr. ST factory load	—	—	2639
225 gr. Hornady SP	MRP	78	2894
	IMR4831	77	2897
	H205	76	2889
	4350	75	2894
210 gr. Nosler SP	MRP	80	2961
	IMR4831	79	2985
	785	83	2971
	H205	78	2992
200 gr. Speer SP	IMR4831	80	3068
	785	85	3041
	H205	79	3014
	4350	77	3024

These loads were all near maximum in the test rifle and should be approached from 4 gr. below.

See pp. 44–45 for note with supplementary information, and for explanation of abbreviations used in charts.

BULLET DROP SIGHTED 3″ HIGH AT 100 YARDS FOR BIG GAME SHOOTING

100 YARDS	200 YARDS	300 YARDS	400 YARDS	VITAL HIT WITH CENTER HOLD
+3″	+3″	−6″	−22″	Antelope 285 yards Deer 310 yards Elk 350 yards Moose 400 yards
All loads similar drop.				
+3″	+4″	−4″	−19″	Antelope 310 yards Deer 335 yards Elk 370 yards Moose 400 yards
All loads similar drop.				
Drop will be similar to 275 gr. Speer handloads.				
+3″	+4″	−3″	−16″	Antelope 325 yards Deer 350 yards Elk 400 yards Moose 425 yards
All loads similar drop.				
+3″	+4″	−1″	−13″	Same as for 225 gr. Hornady
All loads similar drop.				
+3″	+4.5″	−0.0″	−11″	Same as for 225 gr. Hornady
All loads similar drop.				

.340 Weatherby Magnum, M-70 Win. action 23 1/2″ Hobaugh bbl., no free-bore
W-W .375 H&H cases fire-formed, weight 251 gr.
CCI no. 250 primers
Temp. 70° F.

BULLET	POWDER	CHARGE	MV FPS
275 gr. Speer SP semipointed	H4831	81	2741
	N205	81	2760
250 gr. Nosler RP	H4831	85	2901
	N205	82	2902
225 Hornady SP Ptd.	H4831	87	3020
	N205	85	3034
	4350	81	3008
210 Nosler SP Ptd.	H4831	89	3078
	N205	88	3215
	4350	85	3157

All 200 gr. bullets will take same charges as for 210 gr. Nosler, give approximately the same velocity and drop.

BULLET DROP SIGHTED 3″ HIGH AT 100 YARDS FOR BIG GAME SHOOTING

100 YARDS	200 YARDS	300 YARDS	400 YARDS	VITAL HIT WITH CENTER HOLD
+3″	+3″	−5″	−23″	Antelope 290 yards
Similar drop.				Deer 315 yards
				Elk 360 yards
				Moose 410 yards
+3″	+4″	−2″	−16″	Antelope 320 yards
Same drop.				Deer 345 yards
				Elk 385 yards
				Moose 410 yards
+3″	+4.5″	−1″	−12″	Antelope 340 yards
All loads similar drop.				Deer 365 yards
				Elk 400 yards
				Moose 425 yards
+3″	+4.5″	−1″	−11″	Antelope 350 yards
+3″	+5″	0.0″	−9″	Deer 375 yards
Similar drop.				Elk 425 yards
				Moose 450 yards

.340 Weatherby Magnum, Wby. Mark V 26″ bbl., Weatherby free-bore. Weatherby load data with Weatherby cases weight 237 gr. These loads should be used in Weatherby rifles with Weatherby cases.

BULLET	POWDER	CHARGE	MV FPS
250 gr.	H4831	85	2860
	N205	83.5	2850
	4350	76	2800
210 gr. Nosler	4350	86	3172
200 gr.	H4831	90	3137
	N205	91	3210
	4350	84	3210

.375 H&H, Winchester Model 70 24″ bbl.
W-W cases weight 251 gr.
CCI no. 250 primers
Temp. 70° F.

BULLET	POWDER	CHARGE	MV FPS
300 gr. Nosler	N205	87	2758
	4350	84	2704
	N204	83	2718
270 gr. Nosler	N205	91	2872
	4350	86	2813
	N204	87	2861
235 gr. Speer SP Ptd.	N204	91	3015
	4320	78	2987
	N203	78	2977

These loads were all near maximum in the test rifle and should be approached from 4 gr. below.

100 YARDS	200 YARDS	300 YARDS	400 YARDS	VITAL HIT WITH CENTER HOLD

Drop figures will be somewhat more than for those taken from the custom .340 Wby. with the higher velocity possible with the stronger .375 H&H W-W cases.

BULLET DROP SIGHTED 3″ HIGH AT 100 YARDS FOR BIG GAME SHOOTING

100 YARDS	200 YARDS	300 YARDS	400 YARDS	VITAL HIT WITH CENTER HOLD
+3″	+3″	−5″	−22″	Antelope 300 yards Deer 325 yards Elk 350 yards Moose 375 yards
All loads similar drop.				
+3″	+4″	−4″	−21″	Approximately the same as for 300 gr.
All loads similar drop.				
+3″	+4″	−2″	−16″	Antelope 325 yards Deer 350 yards Elk 375 yards Moose 400 yards
All loads similar drop.				

9

Cartridges and Loads for General Hunting

In speaking of cartridges for general hunting of North American big game, we refer not only to cartridges and loads that are suitable for a certain class of big game under certain conditions, but to all classes of game under all conditions normally encountered in hunting them. To put it another way, let's assume the hunter is making a hunting trip for a general bag in one of the western big game states of Idaho, Montana, or Wyoming. On that trip it is possible that he may hunt such assorted animals as antelope, deer—either whitetails or muleys—mountain goats, bighorn sheep, elk, moose, black bear, and possibly grizzly. If the hunt takes place farther north, in western Canada, British Columbia for example, many sections will offer game of similar size. In fact, most of the same species will be hunted in both places, except that there will be no antelope, and caribou will take their place, with a chance at wolf added. Also, the chance for a shot at a grizzly will be much more likely, and the moose will run larger.

Going still farther north to Alaska, the hunting may take on even a wider spread in the size of the game hunted; Alaskan moose are much larger than their Wyoming cousins far to the south, and also run a bit heavier than the Canadian moose, with the exception of those found in the Yukon. Then, in addition to the mountain grizzly, there is the Alaskan brown bear of the offshore islands and coastal areas.

It is obvious that not only the size of the game hunted in any of these areas varies a great deal, but that the ranges at which they will be shot will vary equally. To make the choice of cartridges and loads even more critical in Canadian and Alaskan hunting for a mixed bag, there is the possibility that either the mountain grizzly or the Alaskan brown bear may fight back if it isn't put completely out of commission with the first shot. The possibility of a bear hassle becomes even greater when hunting the big browns in Southeast Alaska along the salmon streams that flow through the unbelievably thick growth of the rain forests, or the hair-thick willows and alders bordering salmon-run streams in any part of coastal Alaska. Of course, it may be argued that one usually hunts brown bears as a single item on a hunt, and, this being the case, the cartridge and load can be suited to hunting brown bears only. This is normally true of spring bear hunts, but certainly is not true of many fall hunts where the hunter may look for a full mixed bag of smaller or nondangerous game on the same trip. Sure, I know that many hunters recommend taking two rifles on every major hunting trip, one for the smaller species like deer, antelope, goat, sheep, and maybe caribou, and a more potent cartridge for elk, moose, and the big bears if present. I've made a lot of hunts in some pretty remote places for a lot of different kinds of game on the same hunt in assorted sizes, shapes, and colors, and I seldom find it either desirable or practical to take more than one rifle. The only reason you ever need two is in case of an accident; barring that, one is plenty if you choose the right cartridge and load or loads.

All-Around Cartridges and Loads

Actually, what we are talking about here is an all-around cartridge; a cartridge for which a load or loads can be worked out that will take care of any game and hunting situation you will come up against on the hunt. I know that many experienced hunters claim that the all-around cartridge for North American big game hunting does not exist and is not likely to be designed. There is some merit to this line of thinking, if you want to split hairs, but, on the other hand, there are some pretty strong examples of proof to the contrary.

For example, consider the cartridges used by some of the most

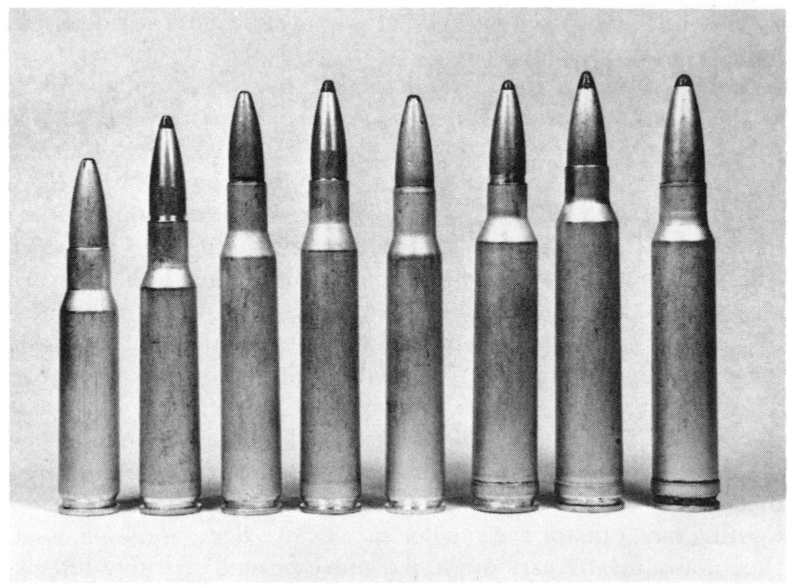

All these cartridges have been considered by some hunters as suited to all-around shooting of most American big game. However, some of the less powerful numbers should not be used for the larger species under all hunting conditions. *From left:* .308 Win.; 7×57 Mauser; .270 Win.; .280 Rem.; .30-06; 7mm Rem. Mag.; .300 Win. Mag.; .338 Win. Mag.

---

experienced hunters and knowledgeable gun people we have today. Take Jack O'Connor and his .270. He has hunted and killed about all kinds of North American big game with one, except Alaskan brown bears, and for that hunting he used a .375 H&H, with good success. Warren Page wandered around over most of the continent knocking off everything that got in his way with a 7mm Mashburn Super Magnum loaded mostly with 175 gr. Nosler bullets. Elmer Keith shot a great deal of big game from Mexico to the Bering Sea, and while he used various cartridges and calibers, it is no news to any gun buff that he favors the .338 cartridges with nothing less than a 250 gr. bullet for everything from mule deer to brown bears.

Then there is the late Grancel Fitz, who didn't claim to know much about guns, but was an outstanding hunter of trophy-class

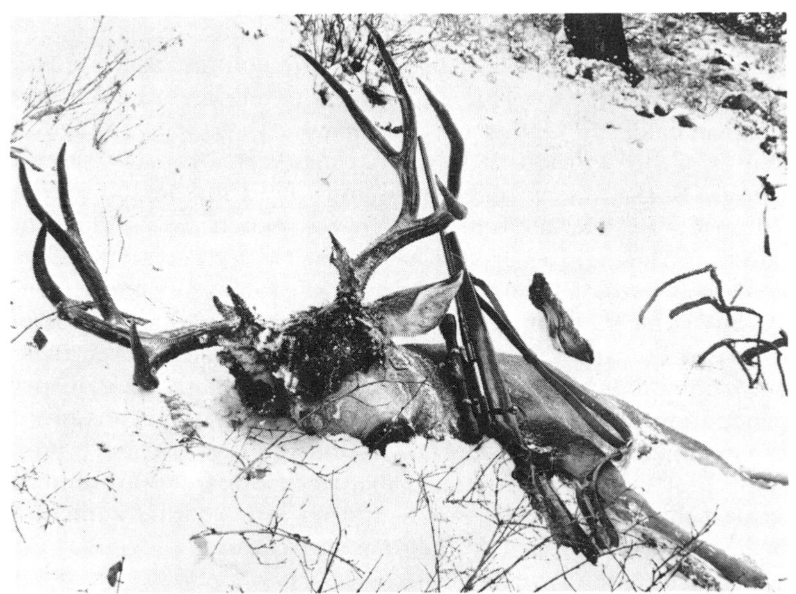

This big buck mule deer was killed with .30-06 and load of 180 gr. Sierra BT ahead of 62 gr. N205 at 2938 fps MV. The old .30-06 cartridge, when loaded to its full potential with modern powders in a strong bolt action like this Weatherby Vanguard—and with the right bullet—makes a good all-around cartridge for nearly any American game.

American big game, and one of the few men who had taken trophy animals of all species of North American big game. You might say Fitz was a "middle-of-the-roader" because, if I remember correctly, he used a battered old .30-06 for all hunting, and I believe with factory ammunition.

What does all this prove? Maybe more than you think. While it is obvious that all these hunters can't be right, it does show that if you use the right load, are a good shot, keep cool when the time comes to shoot, and know where to place the bullet you are using in the right spot to do the most good, you can get by with any good cartridge and load. It does *not* mean, however, that any one of these cartridges, or any other cartridge, stands bullet, neck, and shoulder above all other cartridges, and that it will perform feats that no other cartridge will.

Every so often some joker who portrays himself as an expert expounds on the virtues of some cartridge that are possessed by no other cartridge even though several others may show nearly identical ballistics. One character a few years ago was singing the praises of the .270 Winchester, and claimed that he once stuck a 130 gr. Nosler into a bull moose and found it 6 feet from the entrance hole. He allowed that that was penetration enough to satisfy anyone, and I agree! I have seen Nosler Partition bullets used on everything from pronghorn to Alaskan moose and brownies, and in every diameter in which they are made, as well as in most weights, and I've also followed their path and carved them out if they didn't make exit. They will consistently give deeper penetration than any other expanding bullet that expands properly in the same weight that I know of, but about 36" of penetration is the best I ever observed, and that was from a 175 gr. 7mm. I suspect this fellow got his facts confused with what he wanted to believe. Either that, or that bull moose was as full of wind as the guy punching the typewriter.

The fact is that there is no such thing as "mystic killing power." There is no magic potion inside any case that gives it that "extra something" no other cartridge has. No cartridge will kill any better than the hard, cold ballistics show it will, providing the right bullet is used for the velocity delivered.

Some hunters carry this blind faith in a certain cartridge even further out in left field. I've known a number of hunters who have killed a lot of deer, elk, and maybe some other species of game, who think anyone who uses a .30-30 has lost at least a couple of marbles, yet they believe the .30-06 they use is the greatest cartridge ever spawned for everything from jackrabbits to polar bears. According to their line of thinking, the .30-30 is short on killing power for a big buck muley at 100 yards, yet they tell tales of knocking off deer and elk with a single bullet every time at ranges of 400–500 yards with their .30-06 with factory 180 gr. loads. Assuming that the factory loads for both cartridges give the muzzle velocity accorded them in factory ballistic sheets, the .30-30 delivers the 170 gr. bullet at 100 yards at 1895 fps with 1355 fp of energy. The .30-06 with the pointed 180 gr. Core-Lokt bullet arrives at the 400 yard mark at 1846 fps with 1362 fp of energy (Remington figures). It is hardly logical that the bullet from the

.30-06 will do a better job of killing at 400 yards than the .30-30 bullet does at 100 yards when velocity and energy are that close. There is also the undisputed fact that it is easier to place a bullet from the .30-30 in the right spot at 100 yards than from the .30-06 at 400 yards. It is also a known fact that bullet expansion is not as reliable from the .30-06 at 400 yards with its heavier jacket as with the .30-30 bullet at 100 yards.

The point of all this is that if you intend to use the same cartridge for shooting all classes of game under all hunting conditions, you should realize its limitations and not expect it to perform reliably beyond those limitations, whether handloaded or factory ammunition.

During my hunting career I have killed some form of big game with a variety of cartridges from the .22 Long Rifle, and a number of handgun cartridges, to rifle cartridges ranging from the .25-35 Winchester to the .378 Weatherby, and some larger calibers that were less potent than the big Weatherby. While I own a number of rifles chambered for various cartridges, and have killed a good deal of game with all of them, I seldom use the same rifle two years in a row, and not usually on successive hunts in the same year. In continually testing everything new that comes along from commercial sources, as well as wildcats in many calibers, shapes, and sizes, in the hunting country and through the screens and on paper, one gets a lot of experience he would miss if he got hung up on a single cartridge. In this kind of testing and evaluation of cartridges, loads, and bullets, it eventually begins to sink in that there is no one "best" cartridge, but that there are a number that will give similar results if you use the right load.

Many years ago I discovered that the really small bore cartridges of 6mm, .25, and 6.5mm caliber were far from ideal as all-around cartridges for North American big game shooting, whether they were low or high velocity numbers. Of course, the Weatherby offerings, along with the .264 Winchester, are much better choices than the lesser cartridges if you use the right bullet, but even then they leave a lot to be desired. While Jack O'Connor and a lot of other hunters have proved that the .270 Winchester can be successfully used on nearly any North American big game, this doesn't make it the best choice for the average hunter. If I had to use it for an all-around cartridge for hunting all game under the many conditions encountered, it would be with the 150 gr. Nosler loaded just as hot as the rifle and case used would stand for trouble-free hunting. Even then it seems there are many cartridges better suited to general hunting for all classes of big game found on this continent.

I know I'll get some static here, but my own preference would be the .30-06 in a standard capacity case. The reason for this is that with good handloads in both cartridges using the 150 gr. in the .270 and the 180 gr. in the .30-06, velocity, energy, and drop at ranges out to 400 yards are very similar, and the .30 caliber 180 gr. bullet has the advantage of extra diameter and weight for shock and tissue disruption. (Factory ballistics do not bear this out because the .30-06 is badly underloaded in factory loads on account of some of the old rifles in which it is chambered, while the .270 is loaded to much higher pressures and consequent velocity.) As an example, factory figures show the 180 gr. .30-06 bullet starting at 2700 fps (I have never chronographed any brand that gave that much velocity), but with the right powder it is possible to give that bullet far over 2800 fps at about the same pressure as developed by the .270 factory loads. In fact, as the chart on .30-06 loads shows, I have received 2900 fps from the 180 gr. bullet with some lots of Norma 205 powder, and pressures were mild enough to permit reuse of the cases a dozen times. Then, if the game is big and tough, there are always the 200 and 220 gr. .30 caliber bullets that give the bone-smashing power and penetration required to immobilize them.

These are the same reasons why I prefer the 7mm cartridges over the .270. Perhaps this should be modified to omit the 7×57 Mauser, because it does not deliver enough velocity or energy to outclass the .270 as an all-around cartridge, or even for general hunting if we omit the very largest species. I say this after shooting a great many head of big game from antelope to elk with this good old cartridge in both factory and heavy handloads. It is a good and reliable cartridge, but not as good as the .270 with the best bullets in both cases. If we go another step up the ladder to the .280 Remington, which is a favorite of both Fred Huntington, who has a good deal of experience on American big game, and Jim Carmichel, who has used it some in the past three or four years, there is little doubt that it is a better choice than the .270, because of the heavier bullets available and the slightly increased velocity with all bullet weights. While I've fired many hundreds of rounds from a .280 Remington, I never killed any game with one, but I have killed a large variety and number of big game animals up to elk with the .285 OKH that was its wildcat predecessor. In that cartridge I used several makes and styles of 160–180 gr. bullets. After using that cartridge I can see why Fred and Jim are fond of the .280 Rem., but I did have penetration problems with it on elk with both 160 and 180 gr. bullets of both Barns and the long-discontinued Western Tool & Copper Works brands at ranges under 200 yards. This was no fault of the cartridge or bullet diameter, but of bullet structure. When I started using Nosler 160 and 175 gr. bullets, it performed very well at all ranges out to 400 yards. In fact, it was the use of that wildcat cartridge that led me to having a 7mm Mashburn Super Magnum made up. I haven't killed as much game with it in as many places as Warren Page did with "Old Betsy," but it has seen a lot of country and accounted for a lot of game from pronghorn to Alaskan moose and grizzly, and I found that whatever the .285 OKH or .280 Remington would do, the big 7 will do a lot better. While it is a bit more potent than either the 7mm Remington or 7mm Weatherby, the performance of either of those cartridges is nearly as good.

The same situation holds true where the .30-06 and the various .300 magnums are concerned; the '.06 is a good cartridge for all-around hunting of all game, but the magnums have it outclassed with the right choice of bullets. In fact, it seems that either the 7mm or .30 magnums may be the best bet for shooting all classes of North American big game under all hunting conditions if you choose to use just one rifle, and the .300 magnums at the top of the pile, which includes the .300 Winchester, .300 Weatherby, and several wildcats, which are a little more versatile than the 7mm mags. They'll shoot just about as flat with the right load at all hunting ranges, and with 200 and 220 gr. bullets they do pack a good deal more wallop than does the 175 gr. load in the 7mm magnums.

The only other commercial cartridges that can be considered ideally suited to all-around hunting of all game in this country are the .338 Winchester and the .340 Weatherby. I've used one or the other for shooting most classes of big game under a variety of

This huge Alaskan bull *(Alces gigas)* was shot at edge of willows in semitundra timberline country on Alaskan mountainside, at range of 300 yards. He stood 7 feet at shoulders. Rifle is 7mm Mashburn Super Magnum, and was loaded with 175 gr. Nosler bullet backed by 71 gr. H4831 at an MV of 3130 fps. Bullet landed behind left shoulder, passed through lungs, smashed right shoulder, and left 1″ exit hole. Few bullet designs of any make, caliber, or weight will give that kind of bone-shattering penetration.

hunting conditions and find they do very well, but while they are ideally suited to hunting elk, moose, and the big bears, they are certainly more than needed for any of the smaller species. There is also the problem of recoil that rules them out for many hunters, especially for long shots at small targets.

The reason that these cartridges, or any others that have similar ballistics, are ideally suited to all-around hunting for nearly all North American big game is that they will, with the right load or loads, do a creditable job on game of all sizes at both short and long ranges. Of course, to be fully effective for the great variety of conditions they will have to perform under, the loads for these cartridges will have to be selected with extreme care. It should be

These cartridges are representative of those that can be considered for hunting the heaviest American big game under any and all hunting conditions. There are many other commercial offerings and wildcats that fit into the same general category. *From left:* 7mm Rem. Mag.; .300 Win.; .300 Wby.; .338 Win.; .340 Wby.; .358 Norma; .375 H&H.

obvious that for the largest animals and the longest ranges they will be loaded to full-throttle in all cases. Then, to ensure that the bullet will not blow up and fail to penetrate at close range on these same heavy animals, it must be of controlled expansion design. To complicate things even further, the load used may be called upon to perform well by giving adequate expansion on the light resistance of a mule deer buck or a dall ram in the morning at long range, then penetrate the heavy shoulder bone of a big bull elk or moose, maybe even a grizzly, at close range in the afternoon. Then again, the situation may be completely reversed. At any rate, the bullet must move out fast enough to make a hit reasonably certain on a small animal like a sheep at long range, and expand well when it gets there to ensure a quick, sure kill. Yet, that same bullet, driven at the same speed, will have to have what it takes to break up enough bone to stake a grizzly in his tracks at any range down to a few yards or even feet.

This means that not only does the bullet have to be designed so that it will perform all of these tasks, but that it is of the right shape and correct weight to give optimum results in the cartridge used. These criteria make most factory loads less desirable than good handloads, for two reasons. First, most cartridges are loaded by the factories to less velocity than it is possible to get from full-power handloads while staying within permissible pressures. Second, and of much greater importance, there is no factory-loaded ammunition that uses a bullet which equals the performance of some of the premium quality bullets made by some of the bullet companies. (The exception to this is the Weatherby people, who use Nosler bullets in some of their factory-loaded ammunition.) As pointed out earlier, the pointed Core-Lokt bullets as loaded in R-P ammunition perform the best of any factory-loaded bullet we have ever used on all sizes of game at all reasonable ranges both for penetration and for expansion. There are other factory bullets that will expand faster and to a greater degree, and perhaps at longer ranges, but I know of none that can be depended on to hold together and penetrate as well. These bullets are loaded in the right weight of 150 gr. in the .270 cartridge, and the 150 and 175 gr. in the 7mm Rem. Mag., but in the .30-06, .300 H&H, and .300 Win. Mag., only the 180 gr. is loaded in pointed form, with the 220 gr. not loaded in the latter two, and its round nose makes it undesirable as an all-around load in the .30-06. It would seem that Remington is missing a bet in not making the pointed Core-Lokt bullet in 200 gr. weight in .30 caliber. Such a bullet would be better suited to all .30 caliber cartridges from the .30-06 up for mixed bag hunting in either western Canada or Alaska than either the 180 or 220 gr. It would penetrate better than the 180 gr. and, due to its shape and point design, probably about as well as the 220 gr. In addition, it would shoot about as flat as the 180 gr. at the longest game ranges, and much flatter than the 220 gr. round nose.

As this is being written, Federal Cartridge Co. has just announced a .30-06 load using a 200 gr. spitzer boattail bullet. This bullet is apparently made by Sierra, but is not yet available from that company as a handloader's item. How well it will hold up on big game at close range I do not know, but it will be ideal for long range shooting and will certainly be superior to the 180 gr. BT from the same maker for all-around work where several weight classes of game will be killed.

Earlier there has been mention of a load or loads for the cartridge used for taking all sizes of game under all hunting conditions found on a single trip. To clarify this dual term, it should be pointed out that some rifles, and to a lesser extent some cartridges, will shoot various bullet weights in the same make and style to very nearly the same point of impact at 100 yards, while others will not. As indicated, this situation arises more from the rifle barrel than from the cartridge, so a little explanation is in order.

There is the old tale that a heavy bullet always gives a lower point of impact at any range than does a light one. Nothing could be further from the truth. True, if both bullets are sighted to zero to the same point of impact at 100 yards, the heavy bullet will strike progressively lower as range increases if both bullets are loaded to their full velocity potential and are of the same shape, but this has nothing to do with where they will impact at 100 yards with the same sight setting. As an example, some .30-06 rifles will give several inches' higher impact at 100 yards with a 220 gr. bullet than a 180 gr. when sighted in for the 180 gr. On the other hand, the 220 gr. may land the same amount low, or to right or left. Under the stress created by the bullet passing through the barrel, it vibrates in more or less of a circle at the muzzle, and where a bullet impacts from the line of sight depends on the point of vibration at the time the bullet leaves the muzzle. Thus, it is a matter of the amount of vibration of the barrel created by the bullet and the time the bullet takes to reach the muzzle. If it emerges while the muzzle is at the top of its vibration pattern, it will land high, or low if the muzzle is at the bottom of the cycle. Bullet weight has nothing to do with it whatever.

It is sometimes possible to juggle powder charges with one or both bullet weights and get them to impact at the same point at around 100 yards. And occasionally a change in powders will do the same thing without changing velocity much. If you can make two different bullets give the same point of impact without losing too much velocity with one or the other, it is often possible to use two different bullet weights on the same trip for different sizes of game. If this isn't possible in your rifle, you'll have to settle on a single bullet weight that appears to be optimum for the various kinds of game you'll hunt and the hunting conditions you expect to encounter. And the only way you can find out where *your rifle* will shoot with various loads is to try it. One thing for sure, it is not advisable to try to change your sighting in the field for various loads. And *don't* depend on a marked scope setting for certain loads, because it may not replace correctly. In fact, it is highly unusual if it does.

To use the dual load setup for a single cartridge, you will have to consider the difference in drop at ranges beyond 300 yards or so, which will, of course, depend on the cartridge, loads, and bullet weights and styles used. Obviously, the sure hit range will not be the same on the animal shot at with both bullets.

A good example of this is my 7mm Mashburn Super Magnum with pointed 160 gr. Noslers loaded to 3250 fps MV, and the 175 gr. semipointed Nosler at 3100 fps. With both sighted to print 3″ high at 100 yards (both bullets give the same 100 yard impact with the same sight setting), the 160 gr. is 4 1/2″ high at 200 yards, 1 1/4″ high at 300 yards, and down only 6″ at 400 yards. With the 175 gr. with impact 3″ up at 100 yards, it is 3″ high at 200 yards, right on the nose at 300 yards, and down 10″ at 400 yards. These figures were not calculated but were taken from actual drop tests at an elevation of 4,500 feet on a warm, clear summer day with no wind. There will be some variation at different elevations and under different atmospheric conditions. In practical terms, these figures show that with a center hold on a ram's ribs, the 160 gr. will give a vital hit out to about 400 yards, but the 175 gr. would hit under his belly.

Several .300 Winchester Magnums I've used did the same thing with 180 and 200 gr. Noslers with just a little load juggling, but they did not shoot quite as flat with either bullet weight. There is also a little more difference between the 180 and 200 gr. bullets in drop, due to the poorer shape of the 200 gr. as opposed to the 175 gr. 7mm bullet.

The advantage of using the two different bullet weights when they give the same 100 yard point of impact is that you can use the flatter shooting bullet on antelope on a western-state hunt, and the heavy bullet for elk. On an Alaskan hunt, the light bullet will be ideal for sheep and caribou, the heavy for moose and grizzly. However, either bullet will do a respectable job on both weight classes of game if you run into one while loaded for the other. The main point to consider here is that both bullets will expand at long range on the lightest game being hunted, yet have controlled expansion for deep penetration on the big ones at any range.

If you use the single bullet weight load for one of these trips in an all-around cartridge—and it has advantages, like always being able to use the same hold on any animal—the choice of bullet weight and design is even more vital to success. Here I would draw a line between hunting for a mixed bag in the Mountain States and in northwestern Canada or Alaska. Taking the 7mm magnums and the .300 magnums as examples, the 160 gr. 7mm and the 180 gr. .30 would probably be a better choice for shooting in theMountain States, because they will handle elk well under most hunting conditions, while being better than a heavier bullet on antelope, deer, and sheep. But for hunting in the North, the 175 gr. 7mm and the 200 gr. .30 will come nearer to the optimum for all game. The reason for this is that moose are a good deal larger than elk, especially the Alaska-Yukon variety, and while mountain grizzlies are not especially big—500–600 pounds is a damn big one—you had better break up as much bone as possible while blowing a big hole in the lung area at the same time, and this takes a bullet with plenty of penetrating ability.

There are a number of good 7mm bullets in 175 gr. spitzer or semi-spitzer form that will do quite well, with the Nosler topping the list of those currently available for all kinds of shots on all kinds of game. As pointed out earlier, pointed .30 caliber 200 gr. bullets are pretty scarce. The Bitterroot, if it were available, would be the best for all sizes of game at all ranges, but it isn't, so this leaves the Speer spitzer as the flattest shooting 200 grainer, but a bit fragile for close-in work on heavy game for raking shots. The 200 gr. Nosler with its round point is not the answer to a long range rifleman's dream, but it will do a wonderful job of bone smashing and go on into the vitals. Considering all these points, it is my choice of a single bullet weight for the big .30s for a mixed bag Alaskan hunt, or for the same cartridges if only brown bear is on the agenda.

For a single bullet weight in the .270 Winchester, or the .270

Weatherby for that matter, the best bullet for a mixed bag hunt in any of the areas mentioned would be the 150 gr. Nosler. If the .280 Remington is the cartridge used, the 160 gr. Nosler would be first choice, with one of the 175 gr. pointed or semipointed bullets of several makes as second choice. The reason for the 160 gr. being first is that with the 175 gr. in the .280 case, velocity is not high enough for really flat trajectories over the longest ranges, and you do find a lot of long range shooting in the North, due to most of the shooting being in open country above timber line.

This lack of velocity also probably makes the 180 gr. Nosler the most desirable bullet for all-around use in the .30-06 for all game in all places. Due to the poor ballistic shape of the 200 gr. Nosler coupled with the rather low velocity at which it is possible to start it in the .30-06, the 200 gr. Speer spitzer would be a better choice in that cartridge. With the lower velocity it will not expand as rapidly or as fully as if fired from one of the big belted cases.

My personal preference for a single bullet load in the .338 or .340 for game of all sizes, with the possible exception of brown bear at close quarters, would be the 210 gr. Nosler. The 250 gr. Nosler is great medicine for the big ones at close to medium ranges, but is not ideal for long range work because of its poor shape.

Why Use a Magnum?

Some hunters are bound to question why more emphasis has been put on magnum cartridges for all-around shooting than on the standard capacity cases. There are a number of reasons, and they are all based on the higher velocity delivered by the larger capacity cases. To fully understand the pros and cons of magnum cases for all-around hunting of North American big game, it is well to look at both sides of the coin.

On the technical side, those who oppose the magnum cases see them as far over bore capacity, which, in practical terms, means they are not as efficient as smaller cases because it takes a much larger powder charge to gain a small percentage of velocity increase. This is completely correct as far as it goes, but it applies to all case capacities in small to medium bores from the bottom up.

As classic examples of the fallacy of this line of thinking, the .22 Long Rifle cartridge boosts a 40 gr. bullet along at 1250–1350 fps with 2–3 gr. of powder (depending on who makes the load). In the .22-250 it will take about 37 gr. of powder to start it at 4000 fps. This shows that it takes nearly 14 times the amount of powder to give the 40 gr. .22 bullet slightly over 3 times the velocity in the .22-250 over the .22 LR. But I don't know any varmint hunter who would pick the .22 LR over the .22-250 for shooting chucks at 300–400 yards, or even 100 yards! The same situation exists in the .30 caliber: It takes a little more than twice the powder in the .300 Winchester Magnum to produce only about 1.4 times or 900 fps more velocity with the 180 gr. bullet than the .30-30 gets from the 170 gr., but who would choose the .30-30 over the .300 Win. for long range antelope hunting or shooting grizzlies?

From the pure hunting point of view, it has often been said that whether a hit is made with a .270 bullet or a .30-06 as compared to a 7 mag. or a big .30, the animal never knows the difference. This is quite likely correct if any of the bullets land in the right spot to give a quick kill, and it is equally certain that the animal never knows what cartridge it's been wounded with if it is not killed outright. I've also heard a number of hunters say they couldn't see any difference in the way any of these cartridges killed. If every hunter and ballistic experimenter had adhered to that line of reasoning, we would still be using the .45-70 and the .30-30 because there would have been no reason to develop anything better. Maybe I have an overly active imagination, but after seeing many hundreds of head of American big game killed with about everything that shoots, I find there is a difference when everything isn't just right.

I find the extra punch and penetration of the 175 gr. bullet from a 7mm magnum an advantage over the same bullet from a .280 Remington or the 150 gr. in the .270 Winchester. And the same thing applies to the .30-06 as opposed to the .300 magnums with 200–220 gr. bullets if I have to shoot a bull elk or moose with the point of a massive shoulder or his ample rump pointed toward me; or have to break up a lot of bone to anchor a grizzly or brownie so it won't get into the brush or decide to eat on the guy doing the shooting at close range.

It is also comforting to have the extra helping of velocity to deliver the bullet with the least chance of a miss if a 40″ ram shows up on the far side of a wide canyon and there's no chance to stalk any closer.

All of this does not necessarily apply to the fellow who lives in any of these sections and hunts mostly for meat. He usually is not pressed for time, and, if he isn't trigger happy, can pass up a shot now and then and wait for a better chance. Also, he isn't looking for something special that may offer only one shot under something less than ideal conditions. But for the hunter from the other end or side of the continent, and especially for the trophy hunter, it can be a far different matter.

We'll say, for instance, he makes a trip to Alaska from the Lower 48 after saving for most of a lifetime for the hunt. Seeing that he doesn't make a trip there every year or so, and maybe will never make another, he probably wants to collect all the Alaskan game possible on that hunt. If he hunts in the interior or maybe the country in or around the Brooks Range, which is likely if he wants a mixed bag, he'll surely have dall sheep and caribou high on his list, as well as moose and grizzly. There is a good chance that either sheep or caribou will be shot at long range. Of course, he may sneak up to where the sheep can be hit with a rock, and I've had caribou get curious and prance up and try to smell noses with me, but I've also shot both at 400 yards or so because there was absolutely no way of getting closer to the one I came for. Moose and grizzly may also be shot under ideal conditions at ranges of 50–200 yards or so out in the open, but there is also a strong chance that either may be found in or very near the brush. In that case it is prudent to immobilize the grizzly where he stands, and it won't hurt anything to do the same thing with the moose. If the bull is standing in the wrong direction, it will take a lot more punch to reach the vitals than it will to break both shoulders of even a very large grizzly.

Now, if any one of these animals is in the class the hunter is looking for, and especially if it is record-book material, the success or failure of the whole trip and several thousand dollars can hang on a single shot. To me it makes sense to fire that shot with the cartridge and load that is most likely to do the job with the greatest assurance of success. And considering the advantages the larger capacity cases have in handling heavier bullets at higher velocities,

Alaskan guide Johnny Porter cooks caribou steaks over willow fire in Alaskan caribou camp.

they are the ones best suited to the job. As brought out before, the exception to this is if you can't handle the recoil of the magnums. The only way to find out is to shoot one a great deal before the hunt; then, if you can shoot it accurately, take it; if you can't, take a lighter recoiling cartridge, and use the best bullet available to take care of any hunting situation likely to be encountered. And this is best accomplished by handloading—not only because better bullets are available to the handloader, but because higher velocity and better accuracy usually go with it. There is also the economy aspect to consider, so that more practice shooting can be done prior to the hunt.

In summing up the reasons why the magnum cartridges are the best choice with the right load for shooting all classes of North American big game under the varied hunting conditions where they are found, if you use a single cartridge for everything, the answer is quite simple: If you need the extra velocity they afford for longer sure hit ranges, or the extra punch they pack for heavy animals, you have it; if you don't need it, no harm is done. I have always been highly skeptical of the term *overkill.*

7mm Remington Magnum, Remington Model 700 24″ bbl.
W-W cases weight 241 gr.
CCI no. 250 primers
Temp. 70° F.

BULLET	POWDER	CHARGE	MV FPS
175 gr. Nosler Partition Jacket	H870	77	3022
	H4831	66	2991
	IMR4831	65	3002
	N205	64	2980
160 gr. Nosler Partition Jacket	H870	80	3134
	H4831	69	3115
	IMR4831	68	3145
	N205	68	3150
150 gr. Nosler Partition Jacket	H870	82	3296
	H4831	70	3227
	IMR4831	68	3258
	N205	68	3248
140 gr. Sierra SP	H4831	71	3300
	IMR4831	69	3315
	N205	70	3320
	4350	68	3314
Rem. 175 gr. factory load Ptd.	—	—	2921

These were all near maximum in the test rifle and should be approached from 4 gr. below. Same charges of Norma MRP will give similar pressure and velocity.

See pp. 44–45 for note with supplementary information, and for explanation of abbreviations used in charts.

BULLET DROP SIGHTED 3″ HIGH AT 100 YARDS FOR BIG GAME SHOOTING				
100 YARDS	200 YARDS	300 YARDS	400 YARDS	VITAL HIT WITH CENTER HOLD
+3″	+4″	0.0″	−11″	Antelope 325 yards Deer 350 yards Elk 400 yards Moose 435 yards
All loads similar drop.				
+3″	+4.5″	+1″	−8″	Antelope 350 yards Deer 375 yards Elk 425 yards Moose 460 yards
All loads similar drop.				
+3″	+4.5″	+1″	−7″	Approximately the same as for 160 gr.
All loads similar drop.				
+3″	+5″	+2″	−7″	Antelope 350 yards Deer 375 yards
All loads similar drop.				
+3″	+4″	−1″	−13″	See 175 gr. handloads, above

.308 Winchester, Mark X Cavalier 24" bbl.
R-P cases weight 172 gr.
CCI no. 200 primers
Temp. 70° F.

BULLET	POWDER	CHARGE	MV FPS
200 gr. Speer RN SP	N205	52	2565
	4350	49	2489
	4320	43	2500
	760	50	2536
180 gr. Speer SP Ptd.	N205	53	2664
	4320	44	2620
	760	53	2669
	748	45	2630
165 gr. Speer SP Ptd.	4320	45	2724
	760	55	2821
	748	47	2769
150 gr. Speer SP Ptd.	760	56	2922
	748	49	2902
	H4895	47	2917

These loads were near maximum in the test rifle and should be approached from 3 gr. below. Norma MRP may be used in same charges as N205 for similar pressure

BULLET DROP SIGHTED 3″ HIGH AT 100 YARDS FOR BIG GAME SHOOTING

100 YARDS	200 YARDS	300 YARDS	400 YARDS	VITAL HIT WITH CENTER HOLD
+3″	+2″	−10″	−34″	Antelope 250 yards Deer 275 yards Elk 300 yards Moose 325 yards
All loads similar drop.				
+3″	+3″	−6″	−23″	Antelope 280 yards Deer 310 yards Elk 325 yards Moose 350 yards
All loads similar drop.				
+3″	+3.5″	−3″	−16″	Antelope 310 yards Deer 335 yards Elk 365 yards Moose 390 yards
All loads similar drop.				
+3″	+4″	−3″	−15″	Antelope 310 yards Deer 335 yards
All loads similar drop.				

and velocity. The above charges should be reduced by at least 2 gr. for use in semiautoloading and rear lockup lever action rifles.

.30-06 Sako Finnbear 24″ bbl.
W-W cases weight 192 gr.
Federal no. 210 primers
Temp. 70° F.

BULLET	POWDER	CHARGE	MV FPS
220 gr. Hornady SP RN	N205	58	2650
	H4831	59	2586
	4350	55	2550
	N204	54	2514
200 gr. Speer SP Ptd.	N205	60	2816
	4350	57	2711
	N204	57	2743
	H4831	60	2689
180 gr. Nosler SP Ptd. Partition	N205	61	2900
	H4831	62	2838
	N204	58	2838
	4350	58	2816
165 gr. Speer SP Ptd.	N205	64	2990
	N204	60	2902
	N203	54	2921
	4350	60	2883
150 gr. Hornady SP	N205	67	3103
	N204	63	3071
	4320	55	3095
	N203	56	3128

These loads were all near maximum in the test rifle and should be approached from 3 gr. below. Charges and velocities are somewhat higher than found in most manuals because the manual loads are held to rather mild pressures because of

BULLET DROP SIGHTED 3″ HIGH AT 100 YARDS FOR BIG GAME SHOOTING

100 YARDS	200 YARDS	300 YARDS	400 YARDS	VITAL HIT WITH CENTER HOLD
+3″	+2.5″	−10″	−31″	Antelope 250
+3″	+2.5″	−10″	−31″	yards
+3″	+2″	−11″	−34″	Deer 270 yards
+3″	+2″	−11″	−34″	Elk 300 yards
				Moose 325 yards
+3″	+4″	−2″	−14″	Antelope 320
+3″	+3.5″	−3″	−17″	yards
All loads similar drop.				Deer 340 yards
				Elk 375 yards
				Moose 400 yards
+3″	+4″	−2″	−14″	Antelope 320
+3″	+4″	−3″	−17″	yards
All loads similar drop.				Deer 340 yards
				Elk 375 yards
				Moose 400 yards
+3″	+4.5″	−1″	−11″	Approximately
+3″	+4″	−2″	−12″	the same as for
+3″	+4″	−2″	−12″	180 gr. loads
+3″	+4″	−2″	−12″	
+3″	+4.5″	−1″	−11″	Antelope 350
All loads similar drop.				yards
				Deer 375 yards

some old actions of doubtful strength. These loads should not be used in those rifles. Norma MRP may be used in same charges as N205 for similar pressure and velocity.

.300 Winchester Magnum, Remington Model 700 24″ bbl.
W-W cases weight 242 gr.
CCI no. 250 primers
Temp. 70° F.

BULLET	POWDER	CHARGE	MV FPS
220 gr. Hornady SP RN	H4831	75	2855
	N205	75	2883
	4350	71	2832
200 gr. Nosler SP RN	H4831	76	3012
	N205	76	3038
	4350	73	2993
180 gr. Nosler SP Ptd. Partition	H4831	78	3156
	N205	78	3195
	4350	75	3140
165 gr. Nosler SP Ptd. Partition	H4831	82	3331
	N205	81	3340
	4350	77	3312
150 gr. Nosler SP Ptd. Partition	H4831	84	3471
	N205	83	3478
	4350	79	3457

These loads were all near maximum in the test rifle and should be approached from 4 gr. below. This cartridge is representative of the various .300 magnums, with the

BULLET DROP SIGHTED 3″ HIGH AT 100 YARDS FOR BIG GAME SHOOTING

100 YARDS	200 YARDS	300 YARDS	400 YARDS	VITAL HIT WITH CENTER HOLD
+3″	+4″	−4″	−20″	Antelope 300 yards Deer 325 yards Elk 350 yards Moose 375 yards
All loads similar drop.				
+3″	+4″	−2″	−14″	Antelope 320 yards Deer 340 yards Elk 390 yards Moose 425 yards
All loads similar drop.				
+3″	+4.5″	+1″	−8″	Antelope 350 yards Deer 375 yards Elk 410 yards Moose 440 yards
All loads similar drop.				
+3″	+4.5″	+2″	−7″	Antelope 360 yards Deer 385 yards Elk 425 yards Moose 450 yards
All loads similar drop.				
+3″	+5″	+2″	−7″	Approximately same as for 165 gr. bullets
All loads similar drop.				

.300 H&H and .308 Norma showing somewhat less velocity and slightly more drop. See various reloading manuals for further information.

.300 Weatherby Magnum, Weatherby Mark V 24″ bbl.
Wby. cases weight 229 gr.
CCI no. 250 primers
Temp. 70° F.

BULLET	POWDER	CHARGE	MV FPS
220 gr. Hornady SP RN	H4831	79	2796
	N205	79	2787
	4350	75	2777
200 gr. Nosler SP RN	H4831	80	2892
	N205	80	2882
	4350	76	2860
180 gr. Nosler SP Ptd. Partition	H4831	84	3145
	N205	84	3120
	4350	78	3075
165 gr. Nosler SP Ptd. Partition	H4831	86	3310
	N205	85	3300
	4350	82	3296
150 gr. Nosler SP Ptd. Partition	H4831	87	3326
	N205	86	3320
	4350	83	3376

It will be noted that the velocity is not quite as high for the .300 Weatherby as for the .300 Winchester. The reason for this is that the .300 Winchester with W-W cases is a stronger case than the .300 Weatherby/Norma case. This allows loading

BULLET DROP SIGHTED 3″ HIGH AT 100 YARDS FOR BIG GAME SHOOTING				
100 YARDS	200 YARDS	300 YARDS	400 YARDS	VITAL HIT WITH CENTER HOLD
+3″	+4″	−4″	−21″	Antelope 300 yards Deer 325 yards Elk 350 yards Moose 375 yards
All loads similar drop.				
+3″	+4″	−2″	−16″	Antelope 320 yards Deer 340 yards Elk 390 yards Moose 425 yards
All loads similar drop.				
+3″	+4.5″	+1″	−9″	Antelope 350 yards Deer 375 yards Elk 410 yards Moose 440 yards
All loads similar drop.				
+3″	+4.5″	+2″	−7″	Antelope 360 yards Deer 385 yards Elk 425 yards Moose 450 yards
All loads similar drop.				
				Approximately the same as for 165 gr. bullet

to higher pressures without expansion of the case head and primer pocket. If cases are of equal strength, the .300 Weatherby is capable of higher velocity.

8mm Mauser, Mauser Model 98 24″ bbl.
R-P cases weight 187 gr.
CCI no. 200 primers
Temp. 70° F.

BULLET	POWDER	CHARGE	MV FPS
225 gr. Speer SP RN	4350	56	2500
	4320	49	2460
	H4895	49	2445
175 gr. Sierra SP	4320	51	2725
	H4895	50	2686
	3031	46	2728
150 gr. Sierra SP	4064	53	2935
	H4895	53	2870
	3031	49	2900

These loads were fired in a number of Mauser M-98 rifles and were near maximum in all; should be approached from 3 gr. below.

BULLET DROP SIGHTED 3″ HIGH AT 100 YARDS FOR BIG GAME SHOOTING

100 YARDS	200 YARDS	300 YARDS	400 YARDS	VITAL HIT WITH CENTER HOLD
+3″ All loads similar drop.	+2″	−8″	−29″	Antelope 250 yards Deer 275 yards Elk 310 yards Moosc 340 yards
+3″ All loads similar drop.	+3.5″	−4″	−19″	Antelope 315 yards Deer 335 yards Elk 360 yards Moose 380 yards
+3″ All loads similar drop.	+4″	−2″	−16″	Antelope 315 yards Deer 335 yards

10

Where to Hit Them and How They React

A great deal has been written to the effect that it is much more important where you hit 'em than what you hit 'em with. There is, of course, a lot of truth to that statement; if you hit a buck antelope in the foot with a .458 it is no more likely to kill him quickly and cleanly than if you hit him in the same place with a .25-20, and the same thing applies to a bull moose. But it always seemed to me that this amounts to oversimplification. To put it another way, and to get more to the point we are driving at, *if* you can get a .243 bullet well into the lungs of the bull moose to expand and to tear up a lot of tissue, it will soon stop the breathing process and the moose will die shortly. But the problem is in getting it far enough inside to do that job well.

If the moose is full broadside, a well-constructed .243 bullet in the 100 gr. weight class will normally penetrate one lung and maybe both before it loses steam and stops, but not all moose present the classic broadside rib shot. In fact, even if it is broadside, you may not be able to see the ribs clearly because of intervening brush or trees, but the shoulder area may be clear and tempting. With a cartridge using a larger caliber, heavier bullet of controlled expansion design, the shoulder shot is one of the best to anchor the bull where he stands, but not with the .243 diameter bullet. With bullets of even 100 gr. weight that are designed for deer-size game that have thin jackets that expand rapidly and fully, and with the lighter bullets that are made mostly for varmint shooting, the bone is unlikely to be broken, leaving only a shallow surface wound. And even with the best bullet designs in the heaviest weights, bullets like the 100 gr. Remington Core-Lokt, the Speer 105 gr., and the Nosler partition 95 and 100 gr., there is not enough punch to smash the heavy shoulder bone of a large bull moose and go on inside, or do much damage if they do manage to get there. So, if you insist on using one of the small caliber cartridges of .243, .25, or even the 6.5mm, as well as a lot of others of much larger bore that do not have enough punch to give deep, bone-shattering penetration, you should confine your shooting to broadside rib shots only, passing up any shot that requires deep penetration or the breaking of much heavy bone. What we are really saying is that while bullet placement is highly important with any cartridge and load, it is a whole lot more important with some cartridges than with others.

And while we are on the subject of lung shots, it might be well to bring out some of the myths as well as the facts surrounding both lung and heart shots.

Heart and Lung Shots

First, to try to hit an animal in the heart is not as desirable as many hunters believe. As just pointed out, if you feel you must hunt large animals with small caliber cartridges, or larger calibers with inadequate power or the wrong bullet, or emergency dictates that it must be done, the best place to land your bullet is in the ribs just in back of the shoulder over the center of the lungs. That is about the only place the bullet is certain of getting inside, but this does not mean that the same thing applies to a heart shot.

Many hunters of no great experience think that if the animal is standing perfectly broadside and the bullet lands just behind the shoulder in the lower third of the chest cavity, it will puncture the heart. Not so, unless the animal's leg is far forward. And even then the bullet will have to pass very tight against the elbow joint and within a few inches of the bottom of the cavity. With an animal standing straight with both front legs near the same position and completely broadside, the bullet will have to break the elbow joint to reach the heart. And that joint on a big bull elk or moose sets up a lot of bullet-shattering resistance. On a rear angling shot, it will have to enter several ribs back and drive forward to reach the heart, or in the point of the shoulder and angle back for quartering frontal shots. Either way, it takes more penetration on large animals than most light or thin-jacketed bullets can muster.

But the big disadvantage in trying for the heart, unless you are quite close to the animal, is that to hit it the bullet must land so close to the bottom of the chest cavity. If the range is very great and the bullet drops even 3″ or 4″, it will land too low and only tear through the bottom of the brisket. Worse yet, a few more inches down and the leg will likely be broken, with no internal damage whatever. And while any animal may lie down within a short distance of where it was hit when a leg is broken, it may also go on for many miles without even stopping. If the bullet lands high when aimed for the heart and has plenty of punch and penetrating ability, there is no problem. Also, if it lands too far back, the lungs will be hit. But too far forward will do little damage except to make the animal suffer a great deal before you recover it, if indeed you ever do. Remember that the heart of even a big bull moose or elk is no more than 6″×8″ at the most, and on a deer or antelope only fist-size.

Now, if the bullet does find the heart and penetrates it enough to open it up, the animal it belongs to is very dead, but it may take him a lot longer than you think to find it out. The hunter who thinks a heart-shot animal will collapse in his tracks is usually in for a surprise. A heart-shot deer very often will jump high and far, and leave that place as though he had a bee under his tail. Other game may take off at full speed or just stand there or go walking along as though nothing had happened, but damn few of them will fold up when the bullet lands, as most fiction writers would have us believe. I've actually paced off nearly 200 long steps from where a heart-shot buck stood when hit to where he fell. I'll grant you it didn't take him long to get there, but he still did it. And in some cases if I hadn't followed his tracks I wouldn't have found him, because he was out of sight after the first jump or two.

Most animals react to a lung shot in much the same manner, with the greatest difference being in how they react to different bullet action. The more explosive a bullet is when it gets well inside the lungs, the more likely it is to kill quickly. This is why some hunters get sold on light high velocity bullets that blow up like a varmint bullet—in fact, on cartridges like the .22-250 and .220 Swift, or the .243s and .25s with varmint bullets. It is also why bullets of controlled expansion type, the Remington Core-Lokt in factory-loaded offering, and Nosler and Bitterroot from the bullet companies, are often criticized as being slow killers. They do not expand as violently and they leave a much smaller wound channel. Therefore, they do not tear up as much lung tissue or cause as much hydrostatic shock as the explosive types. Sometimes the animal will drop where hit, but more often it will not. And it doesn't always drop where hit with the explosive bullets, either.

I'll always remember a big buck mule deer I once shot with a .30 Newton on an open hillside at about 200 yards with about 6″ of snow on the ground. The cartridge was chambered in a 1917 Enfield action with original barrel that miked .311, so I was using 172 gr. Western Tool & Copper Works cavity point bullets made for the .303 British in .311 diameter. Those bullets had very thin jackets that were designed to expand at all reasonable hunting ranges in that cartridge and were highly explosive in the Newton at well over 3000 fps.

Anyway, the buck was standing broadside and the bullet landed about a third of the way up the ribs and tight behind the shoulder. When it hit, the buck jumped high in the air, then leveled out and broke all previous records around the steep hillside for about 150 yards, turned straight down for another 50 yards, and smashed head-on into a big Douglas fir, the only tree on the hillside. Obviously, he was running dead on his feet. But the astonishing part was that from the instant he took off, a 3-foot-wide spray of blood painted the snow. I could hardly believe what I was seeing as the blood trail lengthened behind the running buck. Nothing could live and run with the kind of hole it took to spray out blood like that, but there it was and the buck going on and on. Along with the blood, there were several pieces of lung lying on the snow where the buck had been standing. When I opened him up, the heart was also peppered with lead core and pieces of jacket, and there was a 6″ hole in the hide on the off side where the bullet and pieces of rib had made exit.

If most hunters who have seen much game killed will think back over those kills, they will find that a lot more animals traveled at least 50 yards after being hit in lungs or heart than ever dropped on the spot. Most writers seem prone to have all their animals drop in their tracks, however. I'm always pleased when they do drop on the spot, or never get up if lying down, but I'm not upset if they don't, and don't expect them to.

Does Knockdown Power Really Exist?

And this brings up another myth that is highly touted both verbally and in print: so-called knockdown power of cartridge or bullet. The truth is that there "ain't any such thing." At least not the kind hunters talk about, where the bullet slaps the animal flat when it hits him. If it goes down when hit, it is for one of two reasons: either because the spine or the brain is hit or shocked by a near hit, or because of muscular reaction. At times an animal will appear to be literally picked up and turned upside down, but whether it stays there or not, this is not bullet knockdown power but muscular reaction. That is, the bullet doesn't smash him flat as would happen if he got smacked with a 100 pound boulder. I know there are two lines of thinking on "knockdown power": one, that high velocity will do it; the other, that a heavy big bore bullet will do the trick. A couple of instances come to mind that seem to disprove both theories.

In the case of high velocity and knockdown power, I once shot a buck antelope that was running all-out at only about 100 yards with a 7mm Mashburn Super Magnum with a 140 gr. Nosler that left the muzzle at near 3400 fps when boosted by 75 gr. of H4831. The bullet landed in the center of the lungs but that buck didn't even break stride for 75 paced yards, when my hunting partner whacked him in a hind foot and upset him.

I can hear someone bring up the point that the bullet landed in the lungs and exited, thus delivering little of its shocking power. This seems logical but doesn't mean much. In looking back and averaging out the times a bullet stayed inside or made exit, I can't see that it makes much difference in how quick it kills or whether the animal drops or runs on.

What about a hit in the shoulder instead of the lungs? That would probably have upset the running antelope, but it doesn't always work that way either. I know a shoulder hit is supposed to always drop an animal in its tracks, and it often will if it is high up near the spine, but that is because the shock is transmitted to the spinal cord, not because the shoulder is smashed.

An incident that sheds some light on this happened in the Ugashik area of the Alaska Peninsula a few years back. I had stalked a big bull moose to what proved to be 175 yards at the edge of a willow-fringed meadow. I was using a .378 Weatherby Magnum with 270 gr. Nosler bullets backed by 116 gr. of H4831 for an MV of 3131 fps, so it didn't seem to matter much which way the bull was standing. He was quartering sharply toward me, so I split the big shoulder joint with the cross hair and touched it off. When the big rifle settled down from recoil I expected to see the moose with all four feet pointing toward the stars, but he was just standing there looking a little pained but not especially upset. With the scope back on his shoulder, a 2" hole was visible where the bone had blown back through the hide, with a stream of blood running down his leg. It was a little hard to believe, but it didn't seem like it was much use to whack him again. I knew he was dead, but he hadn't gotten the word yet. A minute or so later he tried to take a step and fell on his nose without another kick.

That bullet had smashed the big shoulder joint like a glass rod, poked a fist-size hole through one lung, and penetrated most of the huge paunch before stopping. I was unable to find it in that mess but followed it most of the way through. That bullet had delivered all the shock it carried, something over 2 tons of energy at that range, but where was the knockdown power?

None of this is to say that either the lung or the shoulder shot isn't highly effective, but don't expect animals hit in either place to always go down as if struck by lightning.

The Shoulder Shot

To continue with the desirability of the shoulder shot and how to use it, the first suggestion is not to use it at all on big tough animals unless the cartridge and the bullet it shoots is capable of driving through the heavy bone and muscle and still tear things up after it gets inside. Granting that you have the right cartridge and load, there are times when it is more desirable than the lung shot,

A bullet designed to give deep penetration will break shoulder if placed at + and go on into lungs to give quick kill. If placed at rear of shoulder, it will kill well but go on into forward edge of paunch, making a mess and doing nothing good for the meat.

because you may wish to try to disable the animal so that it is either held where hit or can move only slowly at best. At times all animals will go some distance with one shoulder broken, but it isn't about to go anywhere with both out of commission. Of course, to break both shoulders the animal has to be fully broadside, and it takes one hell of a lot of penetration on a big bull elk, moose, or brown bear to do the job. If you want to make certain the animal drops on the spot or is held to the spot, place the bullet so that it will either hit the spine at the same time or very close below it. If, however, the bullet is placed lower down, say about center, and both shoulders are smashed, the animal is not going to go anywhere, but neither is it likely to die suddenly, except on rare occasions when it dies from shock—not likely with a bull elk, moose, or grizzly. The reason is that the bullet passes too far forward to hit the lungs. It may find the windpipe, which will cause death within a few minutes, but otherwise you'll probably find that it takes a second bullet to dispatch it.

My personal preference, if I'm using the right cartridge and load, is to break one shoulder and tear up the lungs at the same time. To do this, the animal has to be quartering to some extent. If toward the hunter, simply hold on the shoulder and the bullet will pass on into the lungs. If facing away, hold in line with the foreleg on the oposite side, and the bullet will pass through the lungs and smash the shoulder as its final act. One thing that should be pointed out to the average hunter who hunts more for meat than trophies is that any kind of shoulder shot is bound to ruin a lot of meat. It is to be avoided if filling the freezer is the object of the hunt.

Up to this point only the front end of the animal has been covered, and while this is certainly the vital end, and where the bullet should be placed if at all possible, it amounts to only about a third of the total area of the body. A shot anywhere in the paunch area should be avoided like the plague, except on quartering shots from the rear where a bullet will have to pass through the forward edge to reach the lungs. This very often happens even when the hunter thinks he is slipping the bullet far enough forward into the ribs to miss it, but fails to remember that the rear part of the ribs is filled by paunch and liver, and that the lower part of the rib cavity to within a few inches of the tip of the heart is filled with paunch. Anyway, don't try this shot with anything except a load that will penetrate very deeply. That mass of grass, browse, and fluid will stop or blow up a bullet like a sack of sand.

A bullet in the liver is usually quite deadly and many times will drop an animal on the spot to die within seconds, but finding that organ is far from easy and usually is accidental. I've also seen the smaller big game animals killed outright by a paunch hit, but I do not recall seeing moose, elk, or big bears killed by such a hit. When it does kill instantly, which is very rare even on deer-size game, death is caused by hydrostatic shock. And whether this happens or not depends mostly on how much fluid and other matter the paunch contains—something that the hunter has no way of knowing before he shoots.

It should go without saying that a hit anywhere in the rear gut section or hams will normally have only the effect of slowing the animal down, with little chance of recovery. So what does this leave if a shot at the front end is not available? Only the pelvic and spinal area.

Shots from the Rear

I know that some hunters will let off a good deal of oral steam, and probably some written, at even a hint that anyone would consider shooting any game animal in the fanny, but some of these same hunters never bat an eye at taking a shot at a running buck or bull in the open or in the bushes, and they are not overly particular about which end is pointed at them when they shoot. So let's face realities the way they are in the hunting country and not on a typewriter. And let's also consider human nature, and not only the reluctance to pass up what may be the only shot of a long and expensive trip but the fact that most hunters are not as calm, cool, and collected as they would have us believe with a bull's rump staring them in the face from behind a tree.

Actually, if properly executed with the right cartridge and load, the rump shot is one of the very best to anchor any animal to where it was shot. No, it will not kill instantly, and you'll have to get in a finishing shot in head or neck to finish the beast off, but if you are close, as you should be for this shot, very few seconds will elapse before it can be administered. This shot should *never* be tried with any cartridge that is not loaded with a bullet which is capable of smashing up the very heavy bone it will encounter.

There are two reasons for being close to the animal shot in the pelvic-spine area of the hips: as mentioned above, there is the quick finishing shot; then there is the fact that the vital area is very small as compared to lungs or shoulder.

As to the actual bullet placement, if the animal is facing straight away, hold for the root of the tail. A bullet so placed will shatter the spine for several inches and, in some instances, kill the animal without the finishing shot. If quartering away, aim to hit the hip joint and the bullet will also break up the spinal column even if the hip joint is missed. If the bullet lands a little low, it will likely shatter the pelvic section and immobilize the animal anyway. The same thing also applies to the straight-away shot, but that bullet may also go on into the body cavity and reach the lungs if of the right construction and the animal is not too large.

While I'm not advocating that every hunter go around shooting bucks, bulls, and bears in the rump even with the best loads, I will say that I have shot a number of elk as mentioned above, and have never lost one or had one move more than a few feet after being shot. However, I never made a rump shot on a large heavy animal that was moving so there was a chance of poor bullet placement. And I should also make it clear that I never shot one in that place with a cartridge or bullet that I was not completely certain would do the job. To me, the minimum caliber for this shot would be the 7mm, preferably from the .280 Remington up through the 7mm magnums, with the toughest bullets available in 175 gr. weight. And I prefer even larger calibers, the .30-06 and .300 magnums with 200 gr. Noslers or a 220 gr. by several makers with the Remington Core-Lokt, as the first choice. For more certain results, the .338 Winchester and .340 Weatherby are even better with 250–300 gr. bullets, and even these must have heavy jackets for controlled expansion. The 210 gr. Nosler will do very well, however. If you happen to be a .375 fan, it will take care of these shots very well, but only with bullets of sturdy construction—remember the lung-shot Shiras moose. While rump shots are not necessarily suggested, many hunters will try them, so this is to tell them how to get the best results with the least chance of wounding and losing the animal.

A bullet anywhere in the spine forward of the hip area will give very similar results. The target has a very long horizontal area to allow for error, but vertical bullet placement allows for very little. In fact, much less than most hunters think, especially on the high side. As the spine nears the shoulder area, the top spines of the vertebrae (neural spine) become progressively longer, which causes the top line of the back to be farther from the center of the spinal column. This is far more pronounced in some animals than in others, with the moose, American bison, and Rocky Mountain goat being at the top of the list. This is confusing to the hunter who does not know intimately the skeletal structure of the animal being shot. The outcome is that he places the bullet too high and it misses the center of the spinal column and does not break either the bone or the spinal cord. At times the bullet that breaks the top spine but not the vertebra it springs from will induce enough shock to the spinal cord to immobilize the animal permanently, but this is more often not the case than it is. In the great majority of these high hits, the game will go down as if the earth were jerked from under them, but within a few seconds will regain their feet and, unless you can get in a second shot, escape. These animals are especially hard to recover because it is unusual for them to bleed enough so there is a blood trail to follow.

On the other hand, a bullet that lands low and misses the spinal column will also usually let the animal down just as fast as the high hit, and it, too, may get up after a few seconds and take off. Again, there will be little or no blood to follow. The outcome of this is that most hunters firmly believe they only "creased" the back and that little or no harm has been done because there is no blood. In the majority of instances they do not even go to where the animal stood when hit if they see it run off, but assume it will recover. The high hit may or may not bring death later on. If the wound heals without infection, the animal may well survive. But with the low shot that punches through the body hollow but passes over the internal organs, eventual death is almost a certainty, although it may come many days later and miles from where the hit was made. For these reasons, the spinal broadside shot is not desirable under most circumstances.

The matter is far different if the animal is climbing a steep mountainside with its back to the hunter, or is below so that the length of the back is visible. In those cases there is no better shot than to land a bullet anywhere from the base of the neck to the back of the rib cage. If it breaks the spine, it will also go on into the lung section and give an instant kill. If it fails to break the spine but isn't too far to left or right, it will still hit the liver, lungs, or heart and produce a sure kill. That kill will also probably be instantaneous, because the shock to the spine by a near hit will very likely floor the animal and the disruption of tissue in the body cavity will kill it before it can get up.

Neck and Head Shots

This brings us around to neck and head shots, which are believed to be the best game getters of all by many hunters. To me, these are the most overrated shots for sure, clean kills the average hunter can take. My ears are already ringing in anticipation of the blistering remarks of some readers, but I'll stick to my guns and also what long experience has taught me about bullet placement.

There is no argument whatever against the fact that if the spinal cord is broken or the brain penetrated, the neck or head shot is the most deadly of all. Death is sure and instantaneous, but the problem is in breaking the neck bone and the cord or penetrating the brain. Many hunters are convinced that all you have to do is hit an animal in the neck with almost any kind and caliber of bullet and it is a dead animal right where it stands. No line of thinking could be further in error.

For years I had a pair of 117 gr. bullets fired from a .25-35 Winchester M-94 with a 26″ barrel that were taken from two big buck muleys that had rut-swollen necks. Both bullets had gone in and mushroomed perfectly against the bone but failed to even crack it. Both bucks had hit the dirt but didn't stay there and were shot in the lungs as they regained their feet. Increase the size of a buck mule deer to that of a big bull elk or moose, and it will give you some idea of what it really takes to dig in deep enough to reach and break the massive neck bone if the angle is wrong. But this is only a small part of the problem facing the fellow who insists on shooting any kind of game in the neck.

The main problem is in *finding* the bone with a bullet, and hitting it close enough to center to *break* it if you do. Damn few hunters know where the bone is at any given point of a broadside deer, and even fewer know where it lies in an elk or a mountain goat. An elk has a mane on the bottom of its neck, which, together with a somewhat U-shaped neck, puts the bone in the *upper* third of what you see, and to further complicate finding it, the location is not the same for the entire length of the neck. The goat is just in reverse, with the mane sticking straight up on top and the bone in the *lower* third of the profile. The outcome of all of this is that even if you land the bullet exactly where you want it to go, that may not be the right spot to hit the bone. And if the bullet goes low, it is very likely to find the windpipe or esophagus. If the former is hit, the animal may die within a few minutes, or it may live for several hours, depending on the damage done. If the latter is severed, the chances are the animal will not die until it starves to death several days later.

The sad part of all this is that most hunters never know it happened because they are certain that if the bullet hits the neck solidly the kill is instant. If the game falls, then gets up and runs off, they seldom attempt to follow it, because they are convinced that it was only "grazed." And even if they do try to follow, their chances of finding it are slim, because a neck hit normally bleeds but little, nor does it much impede the progress of the animal.

It must also be kept in mind that the neck bone in an antelope is little more than 2″ in diameter, a deer only a little larger, and an elk or a moose gives a sure break area of only about 4″. That is a pretty small target when you aren't even sure of where it is located in a mass of hair and muscle many times its diameter. Actually, it is much easier to hit in an antelope, deer, or sheep than in a goat, caribou, elk, or moose, because the diameter of the bone is so much smaller than the outline of the neck profile of the latter animals.

The head shot is even a poorer bet than the neck shot because the target is even smaller. A deer's brain is only about the size of your fist, and unless you can hit a 3″ target from a hunting position at the range you'll be shooting at the buck, don't attempt it. The brain of an elk or a moose is larger, but so is the head, which makes it harder to locate. Also, the way to get there is not always by the route that it appears to be.

It has also been said that a bullet anywhere in the head from a high velocity cartridge will always kill cleanly. This is no more true than the bullet in the neck that misses the bone. In order to be assured of an instantaneous kill, the bullet *must hit the brain directly,* and not just come close. The shock from a bullet that passes very close to the brain or cracks the brain pan *may* kill instantly, but it may not do more than temporarily stun the animal. Like the neck-shot animal, it will go down, then get up and take off.

A low shot will likely break one or both jaws, or perhaps tear up the breathing or eating plumbing. If too far forward it will either tear up the nasal passages, break one jaw or the other, or even sever the tongue. In any event, the animal will suffer a long, lingering, and unbelievably painful death.

I have seen a number of animals from antelope to elk running around with fearful holes in their noses, an eye blinded by a bullet intended for the brain, or lower jaws hanging. One of the saddest cases I remember was a cow elk.

I was hunting elk at the time and came over a ridge that bordered a little basin. I was pushing through a fir thicket, trying to move quietly, when there was movement down on the basin floor and flashes of tan between the trees as a big cow left her bed and headed for the opposite hillside. By the time I got to where I could see her, she was perhaps 150 yards away, standing in the open and looking back to see what had spooked her. There seemed to be something hanging under her head, but I couldn't make out what it was because of a branch that partially concealed her head and neck. I was suspicious, but was hunting meat and not horns, so I decided to take her—if she was wounded, she would suffer no more; if not, the freezer would be filled. A bullet through the lungs let her down after a couple of steps, and when I was still 50 yards away it was obvious that the hide was stretched over an emaciated carcass with the hip bones sticking out like those of a Jersey milk cow.

Examination showed that she had been shot through the lower jaw about halfway back, and it was held on only by the hide. The tongue was also severed. The wound had been inflicted several days before and she had been unable to eat or drink.

I know I haven't painted a pretty picture, but if it will make some hunters think twice before they shoot at the head or neck, my purpose will have been accomplished. It is incidents like this that have made me turn down all neck and head shots unless I was absolutely certain I could hit the neck bone or brain, and then only with a bullet that was capable of getting there and doing the job for which it was intended.

We have all heard the statement many times that if you aim for the head or neck you will "either kill clean or miss clean." The next time you hear someone repeat this overworked and unrealistic bit of myth, remember the cow elk that was slowly dying from thirst and hunger.

Reaction of Various Animals to Bullet Impact

There is a good deal of difference in the reaction various species of animals show when hit. Some are highly susceptible to shock and react violently to the impact of a bullet, while others show little or no sign of being hit. Antelope and deer both normally react to a hit sufficiently so that the hunter who isn't too excited is well aware that the bullet has made contact. To say that an animal will always react in the same way to a hit in a certain spot is in error. A lung or heart shot deer will usually jump high and take off at full-throttle, but not always. It will also usually sag in the hind quarters or go down rear end first from a hit in the paunch, but this isn't always so either. It is, of course, easy to tell when a leg is broken, but not so easy to tell what the deer will do afterward. Some hunters claim they will never go uphill with a broken front leg; some say it is the rear leg that prevents climbing. Others say they can't go around or downhill. The fact is that they'll go in any direction if that seems the best way to get away from the hunter. There is also the mistaken idea that a wounded animal will *never* go uphill. Don't believe it or you'll often be looking in the wrong direction.

In my experience, sheep react to nearly any hit in much the same manner as deer, except that they usually dash away without the first high jump of the deer when hit in the heart-lung area. It never seemed to me that a ram was especially hard to kill, but I did see a large bighorn ram escape when hit too far back somewhere in the stomach area with a 180 gr. Bronze Point .30-06 bullet. The bullet apparently blew up and did not exit, as there was only an occasional drop of blood. I'm convinced he didn't go very far, but many sheep tracks, broken cliffs, and sliderock made following him impossible without some kind of blood trail.

Goats are an entirely different matter. If any animal is immune to bullet shock, the Rocky Mountain goat is it. In many years of hunting and guiding in goat country I have seen dozens of them killed, and in very few cases did they give much indication of the hit. They'll usually just go on about their business as though nothing had happened, then slowly sit or lie down and die. This, of

This backlighted photo plainly shows the long mane over spine of a mountain goat. This, when coupled with the high neural spines on the vertebrae, serves to put the upper third of the broadside silhouette out of the vital area. If the aiming point is at the center of the shoulder area as it appears to the hunter, and the bullet is at mid-range where it impacts 4″ or so above point of aim, it is likely to go over the spine. For hit in vital area the hold should be at X only about a third of the way up from the bottom. More goats are wounded by being hit too high than from any other cause.

In flat tundra country, caribou are often shot at long range. These two big bulls were approached in broken plateau breaks. The bull on left presents perfect chest shot, while bull on right would be shot with bullet placed in point of shoulder and back into lungs. Even on a caribou, that kind of hit requires a good deal of penetration. The caribou hunter will never go wrong with high velocity cartridge and fairly heavy pointed bullets in calibers from .264 up.

course, is if the spine is not hit. Which brings up a problem in placing the bullet right on a goat that is peculiar to that animal.

The goat has extremely long neural spines that run from the front of the shoulder to well back over the rib cage. To top off this hump there is a long mane that adds several inches of extra height. When you look at a broadside goat, what appears to be the center of the shoulder-lung area is actually very near the spine. A bullet that lands much above center will drive through the long neural fins only, with no damage whatever to the goat except to possibly floor him for a second or two. This situation causes an exception to the center hold with the rifle sighted to print 3″ high at 100 yards. If the goat is anywhere from 100 to 200 yards or so, with a high velocity cartridge, a center hold will land the bullet too high, for goats hold about one-third of the way up from the bottom within the sure hit range of the cartridge on an animal of that vital area size.

I haven't seen enough caribou killed to make any hard statements as to their reactions to any particular hit. I have seen some drop to a lung hit, and others that walked or ran a short distance. None of which is very meaningful.

I have, however, seen nearly 200 head of elk of all sizes killed under every conceivable condition, and have come to the conclusion that few animals show a wider range of reaction to various hits. Occasionally a huge bull will drop where hit from a lung shot with almost any cartridge and bullet; some will take off in high gear and go until they fall. But the majority will either just stand where they were or go on walking or trotting along with not even a flinch. After a few seconds they'll pitch over on their noses with never another kick. But how far they'll go is a little hard to say. Many elk are lost because the hunter saw no reaction and thought he had missed.

There is a great deal of controversy as to how hard elk are to kill. Some hunters contend that any vital hit will do them in and it doesn't matter much what the hit is made with. Other elk hunters of equal experience feel they are never overgunned. The truth of the matter is that *if* the bullet gets to the right spot it will probably kill within a few seconds or minutes, but the size of the elk and the conditions under which many of them are hunted make this less than likely unless the bullet is tough and heavy enough to penetrate a lot of big bone and muscle. If it doesn't find the right spot,

A mature bull elk is a big animal with tough muscle and heavy bone. If shot in shoulders or at an angle from either end, a bullet that gives deep, bone-shattering penetration is required. This big Idaho bull was killed with .300 Winchester Model 70 and load of 78/H4831/180 Nosler at 3150 fps.

an elk can take a hell of a lot of punishment and keep going. And another fact of elk hunting life is that very few hunters are capable of following one 100 yards on bare ground even if they try. And even if they do manage it, the chances of a second shot are very slim.

After forty-five years or so of hunting elk and talking to hundreds of elk hunters from first-timers to lifetime veterans, and after finding dozens of elk carcasses that were not recovered, during the hunting season and after it was over, I feel that as much as 25% of the elk shot are lost. I have also talked to other observers who felt this figure was conservative. This is mostly due to the rough, broken, heavily timbered country where most elk are shot, but this matters little, the loss is still there. When someone asks me about elk cartridges I often think of the title of one of Bob Ruark's books, *Use Enough Gun.*

Moose are much larger than even the largest bull elk, especially those found in northwestern Canada and Alaska. It takes even more penetration to reach the vital machinery of a moose than an elk, and they are often shot in heavy cover where it is extremely difficult to tell in what position they are standing. But all the moose I've seen shot reacted in about the same way and far differently from most elk. I've hit them broadside in the lungs, broadside in the shoulders, and quartering through lungs and shoulders from both directions. I've also seen them shot with everything from the .357 Magnum revolver to the .378 Weatherby. (The .357 was used by a guide to try to finish off an Alaskan mulligan bull that had been wounded with a .308 Winchester. But all it did to the wounded bull was hurry him along into hair-thick spruce, where he was lost. That little bull was hit at least twice with the .308, but only God knows where, and two or three times with the .357, but he kept right on going. Which proves they are not easy to stop once they get in gear.)

I have never shot a moose that went anywhere. But neither have I ever shot one that dropped in his tracks to the first hit. I've heard it said that a moose is too stupid to know when he is hit, and there are times when that seems logical. But the answer, of course, is that moose are just not susceptible to bullet shock. Not counting the smallish Shiras bull shot with the .375 H&H that backed in and out of the beaver pond three times before expiring, I have never had a moose make more than two or three steps after being hit. They just stood there looking kind of stupid, as though wondering what was up, and were either shot again or eventually got the word they were dead and lay down and acted like it. I'm sure they occasionally do drop at the shot, but all I've killed lived for about "one minute and fifty-three seconds" no matter where I hit them or what I hit them with.

This brings us around to bears and where to place the bullet and how they react after it lands. Black bears have been pretty well covered in chapter 6. It doesn't take too much to kill a black, even a big one, but because he is almost impossible to follow on bare ground for any distance, it is a good idea to break one or both shoulders. Like all bears, a black will nearly always hit the deck with any kind of a hit on the first shot—I've even seen them go down from a bullet in the foot—but they may get up so fast it is hard to be sure they were ever down. And they can leave there just as fast. If they don't know where the shot came from, they are apt to run right over you if they come up headed in your direction, which is where a lot of black-bear-charge stories originate.

Mountain grizzlies and Alaskan brown bears are an entirely different matter. The only thing they have in common with the black is that they, too, will nearly always drop when the first bullet hits them, and they can get up just as quickly and go or come just as fast as the black. It is the "come" part that separates the blacks from the grizzly family, and no hunter should ever forget that.

While few hunters who ever tell about killing a grizzly mention one that weighed less than 1,000 pounds, the truth is that a few black bears get nearly as heavy as the largest mountain grizzlies. Of course, when a black gets that heavy it is mostly excess fat, and few grizzlies ever get as fat as the average mature black bear. A grizzly that weighs an honest 500 pounds is a big one, and he is a lot more bear than a black of the same weight. Instead of fat the grizzly is mostly bone and muscle, and the bone is a lot larger than the bone in a black bear. He also has a disposition, courage, and the tenacity to life to go with his physical structure. At the best, he is hard to kill if you don't find the right spot with the first bullet; at the worst, he is decidedly dangerous. And once hit but not killed or completely disabled, it takes a lot of hard hits to put him down and keep him there.

The more bone you can smash on a grizzly, the better off you are. Sure, if you get one out in the open, as is often the case in hunting above timberline in the North, and the land is fairly flat so you can keep track of him after he is hit, a broadside lung shot works fine. This is particularly true if you can shoot from 100 yards or so away. But if you are in close, or the bear is in or near the brush, try to hold him where he stands. To do this, break one or both shoulders. It is fine if you happen to get high enough to break the spine at the same time, but better not try that unless you know grizzly anatomy well. Remember that the hump on his shoulders sticks up high above the spine. A hit there will let him down but not for long. And when he gets up he may show a fit of temper like you've never seen or heard before.

On this kind of quartering shot at Alaskan brown bear, a bullet placed at + will smash shoulder and continue into lungs. If bullet is heavy and performs right, it will immobilize him and give quick, sure kill.

When shooting big bears like this Alaskan brownie, try to break one or both shoulders to immobilize him. If lungs are torn up along the way, kill will be faster. Hit at + will pass through lungs and smash off shoulder if bullet has good penetration ability, and no brownie should be shot with one that doesn't have.

As mentioned concerning the ungulates, if the bullet smashes both shoulders it will anchor a grizzly, but in all likelihood will not kill it outright. Probably the best bullet placement to immobilize a grizzly and give a quick kill at the same time is the quartering shot from either front or rear. A bullet that takes the bear on the point of the shoulder and goes back into the lungs will not only break the shoulder, but will tear a huge hole in the lungs, not just by the action of the bullet but because of the shattered shoulder and rib bones spraying into them. The quartering shot from the rear headed for the off shoulder is not quite as sure or as effective, because a bullet of controlled expansion construction, as it must be to be used effectively for this shot, will not do as much damage to the lungs, and finding and smashing the off shoulder with it is less of a certainty. I have, however, killed both browns and grizzlies with this shot with great success, but always with a cartridge and bullet that was up to the job. As with the rear end shots at elk and moose, the cartridges for shoulder shots on either mountain grizzly or brown bear should pack a lot of wallop and be loaded with heavy, tough bullets. It may sound like a broken record, but again my vote goes to Nosler bullets in full power handloads in calibers from 7mm up, and with emphasis on the magnums. It is in brown bear hunting that the .338 and .340, and the big .35s and the .375, really stand out above the smaller caliber cartridges, with the same bullet structure, of course.

It would seem that if the bear is facing the hunter, a bullet in the center of the chest would be ideal, but if you want to stop the bear in a hurry it is not the best by any means. I saw a rather small female Alaskan mountain grizzly shot in the center of the chest as she faced the hunter at near 150 yards. The 160 gr. Nosler bullet from a 7mm Remington Magnum landed off to one side a bit, barely missing the point of the shoulder just over the bottom of the rib cage. It passed to one side of the heart and just nipped the edge of one lung. Then on through the paunch and back into the intestines, where it was lost near the end of the body opening. That bear ran straight up the mountain through brush and boulders for more than 100 yards and was still going strong when I got a 180 gr. Nosler from a .300 Winchester Magnum through the spine between the shoulders, down into the lungs, and out in front, which ended the affair. Had that bear been coming for the hunter for some reason, it isn't hard to picture what would have happened.

Any shot that is effective on a mountain grizzly is also effective on a brownie. The only difference is that the brown bear is, on an average, larger. It follows that it takes more punch and an even stronger, heavier bullet to be certain of doing the same job. However, there are one hell of a lot more brownies killed that weigh under 700 honest pounds than weigh over that. Especially those killed in the spring, when most brown bear hunting is done. While there are many stories about 1,600–1,700 pound brown bears, those that make the half-ton mark are about as common today as moose that weigh a ton. But be that as it may, the compact makeup of a brown bear that weighs even 700 pounds forms a lot of resistance to even the best bullet. And if you don't want him to get into the brush where you may find trouble in amounts you can't handle, land that first bullet in the right spot to put him down and keep him there.

While discussing vital areas of game animals, bullet placement, and the best load to do the job right, it may be in order to consider what happens when the bullet misses that spot by a few inches. It has many times been said that it matters little what the caliber of the bullet is, or how much wallop it packs, if you land it in the right place. As pointed out earlier, there is some truth in this line of thought, but what if it just lands close to that spot? As an example, we'll say you take a shot at a big bull elk in the timber with a .243 and the best 100 gr. bullet you can find. You are not sure just what part of the ribs you are looking at but it looks to be somewhere near center. But when the bullet lands it may be a little too high, a bit too low, or too far forward or to the rear. Anyway, it hits only a little of the lung somewhere around the edges, or maybe doesn't quite touch it. That little bullet isn't leaving a very big wound channel, and it isn't packing too much energy. It will surely prove fatal eventually, but it isn't likely to be very soon. In the interim the bull can make a lot of tracks.

Now put a bullet from, we'll say, a .30-06, a .300 magnum, or a .338 in the same spot. The wound channel it makes and the shock it delivers are two or three times greater than the .243 could muster. Even though it has penetrated little of the lungs, the size of the wound channel and the shock waves pushing out from the channel will tear up a great deal of tissue, which in turn causes internal hemorrhage and an end to the process of lung function.

It should be obvious even to the hunter of limited experience that the more powerful load is good insurance against wounding and losing the bull.

11

Big Game Bullet Design and Performance

Bullet performance problems have always plagued the hunter, and it mattered little whether he was hunting pronghorn on the plains of the western states, brown bears along the fog-shrouded Alaska coast, or elephants in the African bush. It isn't necessarily peculiar to the modern jacketed bullet either, because efforts were made to improve bullet performance of big bore cast lead bullets long before smokeless powder and jacketed bullets appeared.

One attempt was a bullet cast in two pieces with a rear section of hardened lead to avoid stripping in the rifling, and a front section of pure lead to mushroom into a larger frontal area and deliver more shock. I'm told it wasn't overly successful, because the shank of the front section, which fitted into a cavity in the rear section, often loosened and dropped out before firing.

The cavity point was also used in cast lead bullets many years before most of us were packing rifles. This system worked quite well as far as expansion went, and if the alloy of the bullet was about right. If the bullet was cast too soft, the cavity expanded it too much, and if too hard, not enough. Also, that cavity point cut bullet weight considerably, and the lighter expanded bullet with the larger frontal area failed to penetrate well on heavy animals under adverse angle shooting conditions.

Even though the very large caliber bullets of that day did take care of most hunting situations of that time of lots of game and few hunters, it is apparent that some gun buffs still thought there was room for improvement. But if they thought they had problems in those days of low velocity and lead bullets, they should have been around to see those brought on by high velocity, small bullet diameters, and a lead core enclosed in an envelope of copper alloy.

Actually, the problem of bullet performance of the first jacketed offerings was not great, even with diameters as small as .25 caliber. As long as velocity remained at levels that did not exceed 2200–2300 fps, a jacket that simply enclosed the soft lead core worked very well in most instances. If it was thin enough to expand reliably at the relatively short ranges those cartridges were capable of, expansion usually came to a halt just back of center, giving a perfect mushroom and good penetration. Unfortunately, those old low velocity cartridges were hardly the answer to flat trajectory and ease of long range hits, and neither did they pack much punch at any range. The larger calibers that used very heavy bullets did produce excellent results at fairly close range, giving good expansion with some shock, and plenty of penetration. This is why some big bore enthusiasts still swear by cartridges like the .45-70 for heavy game.

Some of the first real problems arose with cartridges like the .30-06 when hunting bullets started showing up in 150–180 gr. weights. Not only did velocity increase drastically, but to give the lighter high velocity bullets their full potential for long range shooting, the point had to be pointed and not round or flat, as was true of former jacketed slugs. Where the round or flat point had exposed a lot of soft lead core to serve to expand the jacket as it was forced back by impact, the pointed form did not do as well, because of the much smaller opening in the point of the jacket. Also, there was the problem of these small pointed lead points battering in the magazine under recoil (that problem is still with us). Many efforts were made in trying to solve these problems at the same time, but none was entirely successful, although they were unique.

The Newton approach for his high velocity, heavy recoil cartridges was a pointed soft point with a steel wire inserted to stop point battering in the magazine. This system worked quite well as far as point deforming was concerned, but his jacket structure left something to be desired for bullets traveling at Newton velocities. Much later, and to achieve the same end, Winchester developed the old Precision Point. This consisted of a very sharp point of

These are some of the points that have been put on expanding bullets to protect them from battering out of shape in the magazine. *From left:* Remington Bronze Point; Winchester Silvertip; old Winchester Precision or Protected Point. While they do resist deformation in the magazine, performance on game is often erratic. The Silvertip gives the best performance but is inclined to be quite explosive at high velocity.

jacket inserted into a cavity in the main jacket, with three small points of lead peeping through at equally spaced intervals at the point-jacket juncture. The object of this point design was to protect the point from being deformed in the magazine, give it a high ballistic coefficient, and impact would drive it rearward to expand the main jacket. I used many of these in the .30-40, .30-06, and .30 Newton in handloads, and found them very erratic in performance. When velocity dropped off at long range they usually failed to expand at all, especially in the .30-40 and .30-06, and at closer ranges they sometimes blew up completely near the surface, or failed to expand there too.

Several companies made cavity point (HP) bullets in pointed form that worked quite well under some conditions, but problems arose there too. In order to retain high ballistic coefficient, a cavity has to be of fairly small diameter, and if the jacket is a little too thick and hard, there is not enough trapped air or fluid to properly expand it at the retained velocity of all ranges in a given cartridge. On the other hand, if the cavity is large, the bullet loses velocity faster, and if the jacket that surrounds it is too thin, expansion will be too fast and violent. (Some exceptions to this will be mentioned later.)

Probably because the .30-06 then was the most popular of any cartridge among American hunters, it seemed to get more than its share of experimental bullets in factory loadings. There is little doubt that this contributed to the opinion of some hunters that this cartridge did not perform as reliably as some others on all game under all hunting conditions at all ranges. I still know a few old-timers who claim the .30-40 was a better killer of large game because it gave better penetration and consistent performance. They do not know much about ballistics, and have never used enough bullets of different makes and styles in different cartridges to see how others perform. They simply blame the cartridge for performance that is caused by the bullet used. Since the advent of the magnums, this same line of thinking has often shifted to those cartridges because of poor bullet performance. What it all boils down to is that the higher the velocity the bullet travels at, and the more streamlined its shape, the more difficult it is to make it perform properly at all ranges. And this is particularly true of the magnums that carry enough velocity to be ideal for shooting game at the longest ranges. The bullet that starts at 3000–3200 fps may be called upon to give deep, bone-shattering penetration on a brown bear at a matter of a few feet from the muzzle, while at the same time be expected to expand sufficiently on a dall ram at 400 yards or more to give a fast kill. And this isn't nearly as simple as many hunters seem to think.

Before going on to bullet designs in greater detail, it is worth considering the fact that today's hunters are much better off than hunters of even 25–30 years ago if they handload their own hunting ammunition. It is not only possible to use the best of the bullets produced by the ammunition companies for use in their factory ammunition in your own handloads tailored especially to your own requirements, but there is an ever-increasing list of bullets from the various bullet companies. All these independent bullet companies are striving to make bullets that perform better on big game, and at least some of them are succeeding. Not only that, but powders have been greatly improved in the past few years, so that these better hunting bullets can be driven at higher velocity from the hunting cartridge of your choice. Of course, this wide assortment of bullets becomes highly confusing to all except the most experienced hunter/handloader, so the following pages on bullet design and performance are written to help make the right choice easier.

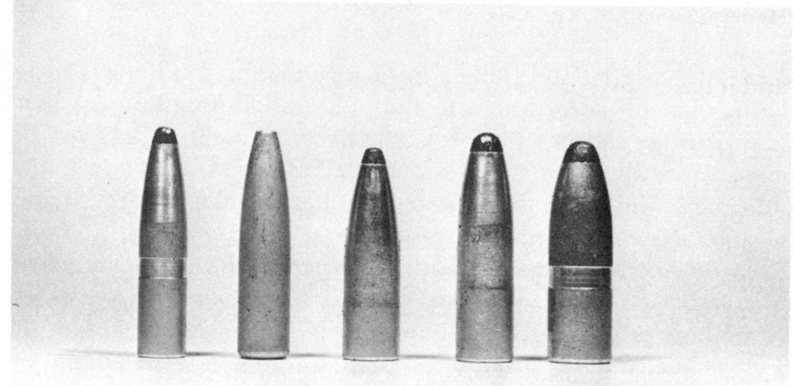

Magnum cartridges have one disadvantage: they often blow up bullets at close range from terrific impact of high velocity. These bullets are designed to hold together for deep penetration at magnum velocities. *From left:* 175 gr. 7mm Nosler; .30 200 gr. Bitterroot Bonded Core; .338 210 gr. Nosler; .338 250 gr. Nosler; .375 300 gr. Nosler. Some Weatherby magnum ammunition is loaded with Noslers, and all are available for handloading.

Let's take a long, hard look at some of the more modern bullet designs that have come along in an attempt to solve these problems and see just how well they have accomplished it.

Modern Hunting Bullet Designs

In factory bullets of more or less nonconventional design that are still in use, we have the Remington Bronze Point. That bullet has been around a long time with little if any change through the years. The point design offers two things on the plus side: no point damage to the point in the magazine under recoil, and very high ballistic coefficient for weight and caliber. The very sharp point is probably actually made of bronze and defies any damage whatever under the heaviest recoil in the magazine. It has a short stem that is set down inside the jacket against the core, and is held tightly in place after final swaging of the bullet. The function of the bronze point is to drive back and rupture the jacket when contact is made with the target. This theory sounds good, but sometimes it works, sometimes it doesn't. I have seen a good many head of assorted game shot with this bullet in 180 gr. weight in the .30-06, and it has given some of the most erratic performances I have ever witnessed. I have always been a bullet digger, and took the time and trouble to carefully follow the path of most of these bullets to see what happened.

Some of the animals shot died instantly from lung shots, while others shot under almost identical circumstances lived to travel long distances and had to be shot a second time after being trailed. Some of them had very small exit holes, others a hole in the hide you could stick your head in, and some bullets never got beyond midway in the lungs of goat, deer, and bighorn sheep. The bullet digging was highly revealing. Some bullets expanded like a varmint bullet on contact with the rib cage, especially if a rib was hit, and blew up completely in the lungs. These gave very fast kills on deer-size game, but wouldn't have penetrated much beyond the hide of a bull elk's shoulder. The ones that left the small exit holes failed to expand at all and were found to have missed the ribs on both sides. The ones that left the great, jagged exit holes did not kill quickly because the bullet had passed entirely through the lungs before expanding on a rib on the off side, leaving practically no wound channel in the lungs, but exploding on the ribs and causing the extremely large exit hole. I know hunters who swear by the Bronze Point bullet, but I feel they have been blessed with good luck, and often wonder how many of those bullets passed through animals without expanding at all, conveying the impression of a miss.

Most of today's hunters do not remember the old Peters Belted 225 gr. .30 caliber bullet, which has long been discontinued, but we mention it here because it eventually led to the development of the Inner-Belted bullet in other weights, and to the R-P Core-Lokt bullet of today that has proved so reliable. The Peters Belted was of round point design with a huge cavity to give immediate expansion on contact. About 1/4" in back of the point there was an *external* belt of heavy metal that was swaged down into the bullet jacket. That extra band of metal was designed to stop expansion at that point, leaving the rest of the bullet shank to furnish the weight to drive the bullet through the heaviest bone and muscle and on into the boiler room of the very largest American game animals. And this it did to perfection. But there was a fly in this jelly too. If that belt had been placed at least halfway back, the bullet would have been a great success for short range work on big animals, but the forward location prevented much expansion, and the bullet performed much like a solid, leaving a very small wound channel and delivering little shock.

The Inner-Belted was about like today's Core-Lokt except that all of them, I believe, were in round point form. The design of the Inner-Belted and Core-Lokt bullet is a very thin jacket at the point that further facilitates expansion by the addition of small notches in the jacket. The jacket gradually thickens to a very thick section near the middle, then thins down in the rear section of the shank. This gives an "hour glass" shape to the tightly swaged core and helps hold it in place within the jacket when expansion takes place. These bullets, especially in the pointed Core-Lokt form, give the best all-around performance of any factory-loaded bullet I know of (Nosler loaded by Weatherby being the exception). The pointed form has good ballistic coefficient, they expand well at all reasonable game shooting ranges, and expansion is pretty well controlled by the thick center jacket section. And unless the resistance is severe enough to split the jacket beyond the heavy section, the core stays in the jacket—something that is extremely vital to deep penetration.

The old Western Cartridge Co., before it became a part of Winchester Arms Co., made some fairly good bullets in one form or another. One of the best was their .30 caliber 180 gr. OPE (Open Point Expanding) bullet. That bullet had good ballistic form and a point cavity large enough to work well as long as velocity was reasonably high. I used some of these bullets on elk and they held together very well and gave excellent penetration even on raking shots, but failed to expand at longer ranges either in the .30-40 or the .30-06. Western also made a 220 gr. soft point that could be classed as a semipointed bullet that had a good reputation for its penetrating ability on heavy animals. My experience with this bullet on elk verified this, but the very small point of exposed lead core made it fail to expand if velocity dropped off very much unless a heavy bone was hit.

I don't recall exactly when the Winchester Silvertip came along in the mid-1940s, but it was hailed as a great improvement by many gun writers. What the Silvertip actually amounts to is a very large tip of lead protruding from the point of the jacket and covered by a very thin sheath of copper alloy covered with a silver-colored coating. This thin cover stops most deformation in the magazine, yet allows the normal action of a soft point. In fact, it allows too much action to take place. If a Silvertip bullet is sectioned, it will be found that the opening in the jacket point is very large, which, in any case I have ever observed, leads to quick and violent expansion. I have seen a great deal of game shot with this bullet in many calibers and weights, running from coyotes to bull moose and grizzly, and I have never been happy with the results. I have been told that the 250 gr. .338 bullets perform well and do not come apart, and that the 300 gr. .375 bullets perform equally well, but I have never seen anything killed with either, so can't say. I have also been told that some other calibers and weights give outstanding performance, but when I tried them I must have been a jinx because nothing was left but the heel of the jacket if heavy resistance was encountered. They give good results on the smaller species of big game and kill quickly because of the explosive action, and they also work well on larger animals on broadside lung shots. But for raking shots on heavy game, all Silvertips that I have used or seen used have been too fragile. They do expand well at long range when velocity has dropped off to where some other bullets do not expand well, and they will also give much better penetration at those ranges. In all fairness to the Silvertip bullets, they may have undergone some improvement in the past few years, but the new ones I've tried in my recovery box still expand too much and lose the cores, and this includes the 250 gr. .338. Neither have I used enough W-W Power-Point bullets to pass judgment on how well they perform on all classes of game at all hunting ranges, but those I have seen used gave about the same level of performance as most conventional soft point bullets from either the ammunition or bullet companies.

I've also killed game, or seen game killed, with a good many bullets of foreign manufacture. As mentioned earlier, the steel jacketed Kynoch bullets proved to be poor performers. Neither have I been any happier with the performance I've seen from Norma steel jacketed bullets. Any I've ever used expanded too much and lost their cores at high impact velocities.

A great many rather odd bullet designs have come out of Germany, and while I haven't tried them all, some have been used to shoot elk. I once loaded a number of the famous H Mantel round nose–soft point bullets in 8×57 Mauser cases. If I remember correctly, these weighed 196 gr. I gave them to several friends who were using these "liberated" rifles for elk hunting just after World War II. The results were invariably the same if the bullet was recovered. The front part of the jacket sheared off when it expanded fully to the partial partition, but the rear section continued to penetrate, leaving a very small wound channel. And even that ended rapidly, because the small section nearly always tumbled. These bullets do not compare in performance to the excellent Speer 225 gr. for the 8mm, or the 200 and 250 gr. CCB.

Performance of the Ackley solid base bullets was much the same as the H-jacket German offering. These were made of copper rod drilled out in the front to receive the lead core and forming a jacket of sorts. This jacket tapered so that it became thicker as it neared the solid rear portion, presumably to give a mushroom effect. In testing these bullets I found that the core left the jacket, with the forward section shearing from the solid rear portion on most occasions. And the solid rear section, being of copper, lacked the weight required to continue penetration. The samples I had were none too accurate, and not many were ever made.

New Bullet Companies Prove Boon to Hunter/Handloader

There were few bullet companies that produced nothing but bullets before World War II, so the handloader was, for the most part, limited to using bullets made by the domestic and foreign ammunition companies. With the close of the war, the stock of factory ammunition and components was very low, and when the ammunition companies got back into civilian production they naturally concentrated on ammunition and not bullets for the handloader. So it came about that a few enterprising shooters got into the act and bullet companies sprang up here and there that offered many calibers, weights, and designs both for target shooters and for hunters. These companies have nearly all survived and prospered, because they not only catered to the demand of the handloader but furnished an excellent product.

Speer was one of the first bullet companies to spring up in the postwar years, and I used a good many of their bullets for big game hunting from the start. Up until recently Speer big game bullets saw little change in structural design. Accuracy has always been good, and performance ran along about the same lines as most other bullets of conventional designs where the jacket is drawn from sheet gilding metal. I have always liked Speer bullets for shooting deer-size game at all ranges, but when I use them for heavy animals it is the heavier weights in all calibers, especially if used in magnum capacity cases.

A few years ago Speer developed a bullet they called the Magnum in 7mm and .30 calibers. These bullets had a flat point to avoid magazine damage, and a tapered jacket that was somewhat thicker toward the rear than their standard bullets. I tested these bullets both in the recovery box and on mule deer and elk, and if they performed any better than the same weight and caliber of their conventional design I failed to see it. The big problem was that they invariably lost the core and, of course, lacked penetration when fired from magnum cartridges. At normal .30-06 or .280 Remington velocities they did quite well.

As this book was being written (August 1976), I received samples of the new Speer 180 gr. .30 bullet christened the Grand Slam. This bullet will be made in at least .270, 7mm, and .30 calibers, and in at least two weights in each caliber. It has the same flat point as the Magnum, but has an 8 caliber ogive instead of 6 or, in nontechnical terms, better point form to give higher ballistic coefficient. The jacket is fairly thin at the point, then tapers back to a heavier body section. It has a dual core with a pure lead front section and a 5% antimony–95% lead alloy. There is a rather deep cannelure that forms a ridge around the jacket on the inside that acts to help retain the core in the jacket, providing the jacket does not expand beyond that point. (See photos of sectioned bullets, p. 247.) There is also a tiny groove around the base at the heel into which the core is swaged. This is there to also help retain the core.

There is no way this bullet can be tested on game before the fall hunting season, but tests in the recovery box did not show especially good penetration or retain weight. A small amount of core did remain in the jacket, but the jacket expanded to within about 1/8″ of the heel. Frontal area of the 180 gr. .30 bullet was very large at .80", which would indicate good shocking power. Impact velocity was 3060 fps from a .300 Win. Mag., so performance would be somewhat better at ranges beyond 100 yards. Speer is headed in the right direction with this new bullet, but they have not yet arrived.

What has just been said for Speer bullets, with the exception of the Magnum and the Grand Slam, will also pretty well cover the performance of Hornady hunting bullets. The design is somewhat different, Hornady using the spire point form, but there isn't enough difference in jacket structure to matter too much in the way they perform. Hornady does make one of the finest solid bullets in several calibers that has ever been developed. Of course, there is no place in the American hunting scene for a solid, but they have piled up a reputation of high success for shooting heavy African game.

Most reloaders think of Sierra bullets more from the standpoint of outstanding accuracy than as hunting bullets in big game calibers. There are a number of reasons why Sierra bullets have never gained any great reputation as big game hunting bullets. For one thing, it appears that Sierra didn't put any great emphasis on the big game hunting angle until recently. This is also borne out by the fact that they did not until quite recently make bullets for some of the calibers used for shooting heavy game, the .338 and .375 for example. Neither did they make heavyweight bullets for some calibers. Another problem I have encountered with some Sierra bullets where deep penetration is needed on heavy game arises from the boattail design of some of them. The core is much more likely to leave the jacket of a boattail than a flat base. In spite of what some gun writers have said about the great advantage offered by the boattail design of the 175 gr. 7mm, 250 gr. .338, and the 300 gr. .375 Sierra spitzer bullets, I would prefer all of them to be of flat base design, with the possible exception of the 7mm when used for specialized work. As we've seen earlier, there is damn little difference between the drop of a flat base bullet and that of a boattail bullet at ranges out to 500 yards, but there is a difference in how well those bullets retain their cores on impact with heavy bone and muscle. And if the core parts company with the jacket, the bullet will not give certain and uniform penetration.

All these bullets are wonderfully accurate, but it takes more than accuracy to make a good big game bullet. The jacket of the 250 gr. .338 bullets I have are a bit too thin and expand too much and too fast at close range where velocity is still high. The new 300 gr. .375 bullet has a very well designed jacket in its final form, but I'd have preferred a flat base to help retain the core. The jacket is tapered from a thin nose section, for reliable long range expansion, to a heavy body section, to control expansion and give deep penetration. I haven't fired any of these latest bullets either into game or into the recovery box, but if by some chance they hold the core, they will penetrate well.

Fred Barns probably built up his bullet business more from the standpoint that bullets were made in several calibers not available from domestic bullet companies than from the standpoint of outstanding performance. Most of his bullets did in fact perform well, but the secret to this was not in design but in great sectional density. These bullets, with the exception of some of the first that had drawn cup jackets, are made from copper tubing for jacket material. This soft copper makes a good jacket if it is heavy enough and if velocity is not too high. I used many of these in 7mm 180 gr. and in 250 gr. .333 in spitzer form. For use in magnum cartridges the .049" jacket thickness gave the best penetration results, but they failed to expand at long range because the jacket was not thinned down at the point and the swaging process made it so thick at the point of spitzer bullets that only a pin-size hole was left. I drilled some of the .333 bullets to form hollow points and they did quite well, but often shed the core. The Barns company has changed hands a number of times, but the most recent owners have changed the name back to Barns Bullets.*

At about the same time that the other bullet companies were putting down roots to support the ever-growing handloading business, another firm came into being as a one-man operation that eventually became one of the country's largest and best-known makers of premium quality hunting bullets. But this bullet-making business was founded on a somewhat different concept: making bullets especially for hunting big game. It was due to the fact that bullets of conventional design and structure failed to give consistent, effective performance, and particularly on big tough animals,

*Located at P.O. Box 215, American Fork, Utah 84003.

that John Nosler designed and built the first experimental bullets that were to become world-famous as the Nosler Partition Jacket bullet.

John knew two things that a lot of us were aware of, but he put this knowledge to use and did something about it, while the rest of us just talked about it. First of the two requirements was that the bullet jacket had to be designed so it would control expansion completely and consistently at all velocities at which the bullet would impact, with cartridges of all velocity levels and on game of all sizes. Second, the jacket design must be thin enough at the point and tapered correctly to expand at the low velocities of long range hits when only hide and meat were contacted, with no bone hit. It might be added here that this is the criterion on which all all-around bullet designs must be based.

The first Nosler bullets I ever used were some of the first produced for sale, and were in 160 and 175 gr. .284 diameter. These were of hollow point design and of true two-diameter style, with the front portion back to just behind the partition being of land (bore) diameter and the rear part of the body of groove diameter. They were of high ballistic coefficient form and gave good accuracy. The jacket was very thin around the point cavity, and I never experienced any difficulty whatever in expansion at ranges out to 400 yards even on coyotes with the .285 OKH I used them in. I killed a number of elk with the 175 gr. in that cartridge and others with the 160 gr. in the 7×57 Mauser. All were killed cleanly at ranges of from 100 to 400 yards, and I don't recall ever recovering one of those bullets.

The design was later changed to soft point, and instead of the two-diameter form, a cut or groove was left over the partition to relieve pressures at that point. These later bullets were formed from bronze tubing with a tiny hole in the partition. The hole didn't make much difference, because the partition effectively stopped expansion, but the bronze was not always of the same high quality in all lots. This occasionally caused the jacket forward of the partition to shear off from the rear section, and even more rarely to rupture the rear section, with the consequent loss of both front and rear cores. When this happened, the penetration for which Nosler bullets have always been famous was lacking. Personally, out of more than 100 kills I've made or seen made with Nosler bullets, I have witnessed only two cases of this, one a sheared front section, the other a rear jacket rupture, and these both came from a poor lot of jacket material. There was nothing wrong with the design.

The latest Nosler bullets are made from gilding metal rod with a cavity formed from both ends, leaving a solid partition. They are of conventional spitzer form with the familiar cut over the partition missing. There is also a tiny boattail where the jacket is folded over the rear core. Accuracy of the new Nosler bullets is excellent, and performance is even better than with the older styles. The new jacket material is more ductile and gives a larger average frontal area, and they nearly always retain a little of the front core, whereas the old ones invariably lost it.

The Nosler claim has always been that their bullets retained approximately 2/3 of their original weight. This is one advertising claim that is completely correct, give or take 3 or 4 gr. I have weighed a great many of them both from the recovery box and from big animals shot at various ranges of from a few feet to nearly 500 yards, and remaining weight is invariably between 65% and 69% of the original weight.

While this was being written, Nosler developed and has started producing a new line of bullets that *should not be confused with the*

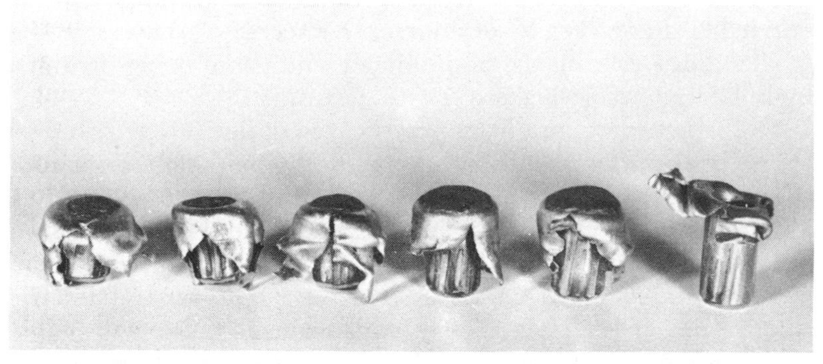

These new style Nosler 7mm 160 gr. bullets show how a good big game bullet should perform at various ranges. These bullets were taken from recovery box described in text at a range of 15 feet from muzzle. They were loaded to give approximate velocity at ranges of 0, 100, 200, 300, 400, and 500 yards when started at an MV of 3240 fps from a 7mm Mashburn Super Magnum. It will be noted that none blew up, and even the bullet at right, fired at 500 yard velocity, expanded quite well.

Nosler Partition Jacket referred to in all other places in this book. The new bullet is called the *Nosler Solid Base,* which means that the base is solid and does not show the exposed rear core as does the Partition bullet. The base of the bullet jacket is very thick, actually of the same thickness as the small boattail. These bullets are in hollow point design in some calibers and weights, but are mostly in soft point spitzer form (pointed), that look very much like the new design Partition Jacket spitzers. The jacket is of more conventional design *without* the partition. They will not give the same performance as the Nosler Partition Jacket, but are made to perform and sell at similar levels of conventional style bullets.

If I have conveyed the impression that I use the Nosler bullet as the criterion by which to judge the performance of all new bullet designs that come along, as well as the old ones, this is completely true. After using them on all classes of game at all hunting ranges in cartridges of all sizes and calibers, I have come to have unlimited faith in their performance.

Because of the many requests I receive for information on the Bitterroot Bonded Core bullet, and just in case it may sometime again become available, we'll cover it briefly. The term *Bonded Core* means exactly that: the soft lead core is bonded firmly to the jacket (do not confuse this with the Speer Hot Core process that *does not* bond the core to the jacket). The process with which the core is bonded to the jacket is, of course, the secret of success of the outstanding performance of the bullet, and is not being divulged by Bill Steigers, the maker.

The jacket is swaged from very heavy copper tubing of up to about .070" thickness, depending on the caliber, and is pure copper, not alloyed with other metals. Expansion is accomplished by a rather large cavity in the point, and the jacket is thinned down at the point and tapered back. All these bullets I have used are in pointed form and have flat bases. The large hollow point and the soft copper jacket give reliable expansion at reasonable game shooting ranges. The fact that the core sticks firmly to the jacket even when fired into the heaviest bone gives these bullets the highest retained weight of any I have ever used, running as high as 98%, and averaging over 90% of the original weight. They usually mushroom back to about the last 1/3–1/4 of the bullet body, which gives a very large frontal area. They deliver great shock and give deep penetration, but do not equal the penetration of a Nosler bullet in the same weight and caliber either on game or in the recovery box. This is because the larger frontal area retards the penetration of the bullet faster than does the smaller area of the Nosler.

As an example of performance of these Bitterroot bullets, I shot a large Admiralty Island brownie with a 250 gr. from a .340 Weatherby backed by 84 gr. of N205 that left the muzzle at 2900 fps. The bear was quartering away at 130 yards. I held for the front leg on the off side and the bullet landed at the rear of the lungs, passed entirely through both, on into the off shoulder, smashing the heavy bone into splinters, and lodged against the hide at the point of the shoulder. It also broke ribs on both sides. Penetration was over 2 feet, and the remaining weight was 209 gr. or near 84%. Part of the core had been wiped off the jacket, probably from a poor bond, but still this was very good performance. Normally, however, retained weight is much better.

I know that some hunters who have killed a lot of game of all kinds pay very little attention to bullet performance, taking the

The author with good Admiralty Island brown bear shot at 130 yards with .340 Weatherby cartridge in custom rifle and 250 gr. Bitterroot Bonded Core backed by 84 gr. N205 at 2925 fps. That load is good brownie medicine no matter how big they come or where they are.

attitude that if the animal was killed it matters little how the bullet performed. This line of thought may sound good to those who don't like the messy, time-consuming job of tracking bullets, but it is hardly the way to find out why a bullet killed well or did not. And if none of us looked to see why a bullet did an efficient job of killing an animal or instead only wounded it, we'd all be offering up a prayer every time we squeezed the trigger.

Poor Bullet Performance and Big Trouble

I was involved in an incident a few years ago that made me highly critical of those who think that one bullet works about as well as another.

This was during one of the periods when a guide was not mandatory for hunting sheep and grizzly in Alaska. The outfitter was tied up hunting sheep with another hunter that day, so I had agreed to tag along with his partner to look for a ram or possibly a grizzly on the slope above the river.

A couple of miles out of camp we saw a grizzly heading down into a side creek, so we decided to see if we could head it off when it hit the high bench above the creek. The hunter was an attorney from a Texas city and not in the best of shape for climbing Alaskan mountains. We managed to make it up the creek to under where the bear should be coming off the slope, and the puffing hunter finally crawled up over the bank in time to get some of his breath back before the grizzly suddenly burst out of the wall of alders into a little opening at what later proved to be 17 yards. It was quartering to us and I told him to take it in the point of the shoulder with his .30-06. When the bullet landed, the bear went down as if the earth had been jerked from under it. But it didn't really stay down. Instead, it came rolling and tumbling end over end down a shallow swale right at us. I waited until he shot a second time and then fired once into the twisting mass of bear, but had little faith the bullet had done any good. By this time the bear was within a few feet of where I stood and it was obvious it would run over me if I didn't move. The hunter was already on higher ground and backing away, so I moved back a bit while chambering another cartridge in the .300 Winchester Model 70. When I moved, the grizzly saw me, straightened out, and came from 15 feet. There isn't much time for precise holding at a time like that, so I just looked over the scope and sent a 180 gr. Nosler, backed by 78 gr. of H4831 at 3150 fps, in the direction of the shoulder. There would be no time for a second shot, so I jumped back, caught my heel on an alder root, and sat down hard in the wet moss. As I worked the bolt, the bear reared up and I remember wondering how it was going to feel when it came down. Then I noticed it had stopped bawling and had a dazed look. Instead of coming down on me, it fell over to one side and tried to crawl groggily along. Before I could get up, the attorney fired into the neck, and then a second time. It was all over, and luckily neither of us had any bear tracks on us, but I was curious to see why the rather small female grizzly hadn't been killed by the first bullet.

We found that the first shot had landed in the neck just below the bone and headed for the off shoulder. This would have been fine and should have broken the shoulder, disabling the bear, but the 180 gr. Silvertip had come apart and failed to even penetrate the neck completely. McKay's second bullet had missed, and mine had found only a front foot of the tumbling bear. My second bullet had landed on the big shoulder joint, shattering the whole shoulder, then sliced every rib on that side and made exit in the flank. That is why the bear had reared up and fallen over on the other side. But the revealing part of the incident was that neither of the last two 180 gr. Silvertips had exited from broadside shots into the neck. And that bear wouldn't have weighed 300 pounds with its belly full of blueberries!

This was clearly not a case of poor cartridge performance but one of poor bullet performance. My .300 Winchester would probably have done little better with the same bullet, but if it had been the 180 gr. Nosler that had landed in the base of the neck at the first shot, there would have been no need for more than possibly a finishing shot for insurance.

Testing Bullet Performance Before Going Hunting

In speaking of bullet performance, I have mentioned the recovery box several times, but the material contained or how it is used has not been brought out. As all bullet manufacturers use some form of recovery material to check bullet expansion and penetration, a brief rundown of procedure and the various materials used is probably worthwhile. No material will produce the same results as living flesh and bone, but it is impossible in testing a great many bullets to try them all on game animals, and they would have to be tried on several animals to come up with solid evidence, so some test medium must be used.

Some of the ammunition manufacturers use gelatin blocks, and some of the bullet makers use wet lap. The latter material is composed of raw paper fibers in 1/8″ thick sheets. To use as a bullet recovery medium, they are placed on edge to a thickness of a couple of feet or so, saturated with water, and, when well soaked, fired into at various ranges and velocities. A similar substance can be made from a pile of water-soaked newspapers held in place in a cardboard box. I have used both, and find they work well to expand bullets and check the velocity at which they will expand, but either is far from ideal in checking bullet breakup.

I have found that nearly any bullet fired into wet lap will give a classic mushroom with very little loss of weight, but fire that same bullet into the shoulder of a bull elk and it may blow up completely. The apparent reason for this is that, much like firing the same bullet into a block of wood, the side pressure serves to hold the bullet intact, and the steady pressure exerted against the expanding point as the bullet drives in prevents the core from leaving the jacket. Therefore, a bullet of conventional design performs about as well as one with completely controlled expansion like the Nosler or Bitterroot.

What I finally settled on is a box about 1 foot square and 4 feet in length. It is filled with a mixture of about 50% sawdust, preferably partially rotted, and 50% fine silt. This mixture is given just enough water to cause it to stick to the fingers, but by no means mud. A piece of heavy truck innertube is placed over the shooting end, and a cardboard spacer placed every 6″ to check expansion and facilitate bullet recovery. The mixture is stirred up between shots, so it does not pack enough to give more resistance for one shot than for another.

As to how well it works, let's take a number of .30 caliber 180 gr. pointed bullets fired from a .300 Winchester Magnum at an impact velocity of over 3100 fps. The Nosler Partition penetrated

24″ and had a remaining weight of 118.6 gr. The Bitterroot drove in 19″ and weighed 157 gr. Conventional design bullets, Speer, Hornady, and Sierra 180 gr., were nearly identical in performance with 15″–16″ of penetration and an average of about 75 gr. of retained weight. All lost the core. The new Speer Grand Slam gave 15″ of penetration, and retained a little of the core in most cases for an average retained weight of about 83 gr.

These tests do not come out like those in the magazine ads, but long experience has shown they come out about the same as when the same bullets are fired into a bull moose or brown bear. And it should tell us something about which bullets will give the kind of performance in cartridges of various velocity levels that it takes to be efficient on game of various sizes. This angle has been covered in one way or another several times in previous chapters, but perhaps not specifically in one place.

As is clear from the penetration tests, all the 180 gr. bullets with conventional jacket design gave almost identical results. The actual penetration and remaining weight figures varied only about 1″ in penetration and no more than 2–4 gr. in remaining weight. Also, former tests in the same test-recovery box show that other bullets of similar design from the commercial ammunition companies, bullets like the W-W Silvertip and Power-Point, the R-P soft point, and bullets loaded in Federal ammunition, give similar results in the same weights. Remington Core-Lokt normally runs between these bullets with conventional jacket design and the premium quality controlled expansion bullets like Nosler and Bitterroot.

There is no doubt whatever that the conventional bullets, Speer, Sierra, Hornady, and those from the ammunition companies, give adequate penetration for deer-size game from nearly any angle in this weight and at this striking velocity, and would also do well on larger game on broadside rib shots. However, it is highly unlikely that they will be called upon to perform at this velocity on game because of the longer ranges involved, and the lower impact velocity at those ranges. It follows that if you load those same conventional design bullets in cartridges in the velocity range from the .300 Savage and .308 Winchester to the .30-06, or from about 2400 fps to around 2800 fps at the muzzle, they will perform quite well on heavy game like elk and moose. The reason is that they will not expand as rapidly or as much, may not lose the core, and therefore give deeper penetration. Even then, it must be remembered that they will not perform the same at all ranges or when big bones are encountered as opposed to only meat and hide. Unfortunately, the hunter has little control over either situation.

What we are trying to point out is that these bullets of conventional design will do a reasonably good job in cartridges that deliver them at the velocities mentioned above, but they are far too fragile for the increased velocity that magnum cartridges give them, especially on large animals.

The same thing applies to bullets of lighter weights that are designed to give higher velocity and flatter trajectory in cartridges of various powder capacities. In .30 caliber this would include the 150 gr. and 165 gr. of conventional design. These bullets, with the exception of the Nosler Partition Jacket, are too fragile to withstand magnum velocities on heavy game, and on deer-size game they are overly destructive, ruining a large amount of meat. They will, however, do a good job for long range shooting of deer, antelope, and other game of similar size, in the lower velocity cartridges. In fact, they are ideally suited to this kind of shooting.

This, of course, does not apply only to .30 caliber cartridges, but to all calibers smaller or larger; the lighter weight bullets (excluding the varmint bullets in the smaller calibers) are designed and should be used for shooting the smaller big game species. And if they are of conventional jacket design, use them in standard cartridges, not in magnums. We do not suggest trying to load magnum cartridges down to the velocity of standard numbers to try to compensate for the use of fragile bullets; instead, use a bullet that will withstand magnum velocities.

To put this another way, the handloader has at his disposal a great variety of bullet designs and weights in every caliber, and experience has shown that he is much better off to suit the bullet to the velocity of the cartridge he will shoot it in, and to the game on which it will be used, than to try to work out a load in the cartridge to suit the bullet design. He will expend a lot less ammunition in the process, and will have a load that will give the ultimate in efficiency instead of a stop-gap measure.

If the photos of sectioned bullets are looked at closely and the bullets of different makes and jacket designs studied, it soon

These bullets plainly show the difference in performance between the premium quality bullets designed to give good expansion coupled with deep penetration on heavy game, and those of conventional design. *From left:* 7mm 175 gr. Nosler from bull elk with 7mm Rem. Mag.; 210 gr. Nosler from bull elk with .340 Wby.; 250 gr. Bitterroot from Alaskan brown bear with .340 Wby.; 285 gr. Speer from bull moose with .375 H&H; 150 gr. Norma from buck mule deer with 7×57; 150 gr. Win. Power-Point from cow elk with 7mm Rem. Mag.; 180 gr. Win. Silvertip from mountain goat with .30-06. Note that only the rear of jacket is left of latter four.

Sectioned bullets showing jacket construction. A close look will reveal one reason why some bullets retain weight better than others when fired into the heavy muscle and bone of large animals. *From left:* Nosler Partition; Bitterroot Bonded Core; Speer Grand Slam; Rem. Core-Lokt; Barns; W-W Silvertip; Sierra BT; Speer Hot Core; Norma steel jacket; Kynoch steel jacket.

becomes obvious why some perform better than others. The first thing I do when a new bullet arrives for testing is to section it and study the jacket structure and test the core hardness. This done, there is little doubt as to how that bullet will perform on various kinds of game under various shooting conditions. Then, if I don't think it will perform well, it is fired into the recovery box with a Nosler used as a control bullet. If it doesn't perform well, I'm damn careful where I hunt with it, and in many cases will not use it on game of any kind.

There are a few final facts about bullets and game of different sizes that it might be well to consider. As previously explained, the bullet that does a good job on deer from most angles, and on broadside lung shots on larger game, may fail to penetrate deeply enough for angle shots at heavy animals. And the bullet that will drive through heavy bone and muscle on big animals and reach the vitals from either front or rear angles, will certainly go on through on broadside shots on heavy game and from nearly any angle on deer-size animals. Some hunters have the idea that a bullet must stay within the animal to deliver all its energy and be fully effective, but obviously this is impossible to accomplish on all sizes of game at all angles and at all ranges. After observing the effect of bullets that stayed inside the animal, and those that made exit, on most species of North American game, I find there is no noticeable difference in how soon it dies or whether or not it collapses where it stands. I have found that a large exit hole that allows the blood to gush out, and the cold air to rush in, will kill just as quickly and surely as the bullet that stays inside. And if the animal runs off after being shot with either bullet, the big exit hole makes it a lot easier to trail!

Last, but by no means least, remember that it is the bullet that does the killing, not the cartridge. No matter how big and impressive the cartridge case looks, it only provides the means of propulsion; it is the bullet that either kills cleanly or wounds the game.

See pp. 44–45 for note with supplementary information, and for explanation of abbreviations used in charts.

Chart comparing drop figures for 180 gr. bullets in spitzer and round point form when sighted to zero at 100 yards as opposed to 3″ high sighting. The drop figures are based on about the average ballistic coefficient of various makes of both pointed and round point bullets. Velocity variation of up to 50 fps either way will have little effect on hold on a big game animal, and can be considered average for most of the .300 magnums with full-power handloads. Drop has been carried out to 500 yards to show more clearly the effect both sighting and bullet shape have on long range big game shooting.

BULLET	MV fps	100 yards	200 yards	300 yards	400 yards	500 yards
180 gr. SP Ptd.	3100	+3″	+4.5″	+1″	−9″	−27″
180 gr. round point	3100	+3″	+4″	−4″	−20″	−51″
180 gr. SP Ptd.	3100	0.0″	−3″	−10″	−24″	−44″
180 gr. round point	3100	0.0″	−4″	−15″	−35″	−67″

12

Hits and Misses

All the ballistic data, and all the pointers on how to place the first bullet in the vital area of the animal being shot at various ranges, have been based on the assumption that the rifle used is *correctly* sighted. That is, sighted so that the point of impact is exactly where it should be, and not just "close." For instance, if you intend to use a 1″ high sighting at 100 yards for a .22-250 and know where the bullets will land at 200 yards, or 250 or 300 yards, the rifle will have to be sighted exactly 1″ high and not 1 1/2″ or maybe only 1/2″. Also, if you want drop figures and mid-range bullet impact above line of sight to come out right, you sight 3″ high with big game hunting loads, and not 4″ or 2″ high. Close is not good enough. You also have to know the exact distance and not place the target just somewhere near 100 yards, like 90 or 110 yards. To do so can cause the vital hit range for a deer to vary by at least 50 yards for even the flat shooting loads.

As for the horizontal or windage adjustment, if you are shooting varmints, sight right on the nose and not 1/2″–1″ left or right. A bullet that is only 1/2″ to one side at 100 yards will miss a standing ground squirrel at 200 yards with a perfect center hold and not a breath of wind. It isn't all that critical with the big game rifle, but be certain the impact point is within 1″ of horizontal center. Remember that if the bullet is off to one side by 2″ at 100 yards, it will be off by 8″ at 400 yards, and that is enough to land the bullet intended for the center of a deer's lungs back in the paunch, or to cause a flesh wound at the front of the shoulder.

Even the worst of the examples just listed, however, are excellent sighting compared to that used by most hunters. Many hunters think that if they buy a new rifle it will be sighted in correctly with any load they feed it. And if they have some sporting goods dealer or gunsmith mount a scope on it and bore sight it with or without the aid of a collimator, it will also do the same thing. They have been led to believe that a collimator will sight the rifle to put its bullets right on the button at about 100 yards, but they never consider that few loads will give the same point of impact in that rifle. Some rifles will collimate very close at 100 yards, while others may be off in any direction by as much as 1 foot!

There is also the fellow who thinks that if the bullet is on the paper it is close enough for game shooting. I'm reminded of a hunter I know who was "trying," not sighting, his rifle the day before hunting season opened. He fired one shot and the bullet landed about center for elevation but about 8″ right at somewhere near 100 yards. When he started to put his rifle back in the case, his companion for the planned hunting trip asked if he didn't intend to make adjustments. "No, that's close enough. I'll just allow a little to the left. . . ."

Then there is the man who takes his rifle on a hunting trip without bothering to check the sighting until somewhere along the way or after he gets there. He picks out a rock of unknown size at an unknown range on a hillside, and takes a shot or two at it. If the bullet hits the rock, he is satisfied that "old meat in the pot" is shooting "right where she looks." Which is probably correct, but where is she looking? The point is that the rock is maybe 1 1/2 feet in diameter, and may be anywhere from 200 to 400 yards away. He has no idea of where the bullet hit the rock, and, not knowing the range, he hasn't the haziest notion of where the bullets will land at any given range.

It is also amazing how many hunters think that if they fire a shot or two at a target and find the bullet is off a few inches, all they have to do is give the scope adjustments the right amount of correction and the rifle is zeroed. Part of this is the fault of scope advertisements, in which all scopes have perfect adjustments. These claims are usually in error and highly misleading. You may adjust for a 6″ change of impact and get 3″ instead, or adjust for 3″ and get 6″, or, in the worst cases, you may get none. You may also get some windage along with the elevation adjustment, or vice versa. Many variable power scopes will also change point of impact considerably with different power settings. Something for the varmint hunter to think about before mounting one on a long range varmint rifle. If you do use one, and many are good, check the various power settings on paper before you go hunting.

Sighting Procedure

Considering that correctly sighting the hunting rifle is one of the most important parts of a successful hunt, and inasmuch as we have explained how the rifle should be sighted to take advantage of the various loads used, perhaps some suggestions on *how to sight* are in order. Nearly anyone of limited experience can eventually sight a rifle if he takes enough time and expends enough ammunition. The following suggestions are offered to help expedite the operation, save ammunition, and make it less frustrating.

The best and most efficient method for starting the sighting procedure is to use a collimator. (This is an optical instrument that fits into the end of the barrel and has a lens facing the rifle sights with either grid lines or an X to adjust the sights to for approximately a 100 yard zero.) As explained earlier, the collimator can't possibly give a perfect 100 yard zero with all bullet weights, or with handloads at different velocity levels even in the same bullet weights, but it will normally come within a few inches of placing the bullet center at 100 yards. Anyway, it will be on the paper, which will show you how much adjustment to make. The advantage of the collimator over bore sighting with the rifle bore is that it can be used in all types of actions where the bolt mechanism is not removable.

For the bolt action rifle, and if a collimator is not available, remove the bolt, place the rifle solidly on sandbags or V notches cut in the top edges of a cardboard box, and center the target or some other object at 100 yards or more in the center of the bore. Make certain that you keep the muzzle of the bore centered with the breech or action end, otherwise you will not get a true line-of-bore sighting. Now, making certain the rifle is not moved, adjust the sights until they zero in on the center of the target. This "bore sighting," if correctly done, should land the first shot on the target so that you will know what adjustments to make and go from there.

If you do not have a collimator, and use a semiauto, slide, or lever action (some hunters also use this method with a bolt or single shot action), it is best to start sighting by firing at a target placed at 25 yards. As mentioned early in the book, it is not advisable to try to finish sighting at any range of less than 100 yards, but the first bullet is almost certain to land on the paper at 25 yards and you can go from there. You can then adjust the sights so that the bullet lands exactly where you want it to go in the center of the target at 25 yards before going on to 100 yards, but remember you'll have to multiply the adjustment calibrations on your scope dial by 4 to give the right amount at 25 yards.

There is no substitute for a benchrest and a good pair of sandbags for steady holding when sighting the rifle, but if they are not available, which they will not be in many cases, use the most solid rest you can find that you can shoot from in a relaxed position. If you rig up a rest and find that the reticle will not stay steadily centered on the bull's-eye, either change it or your position until you can hold rock-steady. You'll never know if you are sighted correctly when shooting from a poor rest or poor shooting position. Some rifles will shoot high from a solid forend rest, some will not, depending on the barrel and bedding, but it is a good plan to hold the forend in the hand placed on the rest for final sighting, then you'll know it is correct for hunting use.

If you are using a new rifle or load and are not certain of the accuracy it will give, it is best to fire three shots so the center of impact will be established before adjusting the sight. This will also let you see what kind of accuracy you can expect from that rifle and load. If this proves the load to be accurate, or you already know the load and rifle are accurate enough to give groups of under 2" at 100 yards, you can fire a single shot and then make sight adjustments, which will save ammunition and time, and avoid heating the rifle barrel. If the rifle or load will not keep the three shots in at least 2", it is best to shoot three shots each time after making sight adjustments so that you can tell exactly where the center of impact is. After bullet impact is where you want it for the kind of shooting you intend to do, fire three final shots to make certain center of impact is exactly right, not just close.

Most iron sights with either open rear or aperture (peep), as well as all scopes, have marked dials or slides to indicate direction and amount of movement of bullet impact. However, the calibrations are not always accurate on iron sights, and there usually isn't anything to tell you how much change of impact they give, so you'll have to try them by shooting to find out at 100 yards. With scope sights the adjustments are usually quite accurate when large amounts of change are needed, but getting that last inch can be highly frustrating. There are a number of causes for this, which we will not attempt to go into here, but one thing that will help is to always tap the scope tube or adjustment screw housing sharply several times with a soft object like a piece of wood or even a cartridge head after making the adjustment and before firing again. This will help to jar the reticle into place in case it sticks. Also, never make an adjustment that you think will correct the right amount without firing from one to three shots to prove it, depending on the accuracy of the load and rifle.

If your scope does turn out to have poor adjustments, you'll just have to grit your teeth, keep your cool, and go right on shooting until you have the rifle sighted in right—there is no cure for bad scope adjustments except to return it to the factory for repairs or a new scope.

There is one more word of warning regarding sighting: Do not finish sighting your rifle when the barrel is hot from prolonged shooting. When you think you have it right, let it cool completely and then try it again. You may find it has changed impact by a few inches. This is because hot barrels often do not shoot to the same point of impact as cold barrels. If impact has changed, make adjustments, let the barrel cool again, and try another three shots to make certain it is sighted right with a *cool* barrel. Remember that the first shot, the all-important shot, is always fired from a cold barrel in hunting.

There is one last point that a big game hunter should keep in mind regarding sighting, and that is what to do when you find your rifle shooting off when you are in the hunting country, either because you missed an easy shot when you knew your hold was right, or if you think it may be off after a bad fall. If this happens, don't be too upset over the possibility of scaring nearby game; go ahead and try your rifle and resight if necessary. Better take a chance on moving the game out of the immediate vicinity by the shots fired in resighting than to miss or wound it if you don't. If you are short of ammunition go ahead and check your rifle anyway. If you have only two cartridges left, it is far better to fire one at a target where you are sure of where it landed, and thereby know where to hold with the remaining cartridge for a vital hit, than to miss or wound with both of them!

In sighting in the hunting rifle, the reloader has a decided advantage over the fellow who uses only factory-loaded ammunition. In this day of extremely expensive factory-loaded ammunition, a lot of fellows will be tempted to quit shooting before their rifle is sighted exactly where it should be. But the handloader, who can fire a shot for a fraction of what a factory round costs, can afford to expend the ammunition to do a good job and get some extra practice while he is doing it. If he is using a premium quality and priced bullet like the Nosler Partition Jacket, the Bitterroot, or the new Speer Grand Slam, he can "rough sight" with a cheaper bullet, then check with the premium bullets and make adjustments if necessary at far less cost. It should be pointed out, however, that final sighting should be done with the bullet you intend to use, because few bullets of different makes and styles will shoot to the same point of impact even if they are of the same weight.

No matter how you cut it, if your rifle is not properly sighted in before the hunt, there are likely to be unaccountable misses. And don't think that just because your rifle was sighted perfectly last hunting season it will shoot in the same place this year. Atmospheric conditions change the moisture content in the best stocks, and the consequent wood movement exerts pressures in different places on barrels and/or actions. This, in turn, causes a shift in point of bullet impact, so sight that rifle in just before you go hunting, and preferably near where you will hunt.

There is one other factor affecting the sighting of a rifle that is of importance to the hunter, and that is the kind of rest that is used to hold the rifle steady when shooting at game. Never rest the barrel against any solid object; better yet, do not let it touch any object. If the barrel rests against something solid, it is very likely to cause bullet impact to shift in the opposite direction. How much at any range is impossible to predict, because barrel and load will govern this point, but it is the cause of many unexplained misses.

Resting the forend solidly on a hard object like a log usually has little or no effect, but it is simple to lay your hand on the rest with the forend gripped in it, which will eliminate any possible change in point of impact.

Pointers on How to Estimate Range

Aside from poor rifle sighting, the greatest cause of misses in hunting country is poor range estimation. This is the reason we have so vigorously stressed the importance of sighting for the longest possible range where the mid-range height of the bullet over line of sight will not cause a miss. But there are many reasons why the distance to an animal is misjudged besides just plain not knowing how far it is from here to there. Probably, though, it would be well to look at that aspect first and go from there.

The average hunter has little or no opportunity to learn anything about judging range where he lives, since it is a little difficult to pace off the distance to a given object on Sunset Boulevard or Park Avenue, but many hunters raised in hunting country do little better, because they never take the time to estimate ranges, then step off the distance to see how close they called it. I'm not bothered greatly by range estimation when hunting new country, because I'm used to it. Even so, the first thing I do when hunting a new area is estimate the distance to some object and then step it off. If I find I'm off very much, I work on it until I correct the mistake. Anyone else can and should do the same thing, instead of guessing when they shoot and wind up missing or wounding the animal.

The first thing to do before you start the estimating-stepping process is to find out how far you step with just enough effort put into it to make the length of step consistent. Don't assume you step an even 3 feet, because few people do. Measure off 100 yards and step it off until you get very near the same number of steps each time, and remember the number it takes. Then, when you start estimating and checking ranges, you'll know you are near right. It does little good to estimate a range at 300 yards, step it off, and verify it, but find out it actually measures only 250 yards because the length of your step was not 3 feet.

One cause of misjudging distance for hunters who are good at it is the difference in altitude between where they live and where they are hunting. High elevations normally have very clear air that gives sharp images. Animals seen there seem much closer than at the same range down near sea level, where humidity and haze are normally much heavier. This, of course, can also act in reverse. Haze can cause the same problem at any altitude, and will especially upset your estimation of distance at high elevations between days it is present and days it is not. The same object will appear farther away on hazy days than on clear bright days.

Haze acts much like fog, rain, or snow, but to a lesser degree. Animals seen through fog, rain, or snow usually appear to be a great deal farther away than they actually are. Even with a properly sighted rifle this illusion of distance causes many misses. If you think a muley buck is 450 yards away and know you will have to hold the cross hair to ride the top of his back for that range, and it turns out he is only 350, the bullet will go over the top. That may sound like a long way to be off in the estimation of range, but few once-a-year hunters come that close even under good visibility conditions. To be on the safe side, take a second hard look at the range on stormy days if you have time; it may not be as far as it first appears.

Another cause of overshooting because the range is less than it appears is when the game is in shadow while you are in bright light. Also, if you are shooting across a canyon that the sun has not fully covered, and the game is in the deep shadow of the canyon side or peak above, and your side is in bright sunlight, it will appear to be farther away than it actually is. Reverse the situation and put the game out in bright sunlight, with your side in deep shadow, and it will appear closer to untrained eyes than it actually is.

Another cause of poor range estimation comes from animals that either blend in with their background or contrast sharply with it. A gray mule deer in sage will appear to be farther away than a black bear in the same place. A white goat or sheep in very light-colored rock or in snow will be indistinct and appear farther away than if it was standing on a slope of dark rock or dirt. And the brighter the light is when the animal contrasts greatly with its surroundings, the better it shows up and the nearer it seems to be. Of course, the dim light of early morning or late evening, which blots out color and softens the outline of the animal to create an indistinct image, gives the impression that the animal is a great deal farther away than it actually is.

In nearly all these cases where there is time to check things out a little, and there usually is time in long range shooting, there are much better ways of estimating distance than by looking at the animal. If the animal appears indistinct and you find it hard to tell how far away it is, look for some other object near it that contrasts with the surroundings and compare the two range estimates. On the other hand, if the animal contrasts sharply with the background—a dark animal on snow, say—forget it and just try to estimate the distance to the area it is in.

Something else that will help a lot where the land between you and the game is mostly visible is to break up the distance in 100 yard increments by picking out objects about 100 yards apart. This works very well if you are reasonably accurate in judging what 100 yards actually is and the intervening land is pretty well on the same plane, but it is of no great help in shooting from one side of a canyon to the other. On cross-canyon shots you'll about have to estimate the distance by how you know an animal will look under the prevailing light conditions, and only long experience can tell you that. Even then, we all goof now and again.

Variations in Bullet Drop in Various Areas

As mentioned earlier under problems that are encountered in long range shooting, there is a good deal of difference in the amount of bullet drop at, we'll say 400 yards, at sea level, and at 10,000 foot elevations. The main problem as far as the hunter is concerned is that it is impossible to predict exactly how much difference. There is actually very little solid information available, and what there is has of necessity been computed. And those computations are only for what might be considered average conditions. As the difference in drop at various elevations is based on air density, any change in atmospheric condition will influence day-to-day bullet impact. These changes are not great but they are there, and there is no way the hunter can compensate for them in hunting country. The best advice we can offer is to check the sighting of your rifle as near as possible to where you will hunt, make corrections if necessary, then use the same hold you normally do at that range. The biggest mistake you can make is to start guessing and allowing what you *think* is the right amount. If you do miss with the first shot high or low, and the bullet impact is visible, correct with the second shot. If you use the 3" high 100 yard sighting and hold midway up the ribs of a ram, the chance of a miss because of bullet drop variations due to altitude out to 350 yards or so with most long range cartridges is very small.

This problem of variation in bullet drop at various elevations, and from one area to another, is one of the best reasons for handloading your own hunting ammunition. While there is no way you can know exactly what elevation you will shoot at, or exactly how much that elevation and the prevailing atmospheric conditions will affect bullet drop, the flatter the bullet travels, the less chance for a miss. If you pick a bullet of high ballistic coefficient and a powder and charge that will give it all the velocity your cartridge and rifle will handle for trouble-free hunting use, the chance of a miss will be greatly reduced over that with average factory loads.

Correcting for Wind Drift

Thinking about hunting in the high country also brings us back to wind drift and how to compensate for it. The problem of judging wind velocity and exact direction, and the difficulty in correcting for it, has already been discussed in connection with varmint shooting at long range (see chapter 2). The difficulty in hitting a chuck, jackrabbit, or even a coyote, at ranges similar to the longest ranges big game should be shot at, is much greater than the difficulty in hitting an antelope or a ram. But a point that is forgotten by many hunters is that if the wind drifts the bullet 1 foot it will miss a chuck completely, with no damage except to the hunter's ego. But 1 foot to either side on any big game from pronghorn to caribou is almost certain to wound it.

Also, except for shooting rockchucks in some of the rough canyon country of the West, most varmint hunting is done on fairly level or rolling land. In this type of terrain, winds tend to blow more or less in one direction over wide areas, and at reasonably steady velocities. But in high, broken mountain country it is as fickle as the favors of bull elk during the rut. It may be blowing north on your side of the canyon, and east, west, or south on the other side where the ram is. If anyone has ever figured out where to hold to correct for wind drift in that kind of situation, I'd like to know his secret. The truth is that more shots are missed, and more game wounded, because the hunter tries to correct for wind drift when he doesn't know how hard it is blowing, or in what direction to the line of the bullet's flight. And neither does he know how much it would drift the bullet he is using at the velocity his rifle and cartridge give it, even if he did know wind velocity and direction. Unless you know a lot about wind deflection and correction for your load, and are equally certain of its approximate velocity and direction, you are much better off to hold on the spot you want the bullet to land than to make a poor guess. It has been my observation that the average hunter, and many of the "experts," overcorrect for wind drift if they correct at all. There is little chance that the wind will be blowing exactly 90° to the line of the bullet's flight, and, as in judging distance, most hunters overestimate wind velocity. So even if you know the drift of your load at a certain range and wind velocity, you'll be better off to cut it in half when you correct. That way, you'll be fairly safe for a hit in the vital area of most big game animals.

The Difficulty in Hitting Game from Below or Above

There is little doubt that the most difficult shot for all hunters is when the animal is at a steep angle above or below them. And as range increases so does the problem of putting the bullet in the right place. There are many reasons for this, and some arise because of the difference between surface distance as seen by the hunter, and the horizontal distance that controls bullet drop. Another part of the dilemma might be considered an optical illusion, while a third part is the difficulty in judging range either up- or downhill as compared with seeing the same animal on the level.

Many people of great ballistic knowledge but little or no hunting experience insist that all misses at steep up- or downhill angles are due to the difference in bullet drop between the true horizontal distance and the surface distance. The point is that if you see an animal above or below you at 350 yards on the surface of the mountainside, and the distance on a level line from the muzzle of your rifle to a point where it joins a perpendicular line from the animal is only 300 yards, the bullet will drop only the amount listed for 300 yards. It follows that if you hold to place the bullet center at the 350 yards it actually is to the animal on the slope of the hill, it will strike high.

To put it another way, and to keep it simple, if the range on the slope from gun to animal is an even 400 yards, but the distance to a point either directly above or below the animal on a horizontal line is 300 yards, and you are using an average pointed 180 gr. bullet in a .30-06 at 2700 fps sighted to zero dead on at 100 yards, it would be about 34″ low at 400 yards, but only 15″ low at 300 yards. Therefore, if you hold 34″ above the point where you want the bullet to strike for the 400 yard surface distance to a deer, it will drop only about 15″, or less than half that amount. The bullet will, of course, pass several inches over the deer's back.

As far as the hunter is concerned, this knowledge is of no great value except to show him that the bullet will land a good deal higher on steep angle shots either up- or downhill than at the same *ground surface range* on the level. There is no way he can be sure of the difference in bullet drop, because he has no way of knowing the angle of the slope in either percentage or degrees of angle to use to establish the exact horizontal distance, even if he did know the exact surface distance. The only thing he has to know is that he must hold lower than he would on the level for the same surface range. If the range is not too long, up to 200 yards or so, and on average slopes of 25°–30°, the difference in bullet drop isn't enough with a flat shooting cartridge to cause a miss with a center-of-the-ribs hold.

The optical illusion part is actually of more importance. We'll say you are looking down a steep slope at a muley buck standing broadside. Seen on the level, his ribs would have a depth of about 20″, but in looking down from above, you see not only his side but his broad back as well, which will be about 10″ wide. You'll also see the top of the rib cage on the far side for a few inches to add to the total area. Unless you are aware of this and keep it in mind, your inclination is to hold in the center of what you see, which would be way up toward the line of the back. The broadside depth of the ribs as seen on the level is actually cut about in half from the high angle of view, which doesn't leave much room for error even if you did hold in the center instead of near the top. The outcome of this is that the bullet that would land 4" high at 200 yards with the 3" high 100 yard sighting would give a certain kill on the level, but would either go over the back or only cause a flesh wound when fired from the steep angle from above.

If you want to prove this illusion as to where center is on the side of an animal when seen from above, as to where it *appears* to be, it is quite simple. Take a cardboard box that is 18"–20" wide and 10"–12" deep and turn it up on one side so that the bottom faces you. Stand over it and look down at a steep angle so that you see all of the bottom and all of the side. You'll note that what appears to be center is very near to the corner between bottom and side. Even a better way, if you have a dog, is to stand and look down at it broadside from above and take a close look at what appears to be center. You'll find it is near where the ribs join the spine.

Yet another situation that is present in shooting at animals from above that few hunters are aware of, and which can also tend to cause the hunter to shoot high, is the inability to judge range. When looking down a long slope from the top to the bottom it always appears to be much farther than if you are looking up from below. And neither one looks the same as on the level; if looking up it appears nearer, and down it seems to be farther. If the animal is actually out near the sure hit range of the load you are using with a center hold, you are inclined to think it is even farther when seen from above, hold up near the back line, and overshoot. The illusion of being closer when looking uphill works to the advantage of the hunter, because if the game appears to be nearer than it actually is, he will still hold for the center of the ribs, and the bullet that would have gone high because of the steep angle of the shot will land about where it should within the vital area. The fact that he is seeing the bottom of the chest along with the ribs from below will also cause him to hold low, which will also compensate some for the flatter trajectory of the bullet on the steep uphill shot.

There is no way that I can tell you how much less drop a bullet will have on either uphill or downhill shots than if fired at the same

This bighorn ram illustrates two points important to the hunter: First, if you spend much time trying to dope the range and where to hold for a vital hit, he won't be there to shoot at. The rifle sighted to land a bullet in the vital area out to at least 350 yards will solve that problem with no guessing. Second, a close look shows you are seeing his belly as well as his side from the position below. But, as the bullet will drop less from line of bore at this angle, hold center anyway.

surface range on the level at the same velocity, because, as explained above, too many factors enter into the problem. I can, however, give you a rule of thumb that will be of great help: If shooting at a steep downhill angle, hold just over the bottom of the chest—no more than 2″–3″ up into the body—and if the animal is within the sure hit range of your load, you'll get a vital hit. If shooting from below, just hold about where center *appears* to be and the bullet will land in the right place at the same ranges. This is another case where a good handload designed to send the flattest shooting bullet at the highest practical velocity will minimize the chances of a miss—the flatter the bullet trajectory, the less chance of a miss either under or over.

The various causes of missing that have been stressed here are those that every hunter will face in some form at one time or another, and over which we have little control except to try to learn to cope with them, but there are a number of others that are brought about by the hunters themselves. Most of these not only cause misses but, worse, wounded game that is rarely recovered. Most of these misses and crippling shots could be avoided if the hunter just used a little common sense and took a firm grip on his nervous system.

One of the big reasons for misses that could be avoided is shooting at ranges beyond the capability either of the hunter or of the cartridge and load used. It seems to be fashionable to tell about knocking off big game at 1,000 yards or so, but the hunter who tries to kill an animal at much more than half of that range is asking for trouble. They seem to think that they will either kill the animal cleanly or miss it entirely. Just remember that any bullet that gives a close miss is even more likely to land somewhere around the edges and wound the animal.

Another reason for many misses that could be avoided is shooting at running game, especially at anything but close range. And for every animal that is missed, at least one is wounded. Sure, I know that if no one ever fired at a running whitetail in heavy cover, few would ever be killed, but this doesn't change the fact that a great many are wounded when fired at when the chance of a vital hit is nearly nil. Let's look at it this way: A good and cool rifleman shooting at a standing animal from a good position at 200 yards can tell you within a couple of inches where the bullet landed, but I have yet to see anyone who could consistently call his shots on a running buck at the same range.

Then there is the matter of shooting position. Some hunters insist on shooting at game from the offhand position at nearly any range, when they can't keep their shots in a 1 foot circle from that position at 50 yards! It is an excellent idea to practice in the offhand position so that if the necessity arises you are ready for it, but if at all possible use a steadier position. My personal feeling is that the only time the offhand position is justified in hunting, if other positions are available or possible, is at ranges under 100 yards on standing game or on running shots at close range. In fact, I prefer shooting at running game from the offhand position at any reasonable range to any other position because it is easier to swing with the animal. For the great majority of shots, take a rest even if it means moving a little to do it. Every hunter will also benefit by learning to use a shooting sling. If no rest is available, the sling is the next best thing when used from the sitting or prone position.

The first and last consideration in shooting at any animal is to do everything possible to make that first shot a vital hit, and not just shoot with the blind hope that it may kill it.

When shooting game at anything except very close range, take the steadiest position available. Much game is wounded and lost because the hunter shot from offhand or other poor position. Don't worry about getting off a lot of shots; make the first one count.

The steadiest position possible under the conditions is none too good for big game shooting. If no rest is available, the use of a shooting sling as illustrated here is the next thing to it, and will produce many solid hits that would not otherwise be possible.

APPENDIX

Reloading Hunting Ammunition

As was mentioned in both the Introduction and in chapter 1, the various reloading manuals give excellent step-by-step instructions on the basic procedures of reloading. They are well illustrated and, in general, are clear and concise. There is little we could add here on the A-B-C steps of reloading for the beginner that they do not cover, but perhaps we can enlarge on some of the more important points to emphasize their significance. We also believe that some of the things that are of prime importance to the reloading hunter have not been stressed strongly enough to bring to his attention some of the problems he may encounter and how to avoid them. These are mostly problems that would be of no great concern to the average varmint hunter or target shooter, but can and do spell trouble for the big game hunter. There are also aspects of reloading as to the why as well as the how, which are more important to the loading of ammunition to be used for big game hunting than for other shooting, which are not covered in most reloading manuals or books on reloading. In this section we will attempt to give the hunter this kind of information so that he may avoid trouble when he is far back in the brush where he can least afford it.

How to Use a Reloading Manual

Please do not misunderstand the title of this section: we do not intend to intimate that the beginning handloader, or the hand-

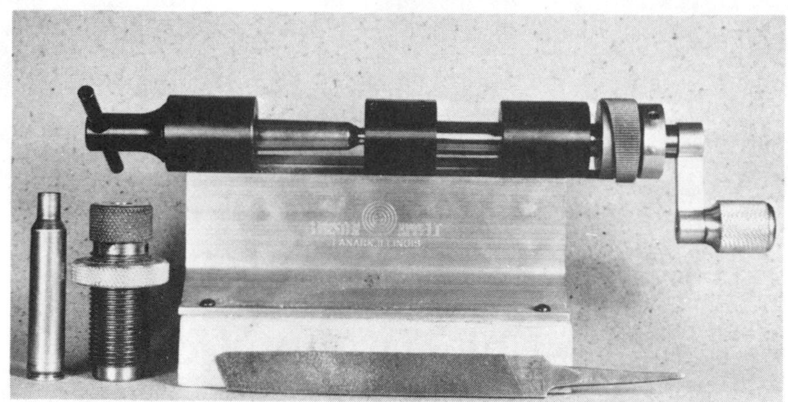

There are a number of ways cases can be trimmed to correct length. Here is the Forster case trimmer, which also can be converted to turn down necks to uniform thickness, as it is set up here; this makes it an extremely good buy for the serious reloader. At left is RCBS die type trimmer, to be used in a reloading press. Case is simply run into the die as in resizing, and the excess neck is filed off level with the hardened die surface.

The advanced reloader will find it very convenient to use a pair of presses in reloading while experimental work or large amounts of ammunition loading are in progress. The author uses the old Super Pacific press at left for priming and bullet seating, and the powerful RCBS Rockchucker press at right for all full length resizing and case forming.

The Bonanza Co-Ax loading press is an extremely versatile tool. The instant die change setup makes it ideal for loading several calibers at one loading session. It also has great leverage for all case forming work.

Here are some of the tools used in charging cases with powder: Redding powder measure; Lyman powder scale with RCBS powder trickler set up to trickle powder into scale pan; MTM powder funnel with long drop tube used to charge cases with compressed loads.

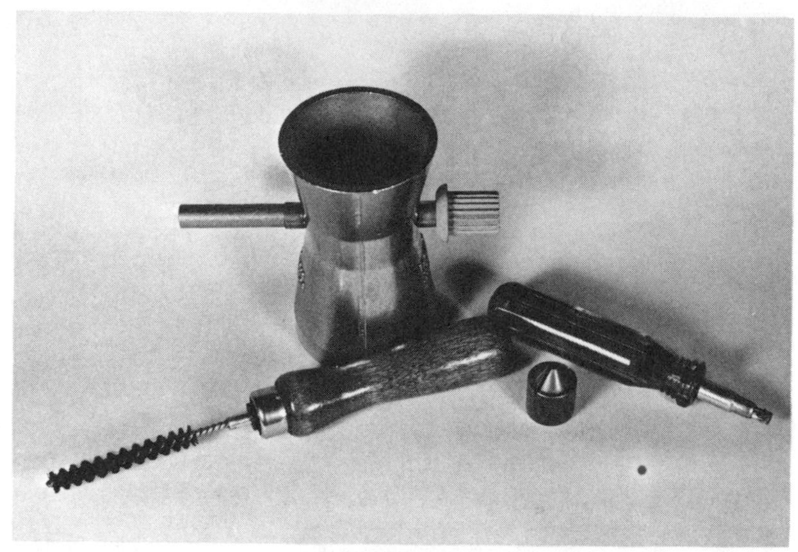

Miscellaneous small tools that are used continuously in reloading. The powder trickler, neck brush, and primer pocket cleaner are from RCBS, and the thimble-type inside-outside neck chamfering tool is from Lee.

loader of limited experience for that matter, is not intelligent enough to know what he is reading; but long association with those starting out to do their own handloading indicates that many of them *fail to read* the instructions and general information the manuals offer. Maynard Buehler's famous saying, "If all else fails, read the instructions," is never truer than when using a reloading manual. All too many beginning reloaders seem to think that if they bother to read what is said by the experts who compiled the text section of the manual, they show some kind of undefined weakness or stupidity. I have been loading my own ammunition ever since the early days of the Great Depression, not only because I could make better loads than I could buy but because I couldn't afford factory ammunition. I used and studied reloading manuals then, and I still study every one that appears, and find much good, solid information in all of them. The best advice I can think of for the beginning reloader is to buy at least one good manual—and better, several—then start with the introduction and read *every* line up to the cartridge load data section, *then reread it* before he loads his first round! That section of the manual will tell and illustrate everything needed to reload those first rounds of handloads. After he has loaded and fired enough of those loads to know all the basics without further outside instruction, he is ready to go on into the other sections of the manual that deal with the more sophisticated aspects of reloading, such as interior and exterior ballistics.

To start with, buy the manual before you attempt to buy reloading tools. Then study the illustrated section on tools and how to use and set them up. Buy good tools but don't go overboard on expensive models. Remember that one of the most important considerations of reloading is the economic angle. And also remember that if you pay exorbitant prices for tools that are out of line with the work they will perform, or get the typical American malady of gadgetitis, you'll have to load more ammunition than most hunters use in a lifetime to break even. Once you get deeply involved in reloading, you will know what tools you require over the basic needs to do a reasonably fast and efficient job, and only then should you add items to the reloading bench that might otherwise almost never be used.

One point that nearly all reloading manuals stress is that reloading is not something to be done when you have a get-together with your hunting buddies. When reloading, you want no distraction of any kind; you need to concentrate on the work at hand—and this applies to the reloader of long experience as well as to the beginner. The old adage "Familiarity breeds contempt" has caused more than one case to be blown. It is much better not to have someone talking to you while reloading, especially if you are doing load development.

Another suggestion made in most manuals is that the reloader develop good reloading habits, which, of course, means some kind of sequence of the various operations. Whether or not you follow those steps explained in the manual is of no great consequence, but if you form the habit of performing one operation after the other the same each time you reload, you will be far less likely to make mistakes. Reloaders normally have an excuse when they blow a primer or freeze the bolt, but if they are honest with themselves they will usually find that the cause was a simple mistake made by not "watching their knitting." I can vouch for the truth of that statement because I've made my share, and always because I let my mind stray to other matters, or some distraction popped up.

One of the best ways to avoid mistakes is *never* to have more than one can of powder on the bench at one time in the loading area. It is a good idea to pour the powder into the measure or dish from which it is dipped into the powder scale pan, then set the can nearby on the bench so that the powder can be poured back in as soon as you are finished with that powder. If two cans are there you can make a mistake either in using the wrong powder or in pouring it back into the wrong can. The results can be disastrous either way. The same thing applies to bullets: never have more than one bullet weight in the loading area at the same time. It is also better not to mix primers, either from one make to another, or from magnum to standard. But accuracy will suffer the most from that mistake, and while velocity may go up or down somewhat, pressure will not get out of hand.

Another mistake made by the majority of handloaders is in picking a load from the manual for the bullet weight they intend to use. It is safe to say that 75% of the reloaders, both novice and veteran, start with the powder charge that is listed as *maximum* in the load chart. Not only that, they usually don't know if the pressure it develops is excessive in their rifle, unless the bolt handle has to be pounded open. (This will be covered more fully later.) *Never* start with the maximum load listed, but always at least 5% below. That is why those manuals give starting loads, and they all tell the reloader that, if he would just read what they have to say and pay attention to it.

It is worth any beginning reloader's time to read the safety tip section on page 17 of the *Nosler Reloading Manual* No. 1. They say most of the things I have said here, with some other thoughts added. I might add that this manual has a very good section on reloading tools and the basic steps the beginner needs to know. The Speer manuals have always had a good beginner's section, and both manuals have top-drawer illustrations.

The Speer and Hodgdon manuals both have sections on powders that list them in the order of approximate burning rate, which is very important to any handloader. The Speer manual is of more value to the handloader who will load for several cartridges than the Hodgdon book, because it lists all the various brands that are normally available to the American handloader, whereas Hodgdon lists only Hodgdon powders.

For those advanced handloaders who lean to hard technical facts, and for the hunter who really wants to know something about the fine points of both interior and exterior ballistics, both the Nosler and Sierra manuals have a great deal of useful information. This information falls under the "Expert's Corner" in the Nosler book, and the technical and supplementary sections of the Sierra manual.

I think it is well worth the time for any big game hunter who leans toward technical facts to study the information concerning the affect of atmospheric conditions and altitude on bullet drop found in the Sierra manual under Exterior Ballistics, page 248. It may come as some surprise to many hunters that the difference in altitude between sea level and 8,000–9,000 feet will have about the same effect as adding 30% to the ballistic coefficient of the average pointed bullet. While it should be pointed out that this is not of great importance to the big game hunter at ranges up to 350 or 400 yards, it does change point of impact by 3″–4″. Couple this with the maximum change caused by atmospheric conditions explained in the same section, and some unaccountable misses may be explained.

The only thing we might add to the basic aspects of reloading, before going into the special techniques we think will prove useful to the serious hunter/reloader, is that the purpose of reloading hunting ammunition is to produce a better load than factory ammunition offers. That, and the economy angle. But don't let the economy angle blind you with dollar signs. If one powder costs a buck or so more per pound but gives the results you need in a certain load that is not given by its cheaper counterpart, then use it; and if a premium quality bullet is better suited to the game being hunted than one that costs less than half as much, use that too. It is poor economy to miss or wound an animal because you tried to save a few cents per round.

Case Preparation and Resizing

The first step in reloading is case preparation and resizing, and the manuals pretty well take care of the preparation end, so let's concentrate on resizing. The main reason why case resizing is much more important to the hunter than to other reloaders is that the ammunition used in hunting must always chamber freely in the rifle it will be used in. This is especially true if the hunter is using a lever, slide, or autoloader action. The bolt action rifle has a great deal of camming power so that when a cartridge is fed into the chamber and the bolt handle turned down to lock up the action, a great amount of pressure is exerted on the cartridge. If the cartridge proves to be a little tight, for whatever reason, it will be forced into the chamber and allow the bolt to fully lock up. It may take some extra pressure to force the bolt handle down, but it will go when the same cartridge would not be fully chambered by any of the other actions mentioned. And if the cartridge is not fully chambered, a misfire will be the result—or should be, if the action is designed right. And even with the best bolt actions, if the cartridge fits tight enough to require extra pressure to turn the bolt handle down, the hunter may not fully seat it and a misfire will also result.

For this reason, neck sizing only is not recommended for hunting reloads. If the body of the case is fitted to the chamber by the pressure of the last load fired in it, the slightest bit of foreign matter in the chamber or on the case will cause it to fit so tightly that it will not chamber properly and will cause a jam or a misfire.

Full length resizing dies are made to resize the case back down to about the original factory dimensions, and they usually size a cartridge case down sufficiently to chamber well in a bolt action rifle, but special dimension resizing dies are furnished by some die makers for lever, slide, and semiauto actions. These dies have slightly reduced body dimensions so that the case will be reduced enough to fit any properly dimensioned chamber freely, so the action will lock up fully with no extra pressure.

However, to make it brief, and to avoid confusing the casual hunter/reloader with technical details, when you resize cases to be used in hunting, try the resized case in the rifle it will be used in after sizing with the die set down in the press so that it just clears the shellholder. If it is the least bit tight, turn down the die just a little and try it again. By repeating this procedure and stopping when the case fits the chamber freely, you will have a cartridge that will give no chambering problems in the field. One word of warning is *not to overdo* this and set the shoulder of the case back enough to develop headspace. This is unlikely with most good dies, because they will contact the shellholder too solidly to allow this to happen, but if a chamber is on the long side it can and does happen. This is the reason we suggest leaving a little space between the base of the die and the shellholder to start with, and screwing the die down *only* if the case chambers hard.

There is one other cause of hard chambering that the reloader should be aware of that no amount of resizing will cure: a neck that is too long for the chamber. Sometimes this is confused with insufficient case resizing. If used cases are kept trimmed down to the length of a new, unfired, factory case, this problem will be avoided. Sometimes a case with a neck that is just slightly too long will chamber quite freely if tried before a bullet is seated, but after seating the bullet it will not chamber, or, if it does, will require a lot of pressure on the bolt handle (it would not fully chamber in the other actions). If this happens it will cause the hunter two problems he can well do without: if it is too long, the cartridge will not chamber at all and may cause him to lose a shot at an animal; if it is just long enough to cause the case to chamber hard, it will crimp on the bullet and will not release its grip on firing. This will cause pressures to rise sharply as well as raising merry old hell with accuracy and the possibility of missing or wounding the game.

Before we leave case resizing, there is yet another problem that often crops up and proves confusing to many reloaders who do have considerable experience. Nearly any reloader knows what headspace is; but if he doesn't, any reloading manual will tell him and illustrate the point. Actually, it is the arrangement by which the cartridge head is held against the bolt face. It may be the distance from the shoulder of the case to the outside face of the cartridge head in a rimless case, the thickness of the rim on a rimmed case, or the distance from the forward edge of the belt to the case head face on a belted case. On a rimless case like the .30-06, we refer to headspacing being "on the shoulder," which means that the case shoulder touches the chamber shoulder, or is very close to touching it, when the bolt is closed. With this arrangement the case is held back against the bolt face when the firing pin contacts the primer, and there is no chance for the case body to stretch and cause a head separation just forward of the web or solid portion of the head. With the resizing die correctly set as indicated earlier, there is no problem whatever, but the belted and rimmed cases are an entirely different matter.

As these cases are headspaced either on the belt or on the rim, the shoulder does not have to touch the chamber shoulder to hold the case head against the bolt face tight enough to fire the rifle. In many instances either or both chambers and cases for these rimmed and belted cartridges are a little on the sloppy side. That is, the cases may be shorter from head to shoulder than the chamber. You can usually fire a case, either reload or factory load, the first time without a head separation, but if you run it through a full-length resizing die set clear down against the shellholder and the chamber happens to be a little long, the case shoulder will be pushed back to nearly original dimension, allowing the shoulder to be blown forward a second time, thereby stretching the case body again. When this is done it is entirely possible to get a *complete head separation* on the second firing, and certainly if you continue to resize the case in the same manner. This is why belted cases have the reputation of being subject to head separations. The truth is that they are no worse than rimless cases if they are resized so that the shoulder is not pushed back more than enough to barely let them chamber. The same thing applies to the rimmed case. But what is important to the hunter is that if he doesn't know this and does not take precautions in resizing, he may get a complete head separation while hunting. The case head will be extracted, leaving the rest of the case stuck in the chamber and rendering the rifle totally useless until the proper tools are found to extract it.

There are only two other problems concerning case preparation that are of major concern to the hunter. The most important is in neck thickness. This is usually of little or no concern to the hunter with a commercially built rifle with the original barrel, but custom rifles or those that have been rebarreled or rechambered can and do cause trouble at times. It is a very good plan to fire a cartridge with the cases you will use in hunting in your new rifle and then try to push a bullet into the case. If it slips in easily, there is no problem, but if it cannot be seated easily with the fingers, you'll have to ream or outside turn the necks of those cases for that rifle. If this is not done, pressure of your loads will be far above where it should be for that load, and accuracy may be extremely bad. At the worst, you may find those reloads difficult to chamber.

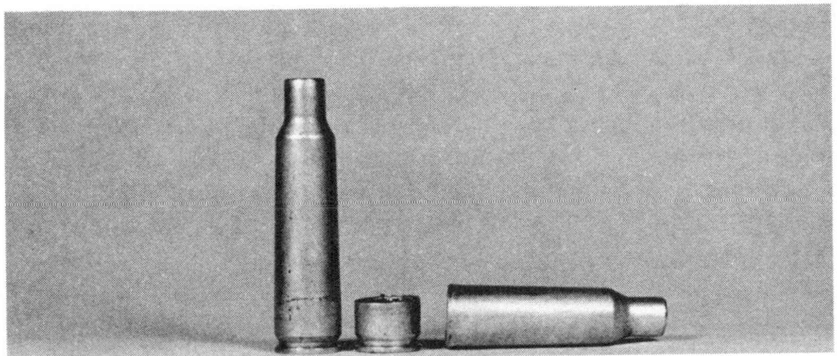

These two .250-3000 cases show partial and complete head separation. High pressure will cause this condition in lever action rifles with rear bolt lockup system. It also occurs with all types of cases, rimless, rimmed, and belted, if case is not properly headspaced on shoulder. This condition usually does not appear until case has been fired two or three times, but it does happen on first firing with excessive headspace.

The second problem that sometimes comes from poor case preparation is primer pockets that have not been cleaned. This can cause the primer to stick up above the face of the case head, making the round very difficult to chamber because it actually changes the headspace. If the pocket is cleaned well, the trouble will usually be eliminated, but occasionally the brand of primers used is too thick for the pockets in the cases being used. When this happens, a different make of primers may solve the problem. A good bolt action will usually chamber cartridges with "bugged" primers even though the bolt is stiff to turn down, but the lever, slide, or autoloader is almost certain to jam or misfire. The answer is, of course, not to use reloads with extruding primers for hunting.

The total and complete answer to all this is to *always try every round in the chamber of your rifle* before you take that ammunition hunting. And *never* borrow ammunition from anyone else to use in your rifle without trying it in the chamber first. If you do run out in the field and wish to try someone else's handloads in your rifle, better have a rod handy, or take it very easy in closing the action. If the case hasn't been resized enough in the body to fit your chamber and you try to force it, chances are you will find it impossible to extract without the use of a very stiff rod.

Correct Bullet Seating for Various Rifles

Bullet seating is a lot more complicated than it sounds, for a number of reasons, and some of them are not covered in the reloading manuals. First, and most important to the hunter/reloader, is the fact that all chambers of the various rifle makes from commercial sources, or from custom rifle makers, do not have throats of the same length or leades cut to the same angle. (The throat is the section ahead of the end of the chamber neck that is smooth and without the lands, and the leade is the taper of the ends of the lands from this smooth section to the top side of the lands, usually 2° to 4°, but it may vary even more on custom chambering reamers or throaters.) If the bullet is seated far enough out of the case so that when the cartridge is chambered it is forced into the leade section and wedges there, and for some reason the cartridge is extracted before firing, the bullet may be left in the barrel. When this happens, the powder charge will almost certainly be spilled into the action and magazine, and if you do not have a rod, which you certainly will not while actually hunting, the bullet is impossible to remove, so the rifle is useless.

To complicate this seating situation even further, some bullets carry their full body diameter or bearing surface farther forward than others. This is, of course, governed mostly by the shape of the bullet's point, but there is no way of knowing for sure how long the bearing surface is without measuring it, and the best way to do that for the hunter's purpose is to seat it in a case and chamber it in the rifle it will be fired in.

To do this, seat it out of the case about 1/8″ farther than a factory-loaded round. Take a match, preferably a wood stick match, or a candle, and smoke the bullet from the end of the case neck about halfway to the tip. Place it carefully in the chamber and gently try to close the bolt. If the bolt shows resistance, extract the cartridge and you'll see the marks of the lands on the smoked bullet. Seat the bullet down 1/32″ deeper, resmoke, and repeat the chambering operation. After the bolt will lock with no extra resistance, there may still be land marks in the smoked area. Continue seating the bullet deeper into the case until the land marks barely show, then seat it down 1/32″ to 1/16″ and you have the right seating depth for that particular bullet in that rifle.

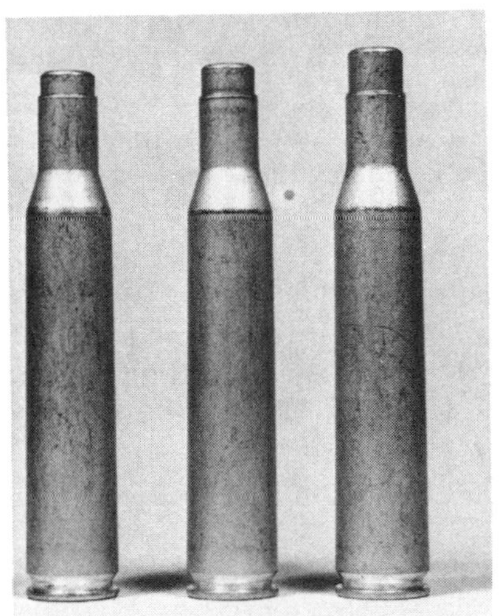

Bullets were seated base-first in these .270 Winchester cases against lands in chamber to show throat length of standard rifles of different brands. Obviously, if bullets were seated to just miss touching lands in rifles for either center or case at right, they would jam far into rifling of rifle for case at left. Pressure would increase drastically, and bullet would probably be pulled if unfired cartridge was extracted, spilling powder in action and leaving bullet stuck in barrel.

These smoked bullets were seated far enough out of case to show land marks in chamber of .264 Win. For correct seating they will be seated deeper until they miss lands by 1/32" to 1/16", which normally gives good accuracy and normal pressure. These two bullets also show why *all* bullet styles in same weight can't be seated to give same overall cartridge length. Load at left is with Speer 140 gr., while the other is with W-W 140 gr. two-diameter bullet. It would be impossible to chamber the cartridge with Speer bullet seated to same depth as the W-W.

There is only one hitch here, and that is if the rifle has a very long throat, as found in some rifles like Weatherby. In those rifles the seating depth will either be governed by the length of the magazine or because there is not enough of the bullet left in the case to hold it firmly under recoil, which requires a depth of approximately the diameter of the bullet. In any event, there is little chance of seating the bullet far enough out of the case to cause it to stick in a Weatherby throat. Also, many rifles have magazines so short that very few bullets can be seated shallow enough to jam in the throat if the cartridge functions through the magazine. There is no way of knowing this, however, with the various types of bullets and throating. To avoid trouble, check out this point before loading your hunting ammunition. Besides the problem of sticking the bullet in the barrel, if the cartridge is fired, pressures will be higher than with the same load with the bullet seated to miss the lands by at least 1/32".

Powder Selection for Hunting Loads

Powder selection for hunting loads is more important than is generally realized. Nearly any of the powders listed in loads for the various cartridges in any manual will propel a bullet of any weight down the range, but some will send the bullet on its way a lot faster than others while developing similar pressure, and may give it better accuracy. Some of the reloading manuals do not, however, list some of the powders for certain cartridges with certain bullet weights that give the highest velocity. We won't give specific instances here, because of the many manuals available and the vast number of cartridges and the bullet weights made for them. In the load charts included here, only the powders that give the highest velocity to the various bullet weights in each cartridge are listed, except for an occasional load for comparison. In some instances powders that have only recently been marketed are not listed, because they were not available at the time the loads were developed. If the reloader wishes to use loads that are reduced in velocity by any great margin, he should refer to the reloading manuals for loading information for whatever velocity level he wishes for that cartridge and bullet weight.

While the loads in our charts with powder charges listed for the different cartridges and bullet weights may not prove desirable in your rifle from the standpoint either of pressure or of accuracy, they do show what velocity can be expected from the various cartridges with these powders and bullet weights. Even if your rifle will not handle these charges without showing pressure pains, the reduction of a couple of grains will not affect velocity a great deal. These are intended as hunting loads, and it is my firm belief that a hunting load should deliver all the velocity the cartridge is capable of at pressures that give trouble-free rifle operation under all hunting conditions.

If the hunter feels he is better off starting a 180 gr. .30 caliber bullet at around 2700 fps for certain shooting conditions, then it should be loaded in a .30-06 case instead of the .300 Winchester or Weatherby and trying to reduce the velocity to that level. Or perhaps instead of using the 180 gr. he might consider loading a 200 or 220 gr. instead in the big case. He will not have to reduce the charge so much to attain the velocity wanted, trajectory will be similar, and killing power will be equally good, with no more damage to the steaks. The heavier bullets would certainly be a better choice for the larger game species.

There is yet another reason why reducing loads and velocity in large capacity cases is not always successful, and this is the accuracy angle. It is generally assumed that if the powder charge is dropped a few grains below maximum, accuracy will be greatly improved. There are certain instances where this does prove true, but is more normal with small to medium capacity cases than with the magnum cartridges, and it doesn't always hold true with the smaller cases either. It has been my experience, after many, many years of test work with magnum cartridges, that with most bullets, especially the heavier bullet weights, the best accuracy comes from loads as hot as the case will stand without causing pressure problems. In fact, I have used a number of magnum rifles that delivered the best accuracy with loads so hot that the case could be reloaded no more than three or four times because primer pockets expanded and became too loose to properly hold the new primer. I do not suggest you use loads this hot, especially for hunting, but it does show why big cases should not be loaded to reduced velocities. Many times a cartridge will give no better than 3″ 100 yard groups with charges dropped 3–4 gr. below maximum for that rifle, but loaded up to all it will handle safely, the same bullet will deliver 1″ groups.

My personal experience has strongly indicated that the hunter, particularly the big game hunter, is much better off to load a bullet of the correct design to perform properly at the velocity the cartridge he is loading will give it at all practical hunting ranges, than to try to load that cartridge to suit the performance of a certain bullet. Chapter 11 explains this in greater detail.

If the reloader will study the various reloading manuals, as well as the charts in this book, he will see what powders give the highest velocity to the different bullet weights in the various cartridges. Some of the reloading manuals also list powders as to their respective burning rates in comparison with other powders. (Speer and Hodgdon, with some information in the Lyman Handbook.)

To sum it up briefly, if you load a lightweight bullet in any given case you will use one of the faster burning powders, and for heavier bullets a slower powder gives the highest velocity. There are, of course, exceptions to this rule. As an example, cartridges like the 7mm and .300 magnums do not do well with any bullet weight with fast or medium burning rate powders. They require one of the slower powders for all bullet weights, but the heavier the bullet the slower the powder that should be used for the best results. This holds true of all cases of large capacity that have bullets of small diameter as compared to the powder capacity. Even the mammoth .378 Weatherby is at its best with very slow burning powders. On the other hand, the .375 H&H, which uses bullets of the same .375″ diameter, but has much less powder capacity than the .378, does better with powders of medium to medium-slow burning rates: that is, powders like IMR4064 and 4350, but not with the really slow numbers like H4831 or Norma 205 or MRP that replaced it. The cases with very little restriction of the case body to fit the bullet, cases like the old .45-70 and the .458 Winchester Magnum, even though they use very heavy bullets, require fairly fast powders like W-W 748 or IMR3031.

Small cases, even though the bullet diameter is small, may not do very well in the velocity department even with heavy bullets with slow burning powders. The reason for this is that the case lacks the capacity to load enough powder into it to build up sufficient pressure to deliver high velocity. And this brings up another question where case capacities and slow powders are concerned.

I receive many inquiries each year from reloaders who are greatly concerned when they find out a charge of slow powder fills the case nearly to the top of the neck, and the same thing happens with small cases and faster powders. They think that if you have to compress the powder when seating the bullet, you are sure to either blow the rifle up or at the best have a load that gives highly erratic pressure and velocity from shot to shot. This is far from true, and many of the loads in the accompanying charts require all the powder compression the bullet can exert without being forced back out of the case. In fact, the only way some of these powder charges, as well as some found in various manuals, can be stuffed into the case is to pour them through a funnel with a drop tube at least 4" long, and then do it very slowly by tapping the powder scale pan on the side of the funnel to sift it *slowly* into the case. Yet, many of these solidly compressed powder charges give high quality accuracy, very uniform shot-to-shot velocity, and make some of the finest hunting loads available. Powder compression can sometimes be avoided by using a powder of similar burning rate that is denser to replace the charge of coarse-grained powder; substituting a fine-grained stick powder like Norma MRP for H4831, or a ball powder like W-W 785. The charge will be similar but not identical, and so will velocity, but with less compression. Consult charts for magnum cartridges.

Also, in regard to powders for loads used for hunting under certain conditions not usually encountered, there is the question of how high or low temperatures affect velocity. This is more normally connected with low temperatures than with high, because most writing on the subject has indicated that as temperatures rise above the normal 70° F. at which most testing is done, the pressure and velocity go up. However, in North America there is more big game hunting done at below freezing temperatures than at 100° F. It has also long been believed that for shooting at low temperatures a magnum primer gave more velocity uniformity and less velocity loss than did standard primers.

I once ran some fairly extensive tests to see if this was true or just theory. Briefly, they show that some powders give much less velocity rise or fall when temperatures go up or down than others do. They also show that any good standard primer is as reliable at low temperatures as a magnum. What this means to the big game hunter is that if you will hunt where the temperature is likely to be from the freezing point on down, don't be overly concerned about the primer used, but picking the right powder will solve most of the temperature problem.

There is very little information on the actual effect that temperature change has on velocity, and none that I know of except my own limited test as given here, which takes various primers, powders, and cartridges into consideration. The only tabulated information I know of that is readily available to the handloader is found in the *Speer Reloading Manual,* and it is plainly stated that the data was not compiled from actual firing tests. My own testing proved this to be an understatement! The greatest discrepancy between actual firing tests and the apparently theoretical data compiled by Speer is that there is no set rule for velocity gain or loss as temperatures rise or drop above the normal 70° F. Speer data shows a fairly consistent gradually increasing rise as temperatures go up, and assumes all powders react the same in all cartridges. My own tests did not come out that way. It should be noted that in *most* instances velocity was actually slightly higher at −20° F. than at 0° F.

To make any test of this type meaningful, all possible variation must be eliminated. First, the only bearing that the temperature of the firing location has on velocity is normal atmospheric pressure changes due to the difference in cold and warm air. Powder and primer temperature is the deciding factor. To assure correct powder/primer temperature, the ammunition must be held at the desired temperature long enough to make certain that temperature is actually attained. Tests proved that rifle barrel temperature has little if any bearing on velocity, so all firing was done inside the chronograph room at the normal 70° F.

Experiments proved that anything over thirty minutes' exposure would bring the ammunition to the correct temperature, but all ammunition tested was exposed for two hours for a great margin of insurance.

For the −20° F. and 0° F. tests, a freezer was set so that an independent thermometer showed −24° F. and −4° F. respectively. The ammunition was placed in an open thermos in the freezer and left for the two-hour cooling period. The lid was then put on the thermos in the freezer and the ammunition taken to the shooting room. Here it was removed a cartridge at a time and fired to assure that temperatures remained constant. The 4° of lower temperature was allowed to cover any possible rise from freezer to firing.

There was no problem, of course, at 70° F.; the ammunition was simply left in the shooting room at 70° F. for two hours before firing.

For the 120° F. tests, a can containing the ammunition was placed in an electric deep-fryer with water surrounding it and heated to 122° F. This utensil was placed right on the shooting/loading bench and a cartridge at a time removed and fired after the two-hour heating period.

These tests are by no means fully complete, as they do not show what can be expected from all powders, cartridges, and primers. They do show more about what can be expected from various cartridges of different case capacities and bores with the powders and primer designations normally used in them.

These charts were originally published in similar form in *Handloader* magazine by the author, and are used here with the permission of publisher Neal Knox.

Velocity/temperature tests
6mm Remington Model 700 ADL 20″ bbl.
R-P cases weight 180 gr.
Sierra 85 gr. flat base spitzer bullet

POWDER	CHARGE	PRIMER	TEMP. (F.)
N205*	47	CCI no. 200	−20°
N205	47	CCI no. 200	0°
N205	47	CCI no. 200	70°
N205	47	CCI no. 200	120°
H450	47	CCI no. 250	−20°
H450	47	CCI no. 250	0°
H450	47	CCI no. 250	70°
H450	47	CCI no. 250	120°
IMR4831†	46	CCI no. 200	−20°
IMR4831	46	CCI no. 250	−20°
IMR4831	46	CCI no. 200	0°
IMR4831	46	CCI no. 200	70°
IMR4831	46	CCI no. 250	70°
IMR4831	46	CCI no. 200	120°
IMR4831	46	CCI no. 250	120°
W-W 760	45	CCI #250	−20°
W-W 760	45	CCI #250	0°
W-W 760	45	CCI #250	70°
W-W 760‡	45	CCI #250	120°

*Note that N205 actually gave slightly higher velocities at temperatures below 70° F. than above. This powder proved almost completely stable in this case with standard primers.

†The tests with CCI no. 250 (magnum) and CCI no. 200 (standard) primers were

See pp. 44–45 for note with supplementary information, and for explanation of abbreviations used in charts.

VELOCITY FPS	REMARKS
3072	Velocity quite normal at all temps.
3090	Temp/velocity change 33 fps.
3082	
3057	
2912	Gradual increase in velocity as temp climbs.
2900	Temp/velocity change 161 fps.
3033	
3061	
2956	Note that mag. primers give 96 fps less velocity
2863	at −20° than standard primers. Temp/velocity
2941	change with standard no. 200 primers 56 fps.
2987	
3010	
3015	
3073	
2978	Velocity jumps drastically at high temperatures.
2962	Temp/velocity change 266 fps!
3060	
3228	

rerun to make certain there had been no mistake, and both tests gave almost identical figures.

‡Tests with W-W 760 were also run twice at 120° F. because of the great velocity increase, with the second test proving the first to be correct.

Velocity/temperature tests
.308 Win. Mark X Cavalier 24″ bbl.
R-P cases weight 172 gr.
Speer 150 gr. Mag-Tip bullet

POWDER	CHARGE	PRIMER	TEMP. (F.)
H4895	45	CCI no. 200	−20°
H4895	45	CCI no. 200	0°
H4895	45	CCI no. 200	70°
H4895	45	CCI no. 200	120°
IMR4064	44	CCI no. 200	−20°
IMR4064	44	CCI no. 200	0°
IMR4064	44	CCI no. 200	70°
IMR4064	44	CCI no. 200	120°
H335	46	CCI no. 200	−20°
H335	46	CCI no. 200	0°
H335	46	CCI no. 250	0°
H335	46	CCI no. 200	70°
H335	46	CCI no. 200	120°

Velocity/temperature tests
7mm Rem. Mag. Remington M-700 BDL 24″ bbl.
R-P cases weight 249 gr.
Sierra 160 gr. BT bullet

POWDER	CHARGE	PRIMER	TEMP. (F.)
H870	78	CCI no. 250	−20°
H870	78	CCI no. 200	−20°
H870	78	CCI no. 250	0°
H870	78	CCI no. 250	70°
H870	78	CCI no. 250	120°
H4831	65	CCI no. 250	−20°
H4831	65	CCI no. 200	−20°
H4831	65	CCI no. 250	0°
H4831	65	CCI no. 250	70°

VELOCITY FPS	REMARKS
2718 2738 2824 2874	Gradual increase in velocity as temperature goes up. Temp/velocity change 156 fps.
2670 2643 2691 2727	Low velocity variation between low and high temperatures. Temp/velocity change 57 fps.
2643 2676 2683 2758 2826	Only 7 fps velocity spread between mag. and std. primers. Sharp velocity increase at high temperatures. Temp/velocity change 183 fps.

VELOCITY FPS	REMARKS
2917 2945 2983 3086 3149	Great velocity variation between low and high temperatures. Temp/velocity change 232 fps. Std. primer gives 28 fps higher velocity than mag. primer.
2842 2840 2878 2957	Not influenced by high temperatures. Std. and mag. primers give nearly same velocity. Temp/velocity change 142 fps.

Velocity/temperature tests
7mm Rem. Mag. Remington M-700 BDL 24″ bbl.
R-P cases weight 249 gr.
Sierra 160 gr. BT bullet

H4831	65	CCI no. 200	70°
H4831	65	CCI no. 200	120°
N205	65	CCI no. 250	−20°
N205	65	CCI no. 250	0°
N205	65	CCI no. 250	70°
N205	65	CCI no. 250	120°
IMR4350	62	CCI no. 250	−20°
IMR4350	62	CCI no. 250	0°
IMR4350	62	CCI no. 250	70°
IMR4350	62	CCI no. 250	120°

Velocity/temperature tests
.340 Weatherby custom on M-70 Win. action Hobaugh 23 1/2″ bbl., no free-bore
W-W 375 H&H cases necked down weight 240 gr.
225 gr. Hornady Spire Point bullet

POWDER	CHARGE	PRIMER	TEMP. (F.)
N205	83	CCI no. 250	−20°
N205	83	CCI no. 250	0°
N205	83	CCI no. 250	70°
N205	83	CCI no. 250	120°
H4831	84	CCI no. 250	−20°
H4831	84	CCI no. 250	0°
H4831	84	CCI no. 250	70°
H4831	84	CCI no. 250	120°
IMR4350	79	CCI no. 250	−20°
IMR4350	79	CCI no. 250	0°
IMR4350	79	CCI no. 250	70°
IMR4350	79	CCI no. 250	120°

2996	
2984	
2977	Gradual velocity increase as temperature goes up. Temp/velocity change 117 fps.
3045	
3059	
3094	
2819	Considerable velocity increase as temperature goes up. Temp/velocity change 195 fps.
2883	
2977	
3015	

VELOCITY FPS	REMARKS
2903	Small velocity change between low and high temps. Temp/velocity change 67 fps.
2902	
2944	
2969	
2779	Gradual velocity gain as temperature increases, but quite even. Temp/velocity change 159 fps.
2834	
2878	
2938	
2752	Very similar reaction to temperature changes as H4831. Temp/velocity change 164 fps.
2742	
2848	
2906	

Pressure

Excessive pressure is something the hunter/reloader should avoid at all times. The main reason is that when pressure reaches a certain point, the case stretches beyond the point where it will be retracted from the chamber wall by its own elasticity. The brass actually starts to give way or stretch as though it were made of lead. When this happens, the head of the case is forced against the bolt face and chamber walls so tightly that it does not release when the pressure drops as the bullet exits from the bore. This causes the bolt to be difficult to open at the best, and makes the action impossible to open at the worst. It is not possible to accurately predict the amount of pressure it will take to cause this problem, because the type of action, and to a lesser extent the design and hardness of the case, will decide that issue. As an example, a lever action may start to get sticky to open with a pressure of 48,000 pounds per square inch (psi), while a bolt action may not show any problem whatever at 55,000 psi with the same cartridge. The concern to the hunter is, of course, that he does *not* want the action of his hunting rifle to be the least bit hard to open when hunting —especially when hunting potentially dangerous game.

The hunter/reloader's main concern is to have some idea of when pressures start to become excessive, and stop increasing the powder charge before it gets out of hand. There are a number of ways of estimating pressure before it becomes excessive without scientific equipment as used by the ammunition manufacturers and a very few independent ballistic laboratories, but even these simplified methods, the ones I use in my own testing, are too complicated for the average handloader who loads only a comparative few rounds a year. So we'll skip all these methods of pressure reading and mention only the physical signs that are obvious to the handloader once he knows what to look for.

Primers have long been considered the best indicators of pressure for the average reloader to use. The visual signs of high pressures are when the primer cup starts to crater (form a tiny ridge) around the indentation left by the firing pin, or when the cup flattens out so that it fills the primer pocket in the case head right out to the edges. These visual signs certainly *can* be indications of high pressures, but this is not always the case.

Let's look at cratering first. It is caused by the pressure inside the case forcing the primer back against the bolt face with sufficient force to extrude the cup into the firing pin hole in the bolt face around the point of the firing pin. The reason that it is not always reliable is that, first, the cups of all primers are not of either the same thickness or hardness in all makes or even in lots of the same make. A soft or thin cup is more likely to extrude than a thick hard cup. Also, and more likely to be the cause of cratering, is a bolt face with a large firing pin hole and/or a small firing pin. A weak firing pin (striker) spring will also allow the firing pin to be forced back into the bolt and cause cratering or even a pierced primer.

These .264 cases were both fired with same charge of powder at very high pressure as indicated by ejector hole mark, but the primer on left shows cratering, while the one at right does not. They were of different brands, which proves that before making judgment of pressures as indicated by primer appearance, the reloader must know what to expect from the primer being used.

Flattened primers are very often caused from thin and/or soft primer cups. The shape of the primer cup and the top edge of the primer pocket also affect primer flatness when pressures are not particularly high. Some primers have a convex surface, while others are already quite flat; the flat ones show a flat appearance at lower pressure than the round ones do. If the primer pocket is quite square around the edge, it will cause the primer to appear flatter than a pocket that has a beveled edge. The only way primer appearance is a reliable indication of high pressures is if the reloader knows well the particular brand and lot of primers, the case, and the rifle. After he knows these things, and only then, he will be able to use the primer as a reliable indicator of pressure. It might be well to add, however, that when the reloader notices any of these visual signs of *possible* high pressure on the primer, he had better take it easy in increasing the powder charge.

A certain indication of high pressure comes when the brass of the case head starts to extrude into the ejector hole or slot in the bolt face. The first indication of this, and you'll have to look closely to see it, is when a line the shape of the ejector hole shows up. With just a little more pressure the brass will extrude deep enough into the hole so that when the bolt is rotated in opening a bolt action, this brass will be scraped off, leaving a bright spot on the case head. Whenever there is the *slightest* mark left by the ejector opening in the bolt face on the case head, *reduce the powder charge until it is no longer visible.* Usually the same charges that it takes to first show the mark of the ejector opening will also start to expand the primer pocket of the case so that the primer no longer fits tightly as it should. Of course, loose primer pockets make cases unfit for further reloading.

When a shiny spot appears on the case head where the brass was forced into the ejector hole in the bolt face, pressures are far too high. Back load off until it is no longer present, usually 2–3 gr. of the slow powders in large capacity cases like this .264. Bolt lift will be "sticky" with this kind of pressure also. Hunting loads should *never* show either of these signs of excessive pressure.

The final sign of pressure that is readily apparent to the handloader is when the bolt handle starts to require more than normal pressure to lift to extract the fired case. (The lever and slide actions will, of course, be difficult to open at much lower pressures.) Whenever this occurs, reduce the charge until it is no longer present. There is always the possibility that some foreign matter like sand or dirt has worked into the action and is causing the stiffness of operation. It is always a good plan to check this out by chambering a case fired in the same rifle at low pressure (a factory load will do very well), letting the firing pin down on the fired primer, and then extracting the case. If the same action stiffness is present, you will know the problem is not high pressure in the load, but lies rather in the action.

Component Influence on Load Performance

The main reason for bringing up the subject of how different components that make up a cartridge influence its performance is that those changes in performance can, and often are, of great importance to the hunter.

Starting with the case, not all cases of the same cartridge designation are of the same weight from different makers, or from different lots from the same maker. If there's a considerable difference in case weight, there will be a difference in the powder capacity of the cases also. This, in turn, will cause the velocity to go up with the heavy case and down with the light one, when using the same bullet, powder, charge, and primer. There is the possibility that bullet impact will be changed somewhat. So don't mix case brands when loading hunting ammunition, and if the cases come from different lots of the same brand, weigh a sample of each lot before loading. In a case like the .30-06, 3–4 gr. will make little difference, but anything over 10 gr. will cause some velocity change.

A good deal has been written here and there regarding the effect of different brands of primers on velocity with all other components being the same, as well as the difference between the so-called standard and magnum primers in igniting large charges of any powder and any charge of ball powder. I have run very exten-

This photo of sectioned 7mm Remington Magnum cases shows why different brands of cases have different powder capacities. Note difference in thickness of web and body wall. *From left:* Remington; Speer DWM (no longer produced); Winchester; Federal. Case weight in the same order is 247 gr., 269 gr., 239 gr., and 235 gr., which affects pressure and velocity to some extent with all other load components being the same.

sive tests of comparison with nearly all brands and styles of primers, and with all types of powders in cases of small to great capacity, and there isn't enough difference between any of them to matter much. The only suggestion here, if you wish to experiment, is that you may find one brand gives better accuracy than another in combination with the other components used to make up your load. If so, use it, and do not change brands in that load when loading for a hunt.

While little has been said about it in any reloading manual, and not much either in books or in magazine articles, there is often considerable variation between the velocity given by one lot of powder and another of the same number. I have found this to be as much as 100 fps for the same charge with all other load components the same. This, of course, can change point of bullet impact by quite a margin at long range, or even short range for that matter. Also, pressures will go from reasonable to too high if you have been using a mild lot of powder for a safe maximum hunting load and then use the same charge from a hot lot that gives the higher velocity. Don't mix powder lots when loading for a hunt.

This brings us to the most important part of the hunting handload—the bullet—and more problems arise from changing bullets without checking the effect on bullet impact than from any other single cause. As has been pointed out earlier, there is a great deal of difference in the point of impact when different bullet point shapes are used at long range, even though the bullets are of the same weight. I think this is already known by most hunters anyway, but what few casual reloaders know is that even though two bullets of the same weight and caliber look almost identical, they may shoot to different points of impact even at 100 yards. I have seen bullets from different makers, both of the same weight and caliber and style, impact as much as 3″ apart at 100 yards. Also, bullets of the same weight and caliber, but in different styles of the same brand, may not shoot into the same group at 100 yards either. As an example, a hollow point and a soft point of similar shape in the same weight and caliber, and of the same brand, may have different points of impact with all other load components being the same.

To sum this up as to the effect it has on the hunter, never assume that because a 180 gr. Speer pointed bullet shoots to a certain point of impact in your .30 caliber rifle, you can substitute a Hornady, Sierra, or any other 180 gr. pointed bullet and have it impact at the same point.

There is no way of knowing whether there will be a change of impact or in what direction or how much it will be if there is, but if you assume that just because the bullets are the same weight they will land in the same group, you are asking for trouble.

Also, even though two different powders may give a bullet very nearly the same velocity from the same case, there is as much chance they will not impact in the same place as that they will.

It should be obvious that while *any* change in load components may affect pressure and velocity, this nominal change in itself is of no great interest to the hunter, but the change of bullet impact that goes with it certainly is. As stated above, this change of impact may be up to 3″ or so, but even assuming an average of 2″, it is not hard to see what it will do to the accurate placing of a bullet at long range. It also makes a lot of difference in which direction the point

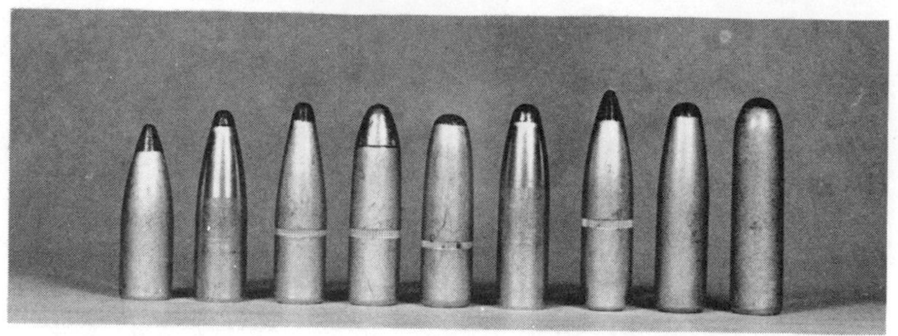

These .338 bullets show some of the many weights and styles made for that caliber. Others, like the .30 caliber, have much larger variety. It is highly unlikely that any two of these will shoot to the same point of impact, and even if of the same weight will not give same velocity and pressure with same powder charge. *From left:* 200 gr. Speer; 210 gr. Nosler; 225 gr. Hornady; 250 gr. W-W Silvertip; 250 gr. Hornady; 250 gr. Nosler; 250 gr. Sierra; 275 gr. Speer; 300 gr. Barns.

of impact is from the sighting used with the original load. If right or left 2″ at 100 yards, the shift in impact at 300 yards would be 6″ and would still prove fatal on a buck deer, but if it is high or low it is an entirely different matter. If the new load impacts 2″ lower than the one for which the rifle was sighted, and the rifle was sighted to group 3″ high at 100 yards, it will now shoot only 1″ high. Conversely, if the new load is 2″ higher than the old one, the point of impact will be 5″ high at 100 yards. It doesn't take a lot of knowledge or serious thought to see what this will do to bullet impact at 200–400 yards. The sure hit range in the vital area of a buck or a ram would be changed so much that it would be like going from a .30-06 to a .300 Weatherby, or vice versa. And a miss or a wounded animal would likely be the result at ranges beyond 150 yards.

The same thing applies to factory-loaded ammunition to an even greater extent, because there is not only the difference in bullets of the same weight and general design, but of all other components. Even though various brands of factory ammunition are almost always listed as giving the same velocity, it is highly unusual if they do.

The main thing to remember is that if you have your rifle sighted for a certain load and need extra ammunition for a hunt, *do not change any component* when you load it. And if you use factory ammunition, do not change brands or take more than one brand of the same bullet weight unless you check the sighting with both brands of factory ammunition or lots of handloads *before* the hunt. Then, if they both shoot into the same group, everything is fine, but if not you will know what to expect.

Hunters have often been advised, for reasons of economy, to sight their rifles with some cheaper bullet of the same weight and point shape when they intend to use one of the high cost bullets like the Nosler Partition or Bitterroot for hunting. This is fine if you sight your rifle with the cheaper bullet and then check it with the premium bullet to make certain impact is in the same place, but if it is not, finish sighting with the bullet you will use on the hunt. Remember that the dollar or two you save in sighting with the cheaper bullets can cost you the trophy of a lifetime if it isn't right for the bullet you hunt with. Also remember that as a handloader you can fire a round of .30-06 ammunition using a 180 gr. Nosler Partition Jacket bullet for about twelve cents less than a factory round if you already have your own cases! If you use the Nosler to sight with, you are still one hell of a lot better off financially than the fellow who must buy factory ammunition.

From the economic standpoint, a box of twenty rounds of factory ammunition for the .30-06 will cost you nearly eight bucks, while the same box of handloads with the same bullet, or another conventional style bullet of similar design from one of the bullet makers, will cost less than three dollars if you have your own cases. The difference is even greater when loading the magnum cases in the same caliber. The only difference in cost to the handloader of the magnum cartridge over the .30-06 is in powder cost, which is only one to two cents per round depending on what powder is used, but the difference between the .30-06 and the .300 Winchester Magnum in factory ammunition is nearer twelve cents per round. This, of course, comes from the price of the new case, but the magnum case will last the handloader just as long as the smaller case if loaded to the same general pressure level.

Another advantage the hunter/handloader has over the hunter who uses factory ammunition is that if he likes a particular factory bullet he can usually buy it as a component part and use it in his own handloads tailored the way he wants them for his own rifle and hunting situation. There are a number of reasons why the same bullet used in the factory-loaded cartridge may perform better in a handload, even though factory ammunition is good.

First, while most factory ammunition gives good accuracy in most rifles, it may be pretty sour in some, and is seldom as accurate as a good handload worked out especially for an individual rifle. You are almost certain to improve the accuracy with a little switching of powders and charges of those powders behind the factory bullet. And if that doesn't work, you always have the option of experimenting with different brands and styles until you find the one that gives the best accuracy in your rifle.

There is also the hard fact that a great many cartridges are far underloaded by the ammunition companies. This is usually more noticeable with cartridges that have been around a long time and are chambered in older rifles of doubtful strength, or in lever, slide, or some autoloading actions. The .30-06 and 7×57 Mauser are examples of bolt action cartridges, and the .308 Win., .284 Win., and .280 Rem. are examples of cartridges also used in lever, slide, and autoloaders. And this is only part of the story because the velocity and energy listed by the factory are, in most cases, more than you will receive from your rifle. For instance, I have run velocity tests on most domestic brands of .30-06 ammunition with 180 gr. bullets and have yet to find one that will give the 2700 fps listed when fired in a 24" barrel of a hunting rifle. In fact, some brands and lots of new factory ammo give the 180 gr. bullet less than 2600 fps. Yet it is no trick at all to start the same bullet at over 2800 fps with the right powder in any modern bolt action rifle at pressures that are perfectly safe and reliable for hunting use. (See .30-06 chart, p. 194. Most reloading manuals also hold velocities down to around 2700 fps because their loads may be used in actions of doubtful strength.) When you do this, you increase both the range and the energy a great deal over the factory-loaded round.

There is also the option of loading your ammunition to lower velocity for some special purpose. And in the small and medium capacity cases, reduced loads with either jacketed or cast bullets can be reduced to velocities suitable for taking small game like rabbits and grouse for the pot, while still retaining very good accuracy if you use the right powder and bullet combination. Both the *Lyman Reloader's Handbook* and the *Speer Reloading Manual* No.

9 show reduced loads for nearly all rifle cartridges listed. I repeat, however, that accuracy is usually a problem when reduced loads are attempted in the magnum capacity cases.

Hunting Load Development and Evaluation

One of the most important aspects of reloading your own hunting ammunition is to obtain a better load than is available in the factory-loaded product. It must be remembered, however, that just because you pick a bullet that is better suited to the kind of game being hunted, then pick a powder and charge from some reloading manual that shows reasonably high velocity, you do not automatically come out with the best load for *your rifle.* The italics are used because no one can tell you what load will give the best results in any individual rifle. And all rifles are individuals even if they come from the same production line. The load that clusters all its bullets into a 1 1/2″ group on the 100 yard target with one rifle may produce 3″ groups with another of the same make and model, while another load may reverse the situation.

When one hunting rifle is a Winchester, another a Remington, or perhaps some import, the likelihood of the same load giving the same results in any two of them is even less. Then, consider the hunter who has a custom rifle chambered for the same cartridge. That rifle is likely to have a barrel by one maker and be chambered by someone else with a chambering reamer of any one of several brands. Those custom barrels, as well as the barrels found on different commercial rifles, may not all have the same rate of twist or the same number of lands, and the lands may also be of different widths, with the grooves of various depths. The bore of those barrels may also vary somewhat in diameter. With all this taken into consideration, it is little wonder that few rifles give the same results with the same load, either from the standpoint of accuracy, of pressure, or of velocity.

To overcome this, the handloader must work out the best load for his rifle for the purpose it will be used for if he wishes to have the best performance that rifle is capable of. To do this he has two alternatives. First, he can take one of the manuals that lists loads for the specific bullet he wishes to use, and experiment with the various loads of powders and charges that manual gives for that bullet until he finds the one that gives the best accuracy coupled with the velocity and energy he feels he needs. The figures given in the manual will almost certainly not be the same as he will receive from his rifle, but they will be somewhere near, probably within 50 fps one way or the other. The second method is to work up his own load after starting with a mild load from a manual and experimenting with both bullets and powders until he finds the combination that gives the best results his rifle is capable of. This is true load development and is what we are concerned with here.

The first thing the reloader will have to know is what kind of accuracy the rifle is capable of with average loads, perhaps including factory ammunition. While he can expect to develop a load that will give better accuracy, he is simply wasting his time if he thinks he can find a load that will make a poor barrel shoot well, or a barrel and/or action that is poorly bedded shoot tight groups. The rifle should be tuned and tested before trying to develop loads that will be accurate as well as potent so you know what you may expect.

Before actual load development begins, the hunting reloader should also consider what he wants and will need from the load. The varmint hunter who will be shooting varmints in the range of ground squirrels to chucks and jackrabbits will need all the accuracy the rifle is capable of with the highest velocity possible for that accuracy level in that rifle. That is, he can hardly afford to accept a load that will not consistently group under 1 minute of angle. If he has to sacrifice some velocity to get it, he is not hurting too much. On the other hand, if his dish is shooting coyotes at long range, he can do with a little less accuracy in favor of high velocity. Sure, the ideal situation is to have both, but the best you can hope for with some rifles is as much as you can get of either without losing too much of one or the other.

The big game hunter is not under the same accuracy pressure as is the varmint hunter, so in many instances velocity and energy are of more importance than a high degree of accuracy. These points have already been brought up earlier, but are mentioned again here as a point of reference to consider while actually doing load development work. The one place where the big game hunter is worse off than the varmint hunter is in bullet selection for a specific use. The varmint hunter has a wide choice of bullets from many makers that perform very well for all varmint hunting, and can surely work out a load with one of them that is highly satisfactory. Not so with the big game hunter. There are only a few bullets that give true controlled expansion coupled with long range expansion assurance, and if they don't happen to shoot well in his rifle he has a load development problem. The only hope of overcoming that problem is in trying all the powders that are suitable to that cartridge and bullet weight, then, starting with the load that proves to be the maximum trouble-free hunting load for that rifle, keep dropping charges to see if accuracy improves. There is a possibility that some powder and charge will give acceptable accuracy, but if it doesn't, the only alternative is to go to a bullet that gives the nearest performance level to the one you wanted to use that does give acceptable accuracy.

A study of the load charts included here for the various cartridges, or the ones found in the manuals for cartridges we do not include, will show which powders give the highest velocity with bullets of various weights. In this book we have included only those powders that give the best velocity with each bullet weight, as these loads are for hunting, not target shooting. There may be some other powders that will do as well as those listed, maybe even slightly better where newer powders are available than were used in the tests, but in most instances the powders used were the best choice when the load data was compiled.

To develop the best hunting load for your rifle, first try a charge of one of these powders that is at least 5% below that given in the load chart for the cartridge and bullet weight. If that load proves to be mild, go on up until you see the pressure signs outlined under the section on pressure (p. 292), then back it off as directed. To expedite and simplify the test work, load three rounds with that charge. Write the bullet make, style, and weight, and the powder and charge, on a small square of paper and slip it under a rubber band around the three cartridges. Do the same thing with the powder charge cut 1 gr. for large capacity cases and 0.5 gr. for small cases. It is a good idea to do this with loads running from the top load down to 3 gr. below—that is, four test groups of cartridges of three rounds each. When you take your rifle to the range to test the accuracy of these loads, sight it to impact about 3″ from the center of the bull with a center hold, high, low, left, or right, it makes no difference. As you fire each group of three cartridges, place the square of paper with the load data on it beside the group with tape. Then rotate the target 90° and fire another group. At the end of the session you will have a record of all loads fired and the potential of the accuracy they are capable of. The information on the target can later be transferred to the reloading record book.

If you have to drive some distance to the range, it is a good plan to have these three cartridge groups made up for three or four of the best powders for that cartridge and bullet weight to save both time and dollars.

The next step is to compare all the groups and see which powders and charges give the tightest groups. At this point it is a good plan to load up three or five rounds each of the loads that show the most promise and try them again; if they do as well as the first group, you will know it was not a fluke and that the load really is accurate. If the groups are studied carefully, it is usually obvious that accuracy is better either with the heavier charges or with the light ones. This will indicate which way to work from the most accurate charge for the best accuracy. If the heaviest charge tried gives the best accuracy, as is often the case with magnum cartridges, you will have to use that load to avoid excessive pressures. If the light load is the best, you may be faced with the decision of whether velocity or accuracy is the most important. Unless there is a wide spread in accuracy between the lighter and heavier charges, the big game hunter is usually justified in using the heavier charge because of the extra punch it packs out where the game is. Only the fellow who is doing the testing and will use the load in the hunting country will be able to make that decision.

Just how far the reloader should go in trying to find the highest degree of accuracy with any powder by juggling the charge is a question not always agreed on by the experts. My personal observation has been that in loading magnum capacity cases in big game calibers, little if anything is gained by cutting charges to finer increments than 1 gr. If better accuracy is ever obtained by changing charges by less than the 1 gr. amount, it will take more shooting to prove it than any hunter will be justified in doing. Even in the .270–.30-06 case capacity range, it is doubtful if 0.5 gr. of any powder makes enough difference to matter to the big game hunter. When you get down to the varmint cartridges, or varmint loads in

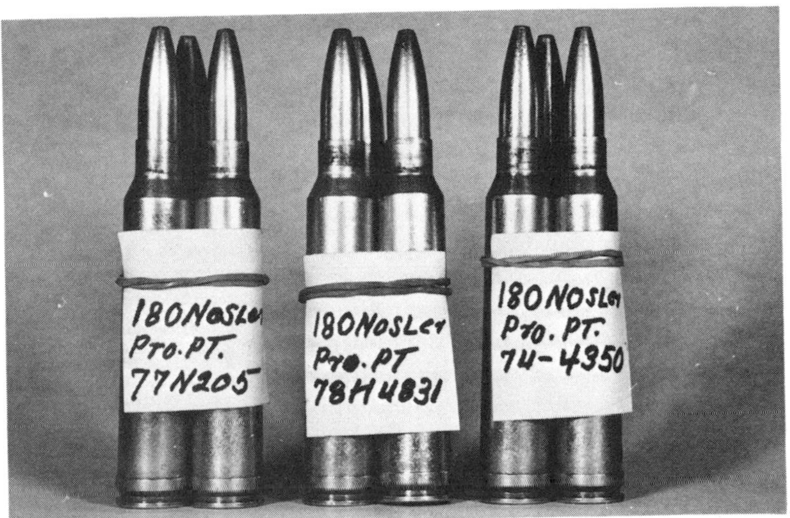

Method of attaching load data to groups of cartridges to be used for velocity/accuracy testing. Tabs are attached to target after each group is fired. If different primer is used for any load, that information is included.

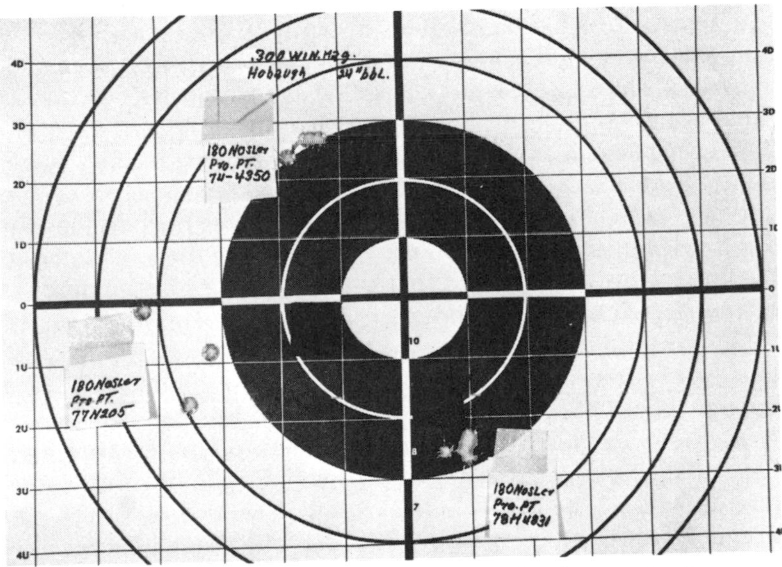

This test target shows method of taping data taken from test loads on target to show accuracy potential of powder and charge, as well as point of impact at 100 yards. Target rotated 90° between groups with center hold used. Point of impact was 3″ high.

some of the larger caliber cartridges like the larger .25 caliber cases, a difference of 0.5 gr., especially of the faster powders, often makes the difference between a good varmint load for all varmint shooting ranges and one that is suitable for only close range work. In the smaller cartridges like the .222 and .223 Remington, and the .17s, even .1 gr. can tighten or spread group size.

As was pointed out in chapter 9, it is sometimes possible for the big game hunter to develop loads with two different bullet weights in the same cartridge for the same rifle that will shoot to the same point of impact at 100 yards. By shifting charges up and down with the two bullet weights, we'll say 180 and 200 gr. .30 caliber bullets, it is often possible to get them to shoot to the same point of impact—or at least close enough for all hunting use on big game. There is very often a difference in impact with the same bullet when two different powders are used. This can work to the advantage of the hunter trying to get two different bullet weights to shoot to the same 100 yard point of impact. He may find that using one kind of powder with one bullet and a different one with the other will do the trick while still developing sufficient accuracy and velocity with both bullets. As an example, Norma MRP used with one bullet weight may give the same point of impact as H4831 does with another weight, whereas no charge of either powder will do the same thing.

In trying to develop loads for two bullet weights to give a single point of impact, the same system can be used to speed things up and save ammunition as described for developing the best load for any single bullet weight. With the data tab from the load taped to the target, you have a record that can be kept for future reference or transferred to the reloading log.

One of the great advantages of developing your own hunting loads for your own rifles is that in doing so you will not only learn a lot of things about powders, bullets, and accuracy, as well as velocity in your rifle if you have a chronograph or access to one, but you'll learn a lot about the rifle itself. You'll also shoot your hunting rifles a lot more between big game seasons than you would otherwise, and this can make the difference between hits and misses, clean kills and wounded game, and the failure or success of the hunting trip.

Index

Note: With occasional exceptions, all bullets are listed under their makers' names—thus, Core-Lokt bullets will be found under Remington, Silvertip under Winchester, etc.